The Kentucky Legislature

The Kentucky Legislature

Two Decades of Change

MALCOLM E. JEWELL
and PENNY M. MILLER

THE UNIVERSITY PRESS OF KENTUCKY

Publication of this book has been assisted
by a grant from the Gannett Foundation

Library of Congress Cataloging-in-Publication Data

Jewell, Malcolm Edwin, 1928-
    The Kentucky legislature : two decades of change / Malcolm E.
Jewell, Penny M. Miller.

    p. cm.
    Bibliography: p.
    Includes index.
    ISBN 0-8131-1668-6
    1. Kentucky. General Assembly.   2. Kentucky—Politics and
government—1951- I. Miller, Penny M., 1943- . II. Title.
JK5371.J48   1988
328.769'09—dc19   88-15552

Contents

Tables

Figures

Part One
Introduction

The theme of this book is legislative change, and the focus is on the Kentucky General Assembly. It is intended for two audiences: those who are interested in the government and politics of Kentucky and those who are interested in the comparative study of American states.

Traditionally, the legislature has been regarded by most Kentuckians as weak and ineffective, less important and less interesting than the governor. No one can understand Kentucky politics today without recognizing that the legislative system has undergone fundamental change. No one can make sense of the conflicts and debates between the governor and the legislature without understanding how and why the relationship between these two political institutions has changed. Kentuckians who have increasing contacts with their state legislators need to understand how these politicians get elected, how they represent their district, how they perceive their responsibilities in the legislature, and what influence they have as individuals in the decision-making process. In order for Kentuckians to understand why taxes are raised or lowered, why the quality of education is improved or remains stagnant, and why environmental problems are solved or ignored, it is necessary to understand how the General Assembly handles the demands made on it by governors, interest groups, and constituents, and how it makes decisions.

This study of the Kentucky legislature should be of interest to students of comparative state government and politics because it offers a case study in legislative change. Since the early 1960s there have been fundamental changes in most American state legislatures. These have been documented in some general studies of the state legislature, but there have been few efforts to study how legislatures evolve over time.

This is not a case study of a "typical" state legislature, nor can it be argued that the process of change in other states has followed the same pattern as in Kentucky. Kentucky is today, as it was thirty years ago, more rural than most states. Kentucky's legislative parties remain much less competitive than those in nonsouthern legislatures. Thirty years ago Kentucky's legislature was one of the least professional in the country, and it is still less professional than most, particularly with respect to the length and frequency of sessions.

But the movement toward legislative reform has had at least as much much impact in Kentucky as in other states. In some respects there are fewer differences across the country today between the most professional and the least professional legislatures because there has been more change in the former group. With respect to such issues as the tenure of members, the strength of the committee system, the effectiveness of budgetary review, and the legislative independence of the governor, the Kentucky General Assembly has changed more than the average state's has.

The more carefully we examine legislative change in Kentucky, the more we recognize the complexity of the process. This change has occurred as a result of national trends, pressures from within Kentucky, and the initiatives of members in the General Assembly. The pace and direction of change have been influenced by particular legislators and staff members, as well as particular governors. Because so many individuals and events are unique to Kentucky, legislative change in this state could not be a model for other states. But an understanding of the complex process in Kentucky might lead scholars in other states not only to anticipate complexity there but to recognize what types of questions to ask and what kinds of relationships to explore.

This volume is divided into five parts. In order to put Kentucky legislative change into perspective, we will introduce the topics covered by summarizing major changes that have been occurring in state legislatures.

1. Studying Legislative Change

In 1966 Alexander Heard introduced a book on American state legislatures by describing the charges brought against them, which he said "often emanate from impeccable sources and are supported by credible evidence." Summarizing these criticisms, Heard (1966: 1-2) said:

> They range from allegations of personal bribery to the doleful conclusion that much of the time these institutions of representative government so conduct themselves that the popular will is thwarted. Even if all the legislators were models of efficiency and rectitude, as indeed some of them are, most state legislatures would remain poorly organized and technically unequipped to do what is expected of them. They do not meet often enough nor long enough; they lack space, clerical staffing, professional assistance; they are poorly paid and overworked; they are prey to special interests, sometimes their own; their procedures and committee systems are outmoded; they devote inordinate time to local interests that distract them from general public policy; they sometimes cannot even get copies of bills on which they must vote. They work, in short, under a host of conditions that dampen their incentive and limit their ability to function effectively.

In the two decades since Heard wrote, there have been fundamental changes in American legislatures. The number of legislatures meeting only every second year has dropped from 31 to 7, and only half as many seriously restrict the length of sessions. Legislatures are much better staffed and have made good use of computer equipment. In most states legislative pay has been sharply increased. Committee systems have been streamlined, with fewer committees, fewer assignments per member, and with more open hearings and decision-making sessions. Legislators have become more experienced and thus more capable of performing effectively; between the 1960s and the 1980s, turnover dropped from 41 percent to 28 percent in the state houses and from 37 percent to 24 percent in the senates. Most of those legislatures that used to be dependent on the governor have grown more independent.

Shortly after Heard summarized the criticisms of state legislatures, Malcolm Jewell (1967: 1) described the weaknesses of the Kentucky General Assembly in similar terms:

> The Kentucky legislature has most of the characteristics that have been criticized in recent years by those who are trying to reshape state legislatures into stronger and more professional institutions. Most Kentucky legislators are inexperienced because the rate of turnover is high and the sessions are short. The constitution limits the legislature to a sixty-day session every two years, unless the governor calls a special session. During that brief period the legislature has little opportunity for careful study of legislative proposals or detailed oversight of the executive branch. The governor is traditionally one of the most powerful in the country, and he has usually dominated the legislative process.

Over the last two decades the Kentucky legislature has also undergone fundamental changes. Although it remains, in some respects, less powerful and less professional than the average state legislature, it has changed as fundamentally in two decades as these other bodies.

The constitution still limits the legislature to a sixty-day session every two years, and the voters have three times (in 1966, 1969, and 1973) rejected a change in the constitution to permit annual sessions. In 1979, however, the voters approved an amendment permitting the legislature to schedule its sixty days of meetings over a three and a half-month period.

In 1968 the legislature established an interim committee system, and since that time the interim system has gradually been strengthened to provide committees with sufficient time to study legislation and hold hearings. In 1968 the committee system was also streamlined, with fewer committees and fewer assignments per member; since that time the committees have become much better staffed and have made much greater use of hearings. The 1979 amendment changed the schedule of legislative sessions so that, following the election, the interim committees could meet for a year before the regular session. With more time and better staff resources, the Appropriations and Revenue committees have begun to review the budget more thoroughly and on occasion have significantly revised it. In the 1970s the General Assembly established several interim committees to oversee the executive agencies; these committees have grown more effective over time.

In 1979 newly elected Governor John Y. Brown. Jr., abandoned the long-established practice of dictating the choice of legislative leaders; partly as a consequence of this step, which would be difficult to reverse, recent governors have lost much of their influence over legislative decision making.

Turnover in the legislature has dropped, from nearly one-half in the 1950s and 1960s to little more than one-fifth, and a number of the legislators have served long terms in office and have become experts in their areas of specialization. This stability and experience of the membership have contributed significantly to the General Assembly's increased effectiveness and independence.

PROBLEMS OF MEASURING CHANGE

This is a study of a legislative institution in transition: the Kentucky General Assembly. Our purpose is to describe the changes that have transformed the legislative system and to try to explain both their causes and their consequences. This study is designed not only to describe what has happened in Kentucky but to shed light on how legislative institutions change.

Political scientists have described the changes that have occurred in American state legislatures, but they have done very little to explain how this process has occurred. Are these changes motivated by outside forces or by the members themselves? To what extent are reforms carefully planned, and how significant are the unanticipated consequences of reform? What are the consequences for public policy if legislators are more powerful, better informed, and more experienced? If gubernatorial control and party discipline have grown weaker, has it become more difficult for the legislature to make decisions?

Political institutions change, sometimes quickly and dramatically, sometimes slowly and almost imperceptibly. The presidency or the governorship may change quickly when a new incumbent takes office. Legislative bodies change more slowly and quietly, in part because no single individual, even a Speaker of the House, can have a sudden and dramatic impact on the institution.

Legislative institutions may change because of amendments to the constitution, decisions of the courts, new legislation or increased appropriations. They may change because the legislature gains office space or modern computers or chooses to hire additional staff. They may change because a generation of legislators comes to the legislature with different goals and skills. They may change because of external factors: a change in the balance of partisan power, the emergence of new interest groups, the appearance of new issues on the agenda, or changes in public attitudes toward the legislature.

We can identify several of the major developments in the 1960s and early 1970s that apparently contributed to change in state legislatures. Court-mandated reapportionment in the 1960s changed the urban-rural balance in legislatures. The gradual decline of urban party organizations led to the election of more independent legislators. A national legislative-reform movement had an impact in some states, contributing to the removal or relaxation of constitutional limits on legislative sessions, the adoption of procedural reforms, the revitalization of the committee system, and increases in pay for members. As the workload of the legislature, and the compensation of members, increased, a growing proportion of members sought (usually successfully) to serve several terms in the legislature. As legislative sessions lengthened and more members served multiple terms, legislators grew more visible and more politically skillful; thus, their success at the polls increased.

It is relatively easy to identify these broad trends that affected legislative change. It is much more difficult to describe and explain exactly how change came to the legislatures of individual states, or to suggest why the patterns of change have differed from one state to the next. Political scientists recognize the importance of change, but they have not been particularly successful in developing the techniques for measuring change in political institutions. In attempting to understand how the Kentucky legislature has evolved, we have very few guidelines to rely on from studies in other states.

There are several reasons for the difficulty of assessing institutional change. If change occurs slowly over two decades, as it has in Kentucky, it is difficult to monitor systematically the characteristics of the legislature over such a long period. There is often a lag time between the adoption of changes in legislative rules or procedures and changes in the way the legislature actually works, because legislators may be slow to react to these innovations. If more staff members are hired or a new computer system is installed, several years may pass before members learn to fully utilize these new resources. Older members who are accustomed to traditional ways of doing legislative business may be slower than new members to adapt to change. When political scientists first studied the consequences of new standards for state legislative reapportionment, they often concluded that the effects on policy were minimal. One reason for this conclusion was that it took several years for the effects to be felt, as newly elected urban members rose to positions of power in the legislature.

It is difficult to measure the motivations of those who initiated changes because these are often varied and sometimes obscure. Similarly, members' assessments of the consequences of change are colored by their perceptions and values. The legislature is often affected by unplanned and unobtrusive changes, such as a growth in the average tenure of membership. By definition, this develops slowly and sometimes unevenly.

It is unrealistic to describe trends in a legislative body without paying attention to the role played by particular individuals, and therefore it is difficult to test general hypotheses about the causes and consequences of institutional change. It can be argued that legislative reform started in Kentucky in 1968 because a national movement was under way to reform legislatures and because, for the first time in more than two decades, the Democratic legislature faced a Republican governor. But in practice the timing and content of the 1968 reforms were determined by a small group of legislators and the staff director of the Legislative Research Commission (LRC). Changes in the tactics of legislative leadership have resulted largely from the personality and political skills of successive leaders. It is impossible to understand how the legislature has gained control of the budgetary process without knowing something about the two men who have chaired the Senate and House Appropriations Committee for a long period of time.

Despite the difficulty of explaining change in legislative institutions, several political scientists have undertaken such studies in recent years. A few of them (Davidson and Oleszek, 1976; Cooper, 1977; Hedlund, 1980) have used concepts from general organizational theory in studying national and state legislative reform. Ronald Hedlund (1980: 15-25), for example, emphasizes the importance of understanding the relationship between the legislature and the political groups and institutions in its environment. These groups have expectations concerning the legislature and what it should accomplish, and if it fails to meet these expectations its status will suffer and it will be under pressure to change. How quickly the legislators respond to these pressures depends on their perceptions and their own viewpoints about the need for change. He emphasizes that "without a commitment by leaders and influential legislators to act seriously and follow through on changing a legislature, any success for legislative change is endangered" (20).

A number of political scientists have tried to measure the relationships between legislative structures and procedures on the one hand and the operation of the legislature and its policy outputs on the other. Hedlund (1985: 359-73) has summarized these findings briefly in tabular form; many of the findings are contradictory and they leave many questions unanswered. Some of the congressional studies and a few of the state legislative studies are cross-time analyses. But many of the state legislative studies are cross-state comparisons; this is particularly true of those in which the dependent variable is policy outputs, which are usually measured in quantitative terms. As Virginia Gray (1976) has pointed out, it is risky to infer from interstate comparisons how change occurs; it is much better to utilize cross-time analysis.

Political scientists who have tried to measure quantitatively the effects of changes over time in legislative rules, procedures, or organizational structure have faced several difficulties. One is the problem of controlling for external variables that may have affected the legislature, such as changes in federal government policies or in levels of party competition. They have sometimes had difficulty in developing plausible hypotheses for testing. For example, there are few if any a priori reasons for expecting changes in legislative structure or procedure to result in more liberal or conservative policies or higher or lower budgetary spending. It is also difficult to measure the effects of change quantitatively because these effects are often subtle and complex rather than simple and direct.

One other point must be emphasized about the limitations of any efforts to use quantitative techniques for measuring and evaluating changes in legislative institutions. It may be possible to conclude that a procedural change in time one contributed to a change in process or a policy output in time two, but it is not possible to explain how the process of change occurred. Political scientists have left unanswered most of the questions about how legislative institutions change.

Hedlund and Hamm (1975), in their analysis of conflict and perceived group benefits from legislative rules changes in the 1973-74 Wisconsin Assembly, note the difficulties of trying to measure the consequences of rule changes in the legislature. What groups are going to benefit from the rule changes? Did a change in rule or structure produce the effect it was intended to have? From interviews with legislators, they find differences between presession and postsession perceptions about which segment of an interest group sector would have an advantage under the new rules. They suggest that future research should concentrate on a learning model of attitude formation and change.

One organizational-structural change that is likely to have a major impact on the operation of the legislature is alteration in committee systems. Legislative committee operations include such organizational variables as activity structuring (task specialization, division and distribution of labor, and formalization), establishment or enlargement of support services, and distribution of authority (centralized or decentralized) (Hamm and Moncrief, 1982: 385-87). Changes in these organizational-structural variables are some of the leading innovations that have taken place in state assemblies during the past two decades; legislative scholars are interested in the effects of these structural changes on committee functioning, policy making, and the operation of the legislature as a whole.

Francis and Riddlesperger's study (1982), using a nationwide sample of state legislators, illustrates the extent to which committee systems in state legislatures have become the principal centers of decision making. Although their comprehensive fifty-state comparative analysis of committees does not focus on change per se (e.g., only includes some over-time data on factional conflict), they find that in recent years the enormous demand for legislation has amplified the need for an efficient agenda-processing system, and increasingly the responsibility falls upon the committee system, which takes advantage of division of labor and economies of scale. Francis (1985) has also explored the relationship between committee and party caucuses and leadership, a relationship that has changed in some legislatures over time.

Hamm and Moncrief's study (1982) illustrates the advantages of cross-state analysis as well as the frustrations of such analysis. The research by these scholars uses six legislative chambers, including Kentucky's, to examine the impact of reforms in committee structure on the performance of state legislative committees. The reforms included changes in activity structuring, distribution of authority, and support services. They found that structural changes had the greatest effect on those aspects of performance that the committees could most readily control—the reporting and amending of legislation. There was less evidence of a change in actions taken on the floor. Obviously, there are a number of other variables that could affect the impact of changes in committee organization, including, particularly, changes in party or factional balance within the legislature or changes in the leadership. In general, their findings do not suggest very dramatic changes resulting from reforms.

In recent years we have learned a lot about both the variety of methods and the difficulties of measuring committee activity and its consequences, mostly from the work of Keith Hamm (1978, 1982, 1984, 1986a, 1986b). This work has shown that there are great differences from one chamber to another, and even from one committee to another, in the way committees operate. This variation results from differences in rules, issues, and political conflicts, as well as differences in the political style and skills of those running the various committees. The sheer volume of Hamm's studies suggests how difficult and time consuming it would be to carry out comprehensive comparisons of committee systems from state to state and over time.

Fifty years ago the few political scientists who were trying to study the legislature in individual states worked in isolation from each other and paid little attention to theoretical issues or the comparative study of legislatures. Today the political scientists who are studying individual state legislatures are guided by common theoretical perspectives. They are asking the same questions in different settings. They are learning how complex and varied the state legislative process is, and they are beginning to understand some of the reasons for this variation.

STUDYING THE KENTUCKY LEGISLATURE

In our study of the changing legislature in Kentucky, we are guided by the same theoretical concerns of scholars in other states. We want to know how this legislature in the 1980s differs from the Kentucky General Assembly twenty years earlier, and why and how it has changed. We want to know how, and why, it differs from other state legislatures and what factors have made the process of change different in Kentucky from that in other states.

We are not trying to test any particular theory about legislative change, because not enough work has been done on this topic to produce a well defined, testable theory. We are not explicitly making use of organizational theory in studying the Kentucky legislature because of doubts about whether such an approach will enhance our understanding of legislative change.

We have chosen the Kentucky legislature as the focus of this study for several obvious reasons: there has been no book-length study of the Kentucky legislature in modern times, this institution has changed fundamentally in the last two decades, and we have been observing the legislature throughout this period of change.

A few words are appropriate about our research methods. For factual descriptions of legislative developments since the early 1960s, we have relied heavily on newspaper clippings, particularly the excellent reporting of the Louisville *Courier-Journal*. During the 1960s Malcolm Jewell wrote several articles and chapters about the legislature and was also active in the Kentucky citizens' group that sought legislative reform. We have observed the legislature through the years while teaching about it and interacting with legislative interns.

We have also carried out more systematic research. In 1967 Malcolm Jewell interviewed Jefferson County legislators as part of a multistate study of districting. In 1978-79 he systematically interviewed a sample of House members as part of a multistate study of representation. In working on this book, we utilized questionnaires from about half of the members. We also interviewed a number of members, particularly leaders and committee chairmen; staff members of committees; and a substantial number of lobbyists. Most of our interviews were tape recorded and transcribed. We promised the legislators anonymity, and consequently we have not identified members by name in quotations used in the book. We have also made use of documentary records, particularly those on committee membership and activity and roll-call voting.

There is an acute shortage of published research on the modern Kentucky legislature. We have, however, utilized several valuable doctoral dissertations done at the University of Kentucky, by Gary Cox, Gary Moncrief, and Patricia Griffin. One of our goals in writing this book is to stimulate interest in, and research on, the Kentucky legislature. In the years we have been observing the General Assembly, it has become a much more interesting and important body. It deserves more extensive scholarly attention.

This book is divided into three major parts. Part Two focuses on the individual members. Chapter 2 explains how they get elected; chapter 3 describes the characteristics of members and how these have changed in the last two decades; and chapter 4 explores the various ways in which members represent their districts.

Part Three is devoted to "the new legislature," the revitalized committee system that operates both during the sessions and in the interim. Chapter 5 concerns the operation of committees, as well as the role of chairmen and members. Chapters 6 and 7 describe the budgetary process and legislative oversight of the executive branch.

Part Four deals with politics and policy making. Chapter 8 focuses on legislative leadership and parties. Chapter 9 describes the traditionally strong role of the governor and explains how that role has been diminished. Chapter 10 examines the lobbyists and the organized interests that seek to influence decision making. The final chapter is an assessment of the causes and consequences of legislative change in Kentucky.

Part Two
A New Generation of Legislators

Thirty years ago most members of most state legislatures were amateurs, in almost every sense of that word. Most served for only a few terms; in fact, every two years four out of ten were replaced by new members. Because of this brief tenure and because legislative sessions in most states were relatively brief, most members did not develop expertise as legislators, nor did they become specialists in such fields as education or taxation.

Most legislators were also political amateurs. They did not perceive themselves as career politicians. In counties where party organizations were strong, legislators often owed their nomination to the party. Most legislators owed their election to traditional partisan voting patterns in their district, or sometimes to state or national political tides. In other words, most legislators did not get nominated and elected because of their own political skills.

There was little incentive for members to devote time and effort to their districts—either to building a political base or servicing constituent needs. Some represented large, multimember districts where such efforts were difficult. Most lacked the visibility to attract the attention of constituents. Members who planned to serve a short term in politically safe districts had no incentive to build political organizations or gain public attention by constituency contact and service.

Although there were obviously exceptions to these generalizations, the typical legislator had little experience, few if any political goals, modest legislative and political skills, little visibility, and often no incentives to change.

Over the last thirty years, there has been a dramatic change in the characteristics of legislators, and some of these changes have been more dramatic in the legislatures that used to be least professional. Legislators have become more professional—they serve longer terms, acquire more expertise, develop political skills, often plan political careers, and devote much more attention to their districts. Most legislators probably devote at

least half time to their job; in some of the larger states, a substantial proportion of them devote most of their time to the job and perceive themselves
as full-time legislators (Rosenthal 1985).

In recent years the turnover rate has dropped to only about one-fourth
of the membership, and a substantial part of that change is caused either by
electoral defeat or by members running for other offices, rather than by
members retiring voluntarily to private life (Niemi and Winsky, 1987; Calvert, 1979). Although comprehensive data are lacking, it appears that in most
states there has been a drop in the proportion of members seeking renomination and reelection who get defeated.

Most legislatures today have a substantial proportion of veteran members—those who have served five or six or more terms. There are several
more reasons legislatures include a larger proportion of experienced members who are specialists in particular areas. Legislative sessions are longer
and are held annually in most states. There is some evidence of greater
membership stability on committees, particularly the most important ones,
such as appropriations and revenue. Increasing staff resources also helps
members acquire more expertise.

There is no comprehensive set of longitudinal data to prove that today's
representatives pay more attention to the district than their predecessors
did, but it seems reasonable to draw such a conclusion. There has been a
sharp decline in the number of members elected from large multimember
districts (those with four or more members) where constituency service
would be difficult. Interviews with legislators in a number of states support
the thesis that attention to the constituency and its needs is growing. An
increasing proportion of legislators have at least one professional staff assistant who is often given particular responsibility for constituency service.
More states are providing resources for newsletters, surveys, or even district
offices—all amenities that facilitate constituency service (Jewell, 1982).

These trends in the characteristics and roles of legislators are interrelated. As legislators have grown more professional and more political, they
have learned the importance of working harder at constituency service. All
of these developments help legislators discourage serious challenges at the
polls and win reelection. Experienced legislators recognize that their activities in the district between campaigns are more important than their campaign efforts in forestalling serious opposition and upsets at the polls.

In some respects Kentucky appears to be a poor choice to illustrate the
trend toward more professional legislators. The Kentucky legislature meets
for a shorter period than the chambers in most states, few of its members
consider themselves to be full-time members, and they lack the personal
staffs that are becoming important in many state legislatures.

But, over the last twenty years or so, the Kentucky legislature has
changed as much as or more than those in other states. There has been a

dramatic decline in turnover, mostly because of changes in voluntary turnover. Consequently, a much larger proportion of members have extensive legislative experience. Although regular sessions are limited to three and one half months every two years, an extensive system of interim committees keeps conscientious members busy throughout most of the two-year cycle. On the average, throughout their term most members devote half of their time to legislative, political, and district work. Though they lack personal staff help and resources, many members devote considerable attention to communication with, and services for, their constituents. Kentucky legislators may still be more amateur than most, but they have become much more professional and have grown more politically effective in the last twenty years.

2. Getting Elected to the Kentucky Legislature

Like most states, Kentucky elects its representatives every two years and its senators every four years. Unlike any other state, Kentucky elects its legislators at a different time from its election of the governor and other statewide officers. Kentucky is one of the very few states that chooses its governor in odd-numbered years (1979, 1983, 1987), and until very recently legislators were also elected in odd-numbered years. A constitutional amendment adopted in 1979 moved the legislative elections to even-numbered years (coinciding with presidential and congressional elections) and left the gubernatorial election unchanged. This means that state legislators can run for state offices (but not for Congress) without risking their legislative seats. (During the transition to a new election schedule, representatives elected in 1981 served a three-year term until the 1984 election, and senators served a five-year term.)

There are several questions that need to be answered about legislative elections. What proportion of legislators seek reelection, and how many succeed? What proportion of legislators face serious opposition? Is the primary or the general election the most serious obstacle faced by incumbent legislators? What determines the outcome of legislative elections? Is it the traditional Democratic or Republican voting patterns in the districts? Is it the ability to raise money? If incumbents have a major advantage, is it because they are well known, they have better financing, or for other reasons? Finally, we want to know what trends are occurring.

PATTERNS OF COMPETITION

Turnover of Incumbents. We begin by looking at the electoral fate of incumbent legislators (table 1). The most dramatic change from 1947 to 1986

Table 1. Electoral Fate of Incumbent Legislators

Years	Reelected (%)	Retired (%)	Lost Primary (%)	Lost General Election (%)	Winners as % of Those Who Ran	Number
		House of Representatives				
1947-65*	41.0	44.0	11.0	4.0	73.2	900
1971-77	66.5	22.0	9.0	2.5	85.3	400
1979-86	79.0	11.8	6.2	3.0	89.5	400
		Senate				
1947-65*	32.2	52.0	14.6	1.2	67.1	171
1971-77	46.1	32.9	14.5	6.5	68.6	76
1979-86	69.7	19.7	6.6	4.0	86.9	76

*The 1947-65 data exclude the 1963 election, the first election after reapportionment.

was an increase in the proportion of legislators who seek reelection. From the mid 1940s to the mid 1960s, an average of 44 percent of the House members retired every two years, and losses at the polls raised the turnover rate to almost 60 percent. In the Senate over half of the members whose terms expired retired every two years; the turnover rate was just over two-thirds.

There has been a significant drop in voluntary (nonelectoral) retirement from the legislature in very recent years: from 1971 to 1977 only 22 percent of the representatives retired; during the 1979-86 period, the proportion of retirees fell to 12 percent. There have been similar changes in the Senate. The retirement rate for members of the Kentucky House now approximates that in the U.S. House, which was 9 percent for the years 1976 to 1984.

One important but little-known reason for the sharp drop in the retirement rate is the disappearance of rotation agreements. During the 1947-65 period, more than one-third of the representatives and almost one-fourth of the senators who "voluntarily" retired had been elected from districts having rotation agreements. These were found in House districts with two counties (the maximum number) and Senate districts with two or three counties. The agreements were made between the various county committees of the dominant political party, and they specified that the party's nomination was to go to a person in another county after a member had served one or two terms. These were only effective in those districts dominated by a single party. Although some legislators from these districts might have have retired as quickly in the absence of rotation agreements, the effect of these agreements was clearly to compel members to retire after relatively short legislative careers, although some served again when their county had its next term. These agreements collapsed quickly after the mid-1960s because the

Table 2. Winning Margins for Incumbents in Primary Elections, 1973-
1986

Winning Margin (%)	Democratic Primary			Republican Primary		
	Incumbent			Incumbent		
	Won (%)	Lost (%)	None (%)	Won (%)	Lost (%)	None (%)
House of Representatives						
Under 50	6	35	46	6	87	19
50-60	12	43	18	9	7	19
61-70	14	19	15	11	7	3
71+	14	3	5	4	—	22
100	55	—	15	70	—	38
Number	(420)	(37)	(78)	(118)	(15)	(32)
Senate						
Under 50	9	18	44	4	—	33
50-60	14	64	24	4	—	11
61-70	17	18	12	9	—	—
71+	14	—	8	4	—	11
100	46	—	12	78	—	44
Number	(65)	(11)	(25)	(23)	—	(9)

new rules for reapportionment required that some rural districts (particularly in the Senate) be larger and that more of the district boundaries cut across county lines to achieve equality.

Incumbents seldom lose when they seek reelection, but today's incumbents are somewhat more successful than those in the earlier period. The rate of success at the polls for those incumbents who run has increased from almost three-fourths in the 1947-65 period to about seven-eighths in the 1971-86 elections in the House, and from two-thirds to over four-fifths in the Senate (table 1). Incumbent representatives are three times more likely to be defeated in the primaries than in general elections, a ratio that has not changed since the earlier period. (The small number of senatorial defeats occur less exclusively in primaries than in the past.)

Levels of Primary Competition. To explain the electoral success of incumbents, we must examine separately primary and general elections, beginning with the former. The advantage enjoyed by incumbents is most evident in primary elections. In the elections from 1973 through 1986, fewer than 10 percent of the legislators seeking renomination were defeated (table 2). In more than half of the primary elections in which incumbent representatives and senators ran, there was no opposition. Republican incumbents were even less likely to have opposition than Democrats. Only 17 percent of the winning representatives and 19 percent of the senators had margins of 60 percent or less. On the other hand, when incumbents were defeated in the primary, the margin was usually close. (Similar results have been found in studies of primary competition in other states; see Grau [1981] and Jewell [1982: chap. 2].)

In the absence of an incumbent in the race, primary competition (in the incumbent's party) becomes much closer; the proportion of uncontested primaries is only 22 percent in the House and 21 percent in the Senate. More of the primaries without incumbents are closely contested; over one-third are won by less than a majority and over half are won by under 60 percent. This primary competition is much stronger in Democratic than in Republican primaries.

One reason there is often strong competition in Democratic, nonincumbent primaries is that the winner faces little or no Republican opposition. This makes the nomination more valuable and attracts more candidates; moreover, the Democratic primary is the only practical route to political office. In most of the districts held by Republicans, the party is less dominant; this may explain why there is less competition in Republican nonincumbent primaries.

In both parties there is much more likely to be competition in the incumbent's party primary when the incumbent retires. Potential candidates who are reluctant to run against the incumbent wait more or less patiently for his or her retirement and then rush to enter the race. Now that incumbents are serving longer terms, a race without an incumbent is less frequent and is likely to attract even more contestants.

For the party out of power in a district, it is often difficult to find one candidate to enter the race, and primary competition is less common. During 1973-86 in Democratic House districts, the Republicans ran no candidate in 58 percent of the cases and only one candidate in 34 percent, leaving only 8 percent with primaries. In the much smaller number of districts held by Republicans, the Democrats had no candidate in 38 percent of races, only one in 37 percent, and a primary contest in 25 percent.

Almost half of the Republican primaries in Democratic districts occurred in Jefferson County, along with one-third of the Democratic primaries in Republican districts. The two parties are better organized in Jefferson County, and there are a larger proportion of close districts, providing minority party candidates with more incentive to run.

Generally, there was most likely to be primary competition in the opposition party when there was some realistic possibility of winning the general election. One-third of these primaries occurred when the incumbent was not seeking reelection; the opposition had primaries in 26 percent of the elections with an incumbent retiring and in only 9 percent of the cases with an incumbent running. Remarkably, there was an opposition primary

Figure 1. Seats Contested by One or Both Parties in Legislative Races (percentage)

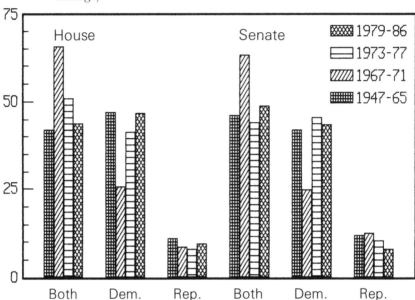

in over 60 percent of the cases when there was partisan turnover in a race. The proportion of opposition primaries was one-third in districts where the majority party won by 55 percent or less, and it dropped to less than one-tenth in districts where the majority party had over 70 percent.

Patterns of General Election Competition. In roughly half of the general election contests, only one party runs a candidate. There have been few changes in that pattern over the last forty years (figure 1). During the 1947-65 period, 47 percent of the House seats were contested only by Democrats and 11 percent only by Republicans. During the most recent period, 1979-86, 47 percent of the House seats were contested only by Democrats and 9 percent only by Republicans. The chart shows comparable figures for the Senate. The only significant change in the pattern occurred in the 1967-71 elections, during and immediately following the Republican administration of Louie Nunn, when the Republicans made a greater effort to recruit candidates; the proportion of seats contested only by Democrats fell to one-fourth in the House and the Senate.

Only 19 percent of all House elections in the 1973-86 period are won by 60 percent or less of the two-party vote, and only 11 percent are won by 55 percent or less (table 3). The proportions of close Senate races are comparable. There are important differences between the two parties. In both houses only 8 or 9 percent of Democrats are elected by 55 percent or less,

Table 3. Electoral Margins in House and Senate General Elections, 1973-1986

Winning Margin (%)	All Races (%)	Democrat Won (%)	Republican Won (%)	Incumbent		No Incumbent	
				Won (%)	Lost (%)	Same Party (%)	Partisan Change (%)
			House of Representatives				
50-60	19	14	41	15	100	21	80
61-70	16	16	15	16	—	19	10
71+	11	13	6	12	—	11	—
100	53	58	38	57	—	49	10
Number	(700)	(538)	(162)	(530)	(19)	(141)	(10)
			Senate				
50-60	19	14	46	13	100	14	100
61-70	18	17	20	16	—	21	—
71+	11	12	7	10	—	14	—
100	53	58	37	60	—	51	—
Number	(133)	(103)	(30)	(82)	(6)	(43)	(2)

compared to about one-fourth of the Republicans. At the other extreme, 58 percent of winning Democrats and 38 percent of successful Republicans are elected without partisan opposition. When partisan change occurs in the House, the margin is usually close.

When an incumbent wins the general election with little or no serious opposition, it may be because the district is safe for one party or because the incumbent is well known and popular. A close examination of table 3 indicates that partisan domination of most House districts is more important than the political strength of incumbents. When there is no partisan turnover, the distribution of victory margins is about the same whether an incumbent is running or not. A party's chances of winning are greater, however, when it has an incumbent in the race. When an incumbent is running in the House, the other party runs a candidate only 45 percent of the time compared to 54 percent when there is no incumbent. Moreover, partisan turnover in the House occurs only 3.5 percent of the time with an incumbent, compared to 6.6 percent when no incumbent is running.

We have seen that in most elections to the Senate and House, half or more of the districts are contested by only one party. This is because most areas of Kentucky, outside the major metropolitan counties, are dominated by one or the other political party—especially in state and local elections. Consequently, there are many Democratic legislative districts and a few Republican ones that are won consistently by one party with little or no opposition. Patterns of one-party domination in House districts are consistent for the elections from 1973 through 1981, a period when district boundaries were largely unchanged (table 4). In 22 of these districts the dominant party was never challenged; in 41 districts (36 Democratic and 5 Republican) it was challenged never or only once. In 84 districts the same party won the district in all five elections; in only 16 was there any turnover.

By far the highest level of competition is found in Jefferson County. Of the 22 House districts in Jefferson County, 19 had partisan competition in all five elections and 3 had such contests all but once. Of the 16 districts that had some partisan turnover in the five elections, exactly half were in Jefferson County; two were in other metropolitan counties, four in eastern Kentucky, and two in west-central Kentucky.

Fayette County, the other major metropolitan county, had a much less consistent pattern of competition. In the six House districts entirely or partly in the county, there was a partisan contest in only 16 of 30 possible times; in 1979 there was party competition in none of the six Fayette districts (five Democratic and one Republican).

The areas where legislative competition is rare coincide with the areas dominated by one party in other elections. Figure 2 shows the House districts in which one party ran unopposed in four or five elections from 1973 through 1981. Figure 3 shows the counties dominated by one party in the presidential, U.S. senatorial, and gubernatorial elections from 1967 through 1980. Although the overlap between the two maps is not perfect, it is relatively close. The 41 districts that rarely if ever have partisan competition are ones containing counties that vote with great consistency for one party in statewide elections.

EXPLAINING ELECTION OUTCOMES

In legislative districts dominated by a single party, the outcome of legislative elections can be explained almost entirely by traditional partisan loyalties, the weakness of the opposition party organization, and consequently the shortage of viable opposition candidates. In districts where there is stronger two-party competition—or occasional partisan turnover—we should explore other explanations for the outcome. Similarly, in primary elections, where partisanship is not pertinent, we look for clues to explain the outcome.

How big an advantage do incumbents have? How important is campaign funding? When there is an upset in legislative elections—a partisan turnover or the defeat of an incumbent in the primary—what is the explanation? Why are most incumbents not seriously challenged in legislative races?

Funding Legislative Races. What does it cost to get elected to the legislature? If it costs only a few hundred or a couple of thousand dollars to run a

Table 4. Party Domination in House Districts, 1973-1981

	Democratic	Republican	Total
Dominant party never challenged	21	1	22
Dominant party challenged once	15	4	19
Dominant party challenged more than once, no party turnover	31	12	43
Party turnover at least once	—	—	16
Total	67	17	100

competitive race, then anyone who is a plausible candidate should be able to pay for the campaign from his or her own resources and from those of friends and associates. If it costs a lot more to be a competitive candidate, then it becomes much more difficult to defeat an incumbent, who usually has greater opportunities and more experience in raising money. A challenger must have either substantial personal resources or the support of an effective party organization or other organized groups.

Studies of congressional races have shown that the success of a challenger depends very heavily on that individual's ability to raise large campaign funds (Jacobson, 1980). Congressional incumbents are relatively well known, whereas challengers are often nearly invisible to the average voter at the start of the race. Challengers must mount an extensive campaign to gain name recognition and develop the themes of their campaign. It is expensive to carry out a campaign that will reach the voters in a U.S. House district that has an average population of 550,000. Generally speaking, incumbents are able to raise as much as is necessary to match or exceed the spending of challengers.

State legislative races are not simply small-scale congressional races. For several reasons we might expect money to play a smaller role in legislative races. There may be a smaller difference in visibility between incumbent and challenger. State legislators are not usually as well known or as successful in generating media publicity as are congressmen. Although most legislative challengers are not experienced politicians, some of them have been active enough in community affairs (as church leaders, Little League coaches, or business persons) to become personally known to as many persons as an incumbent legislator.

Giles and Pritchard (1985), in their study of funding for legislative races in the Florida House between 1972 and 1980, found that in most election years candidate spending has a significant effect on outcomes, but the effects of incumbency, partisan balance in the district, and short-term party trends are so great as to overshadow the effect of spending differences. The effects of spending on outcomes are much greater for challengers than for incumbents, a finding that coincides with congressional research. Research focusing

Figure 2. Legislative Districts in Which One Party Ran Unopposed in at Least Four of Five Elections, 1973-1981

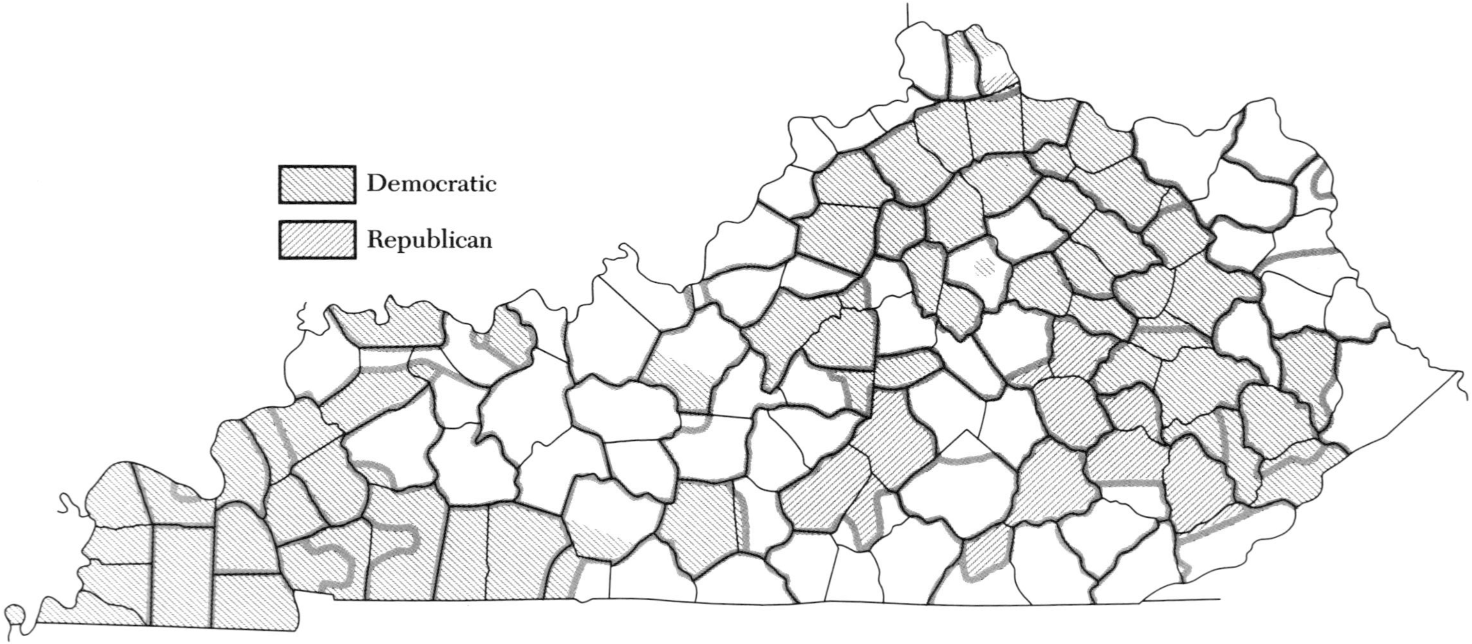

Democratic

Republican

25

Figure 3. Counties Heavily Favoring One Party in National and State Elections, 1967-1980

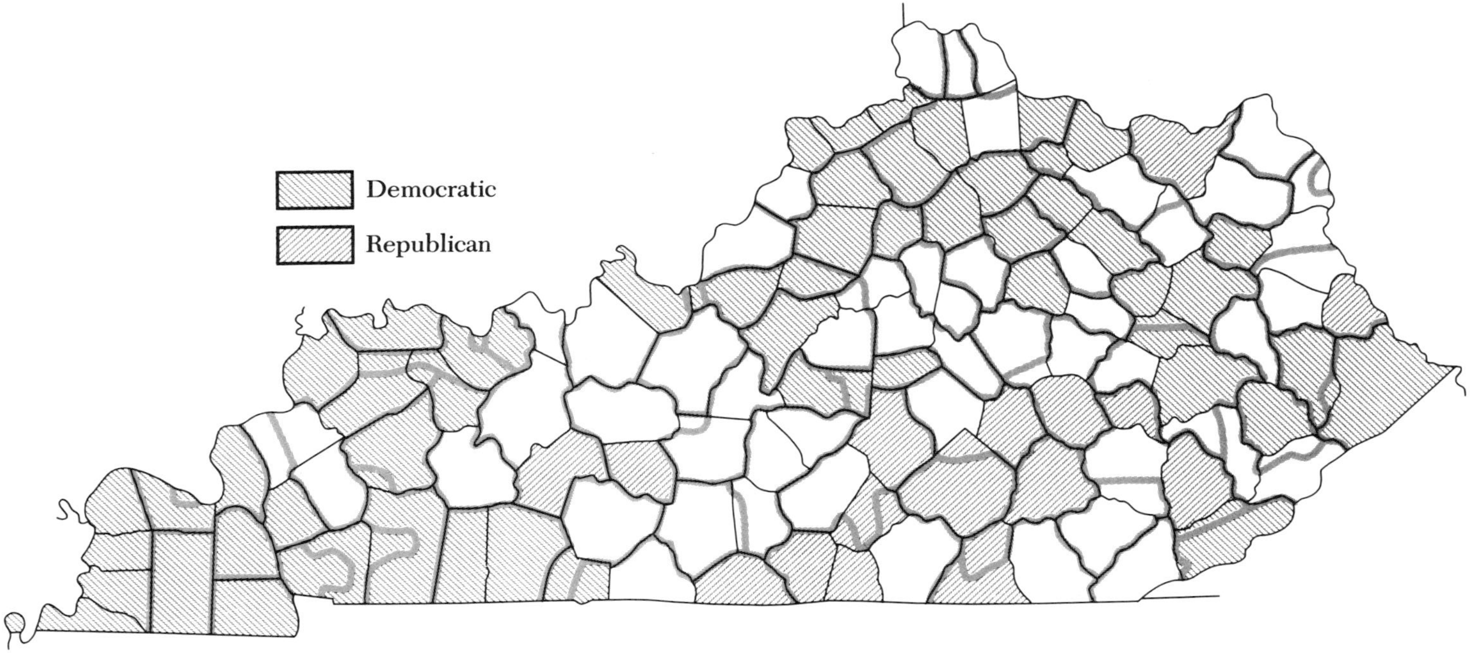

Democratic

Republican

on the United States House and Senate (Jacobson, 1980) and on a handful of state legislatures (see Glantz, Abramowitz, and Burkart, 1976 [California Assembly]; Boyd, 1982 [Houses of Georgia and Wisconsin]; Jones and Borris, 1983, 1985 [Minnesota House and Senate]) has consistently found campaign contributions to be linked to electoral outcomes and the effects of campaign contributions to be greater for challengers than for incumbents.

In some districts campaign costs are relatively low because the use of television advertising may not be feasible. Moreover, it is possible to reach many voters by inexpensive means: door-to-door campaigning, speeches to community groups, yard signs, and similar techniques. Campaign costs might also be low simply because there are not enough contributors who are willing to contribute generously to a race at that level.

In theory, then, we would expect legislative races to be relatively inexpensive, with money not having a crucial impact. In practice, what can we learn about the role of money in the Kentucky legislative races?

The total costs of winning election to the legislature in contested races are summarized in table 5. Some winners have opposition only in the primary or only in the general election, whereas others are opposed at both levels. It usually costs more to win when both the primary and general election are contested. The median cost of winning two contests is less than twice as much as the cost of winning just one election—presumably because few winners have strong opposition in both the primary and the general election. (Some candidates with opposition only in the general election spend money during the primary; this is included in the total because it may help the candidate in the fall election.)

The most obvious finding in table 5 is that the cost is so much more to be elected to the Senate than to the House. There are about 100,000 people in the average Senate district and 38,000 in a House district, a ratio of 2.6 to 1. It has generally cost from two to three times as much to run successfully for the Senate, though the small number of Senate races in any one category makes precise comparisons impossible.

The most striking finding is that the cost of winning elections is rapidly increasing. Between 1975 and 1984 the median costs of running in a contested general election or primary and general election increased by five to six times; the increase for just contested primaries was only two and a half times. The increases in the costs of Senate races are nearly as dramatic, though the small number of races in each category makes exact comparison difficult. If we combine all types of contested Senate elections, the median cost of winning rose from about $5,600 in 1975 to about $24,700 in 1983, an increase of 440 percent. Another way of measuring change is to compare the proportion of expensive races. In 1975 only one winner of a House race spent over $10,000; in 1984 there were 39 winning candidates, over half the total

Table 5. Cost of Winning Election to the Legislature

	Elections with any Opposition					
	Primary and General Election		Only Primary		Only General Election	
Year	Median ($)	Maximum ($)	Median ($)	Maximum ($)	Median ($)	Maximum ($)
	House					
1984	13,783	73,839	6,434	22,715	12,271	41,997
1981	7,955	25,435	4,331	17,910	6,138	30,231
1979	5,134	12,127	4,390	26,167	3,542	13,605
1977	4,075	13,938	2,090	19,820	3,153	11,676
1975	2,482	6,584	2,395	13,417	1,870	8,688
	Senate					
1983	28,483	89,751	23,075	22,802	26,311	31,170
1981	26,397	35,762	16,766	22,193	16,332	27,821
1979	9,192	12,613	7,636	66,578	7,089	28,997
1977	13,699	20,166	7,254	12,161	10,914	20,918
1975	4,125	15,052	5,623	29,947	6,510	8,441
	Constant Dollars: House					
1984	7,141	38,259	3,333	11,769	6,358	21,761
1975	2,482	6,584	2,395	13,417	1,870	8,688
	Constant Dollars: Senate					
1983	15,398	48,514	12,473	12,325	14,222	16,849
1975	4,125	15,052	5,623	29,947	6,510	8,441

in contested races, spending that much. The number of Senate races costing over $20,000 rose from two in 1975 to twelve in 1983.

A major reason for the increased cost of campaigns, of course, is the rise in the cost of living; the consumer price index nearly doubled between 1975 and 1984. Has the cost of campaigning for the Kentucky legislature risen faster than the cost of living? In most cases it has. If we recalculate campaign spending using constant (1975) dollars (the last four rows of the table), we find that the median cost of most categories of races doubled or tripled over a period of five elections. The maximum cost of an election rose substantially in most categories, but fell in cases where the only competition was in the primary.

Many of the most expensive winning House races are found in the two largest counties; in 1979 and 1981, 13 of 22 House races costing over $10,000 were in Jefferson or Fayette counties. But only two of eleven Senate races in those years costing over $20,000 were in those two metropolitan counties. In 1984 the most expensive successful House campaign, costing almost

$74,000, was in Fayette County (the losing Democrat in the primary and the losing Republican in the general election spent another $70,000). In 1983 the most expensive Senate campaign was in a district largely in Pike County; the winner spent over $84,000 in the Democratic primary (beating a candidate who spent almost $77,000) and another $5,400 in the general election.

It has become expensive to run a competitive race for the Kentucky Senate and in some House districts. Unless they are wealthy, candidates who must raise $15,000 to $20,000 or more must devote considerable effort to fund raising, and in most cases must have the support of local party leaders or other organized groups. The cost of mounting an effective challenge to an incumbent senator is a serious obstacle to any challenger. When no incumbent is running, the higher level of competition is likely to increase campaign costs.

How important is campaign funding to an explanation of legislative election results? One rather simple way of answering this question is to find out what proportion of times the winner was not the candidate spending most in a primary or general election campaign. Figure 4 shows that the winning candidate was not the highest spender in about one-fourth of the general elections and one-third of the primary races. Except in the case of senatorial primaries, lower spenders win most often when an incumbent is upset and least often when an incumbent runs and wins.

These data suggest several conclusions about the role of money in legislative races. Because so many districts are dominated by one party, it is unusual for the minority party to raise more money than the majority party, especially if an incumbent is running again. In primary elections a challenger is somewhat more likely to spend more money than the incumbent. About 40 percent of the time that a challenger beats an incumbent in either a primary or general election, the challenger spends less than does the incumbent—a somewhat surprising finding.

These data on high spending and electoral success do not tell us much about the impact of money on legislative races. They do not distinguish between large and small differences in spending levels, and they do not measure the relative impact of campaign spending, traditional party loyalties (in general elections), incumbency, and other variables that might influence election outcomes.

The best way to separate the effects of spending from other campaign variables is to use a multiple regression analysis. In analyzing general elections, there is little point in trying to explain the effect of money on results in those districts that are completely dominated by one party and where the other party either runs no candidate or provides a candidate with little support. For this analysis we have included only 29 of the 100 House districts: those that either had some partisan turnover in the elections from 1973

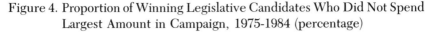

Figure 4. Proportion of Winning Legislative Candidates Who Did Not Spend
Largest Amount in Campaign, 1975-1984 (percentage)

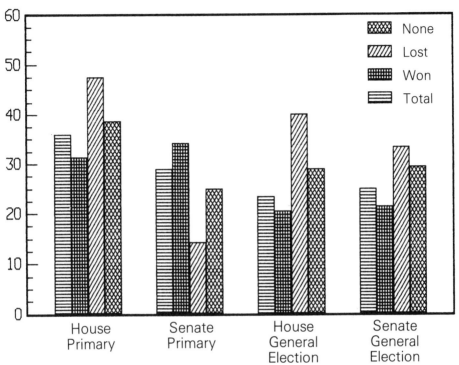

through 1981 or had a partisan electoral margin under 60 percent in at least
two of those five elections. These are districts where both Democratic and
Republican candidates have a plausible chance of winning and where substantial increases in campaign funding might be expected to make a difference
in the vote. The analysis is conducted for each contested general election
in these 29 districts for the years 1975, 1977, 1979, and 1981.

The dependent variable in the multiple regression analysis is the percentage of votes won by the Democratic candidate. The independent variables are the average Democratic vote (in contested races) for the five
elections 1973-81, a dummy variable for a Democratic incumbent running,
a dummy variable for a Republican incumbent, the amount spent by the
Democratic candidate, and the amount spent by the Republican candidate.

In a stepwise multiple regression analysis, the average Democratic vote
proves to be the only significant variable, explaining 65 percent of the variance. This suggests that traditional voting patterns largely explain the out-

come of the legislative races. If the average Democratic vote is omitted from the regression analysis, the presence of a Democratic incumbent becomes the most important variable, explaining 32 percent of the variance; spending by each of the candidates has a significant effect but raises the proportion of the dependent variable explained to only 38 percent. (If the difference between the Democratic percentage and the average Democratic vote is treated as the dependent variable, none of the independent variables is significant.)

How can we interpret such an analysis? It appears that spending patterns occasionally can affect the election results, but they are usually overwhelmed by two much more important variables: the traditional voting pattern and the presence of incumbents in the race.

In order to understand why campaign spending has little effect on general elections, we need to know more about spending patterns. Much of the time there are not large differences between the two candidates. In the 1975 and 1977 elections in these more competitive districts, the difference in spending between winners and losers was less than $1,500 in 59 percent of the races, though in 1979 and 1981 that figure fell to 30 percent.

When there are substantial differences in spending levels, they usually reflect the dominant partisan loyalties of the district. The minority party candidate seldom spends a lot more than the majority party candidate; when this does occur it seldom has any dramatic effect on the majority party's margin.

Explaining Upsets in General Elections. The normal pattern in Kentucky legislative elections is for incumbents to win renomination in primaries without strong opposition, and for each party to maintain control of those districts that it has controlled in the past. Occasionally, however, an incumbent gets defeated in either the primary or general election. By examining these exceptions to the rule, we may learn more about the patterns of legislative elections and the potential for greater primary and general election competition. When incumbents lose, is it because of their ineffectiveness as legislators or candidates, the importance of issues, changes in traditional voting patterns, factional politics, or for other reasons?

In Senate elections from 1979 through 1986, only three incumbents lost a general election; in House elections from 1979 through 1986, there were twelve defeats of incumbents in the fall elections. One losing senator in 1979 was Donald Johnson, a Republican serving his fourth term, who shifted to the Democratic party and then narrowly lost to Republican Jim Bunning (who subsequently ran for governor). Presumably, Johnson's defection upset constituents in the normally Republican district. The two other losing senators, McGee in 1983 and Middleton in 1986, were narrowly beaten in close districts in metropolitan areas.

Six of the twelve defeats of House incumbents during these four general elections occurred in Jefferson County. Districts in this county are among the most competitive in the state for several reasons: a number of them are closely balanced in partisan terms, voters in the county may vote more independently than do most voters, and the two parties make a relatively strong effort to recruit candidates in most of the districts.

The best example of a competitive Jefferson County district is the 38th. An incumbent Republican, Dexter Wright, was beaten by 52 percent in 1973; he came back in 1975 to win by 58 percent, and was reelected in the next two elections by 55 and 52 percent; in 1981 he was defeated by 51 percent, and lost a comeback effort in 1984 by the same margin. Similarly, in the 27th district, the Democrats won control by a small margin in 1973, and the Democratic incumbent lost narrowly in 1981. In 1984 redistricting produced a merger of the 27th and 28th districts; the freshman incumbent Republican in the 27th defeated an entrenched Democrat in the 28th.

Even in districts that are marginal in partisan terms, it is possible for an entrenched incumbent to be reelected by comfortable margins. An incumbent who is well known and hard working can win votes from both parties, and the more entrenched he or she becomes the less likely the other party is to recruit a strong challenger. For example, Democrat Bob Benson had carried the 33d district in several elections, usually by comfortable margins. He was an effective legislator and chairman of the Jefferson Democratic delegation. But in 1979 he was upset by Republican Bob Heleringer, who was prominent in the antiabortion movement and campaigned vigorously. Heleringer has subsequently been reelected by large margins. In the 32d district, Republican Bruce Blythe served ten terms in the House and appeared to be a conscientious legislator who was skilled in the use of the media. But during the 1970s his electoral margins were relatively narrow, 55 to 61 percent, reflecting the close partisan balance of the district. In 1981 he was defeated by Fred Cowan, a young lawyer who campaigned hard, won by a 55 percent margin, and defeated Blythe again in 1984 by the same margin.

Two defeats of incumbents provide good examples of the impact that intraparty factionalism can have on general elections. In both cases an incumbent was defeated in a primary, giving the minority party a chance to win the seat, but two years later the new incumbent was beaten in the general election. One example occurred in the 22d district, which includes Monroe County (heavily Republican), Allen County (narrowly Republican), and part of Simpson County (Democratic). The district is normally Republican, and that party has rotated the seat for four-year periods between Allen and Monroe. In 1977 the incumbent Republican, Richard Turner, trying to extend Monroe County's control of the seat beyond four years, was challenged by three opponents in the primary and lost by 120 votes out of almost

6,800. The primary left the Republican party deeply divided, and the candidate who defeated Turner lost the general election; he won only one-third of the vote in Allen County, and his total of 4,232 votes was less than two-thirds of the votes cast in the party's primary. The winning Democratic, Buel Guy, worked hard to provide constituent services and build a strong political base during his two-year term. But in 1979 the Republican party was united; Turner easily won the Republican primary and defeated Guy by 2,000 votes in November.

The other case was in the normally Democratic 76th district in Fayette County where a veteran incumbent, Jerry Lundergan, lost a hotly contested Democratic primary race in 1984 to Shirley Cunningham. In the general election Cunningham, who is black, was defeated by by Republican Marjorie Stewart in a race that had racial overtones. Two years later Lundergan staged a comeback, winning the primary and defeating the Republican incumbent by a comfortable margin.

Most of the other defeats of incumbents outside of Jefferson County occurred in districts where there is relatively close two-party balance. In 1981, for example, in the 96th district, which included a Democratic and a Republican County, the Republican incumbent was defeated by a Democrat who was able to win a larger majority than usual in the Democratic County.

Explaining Defeats of Incumbents in Primaries. Five incumbent senators lost primaries from 1979 through 1986, and 25 representatives lost primaries from 1979 through 1986 (11 of them in 1984). There is no single, simple reason for these defeats; there are doubtless as many explanations as there are races. We will look at cases that illustrate some of the conditions under which upsets are likely.

The advantages of incumbency obviously disappear when redistricting forces incumbents into the same district. Two of the 11 incumbents who lost primaries in 1984 were forced to run against other incumbents (in addition to one—already mentioned—who lost in the general election). These forced confrontations all occurred in Jefferson County, which lost population relative to the state as a whole. There were major population losses in the central city, and as a consequence there were two primary contests between white and black incumbents. Both of the blacks were defeated, one by a single vote. (An alternative districting plan, which would have forced the two black incumbents to run against each other, had been opposed by black groups in Louisville.)

Redistricting may be harmful to incumbents even when they are not forced into contests with other incumbents. If the boundaries of their district are changed drastically, they must campaign in unfamiliar areas and seek electoral support from constituents who may never have heard of them.

Moreover, when redistricting weakens the incumbent's normal advantages, strong challengers may have a greater incentive to enter the race.

In 1984, the first election year after redistricting, more incumbents were defeated in the primary than had occurred for some time. Did redistricting contribute to some of these defeats (beyond the two who lost to other incumbents)? This does not appear to have been the case. There were changes in some of the districts of defeated candidates, but for the most part they were not drastic ones.

Prior to the mid-1960s, when Kentucky was forced to conform to judicial standards for districting, many rural counties used rotation agreements (discussed earlier in the chapter), which normally provided that every four years a seat be rotated between the two House districts or among two or more Senate districts. (We noted that the remains of such an agreement has persisted in Monroe and Allen counties.) The purpose of such agreements was to give each county its own legislator a share of the time. The strong county loyalties that inspired such agreements continue to be found in some county elections.

Where local loyalties are strong, the winner of a primary may be largely determined by the number of candidates running from each district. A good example is the 84th district, which during the 1970s consisted of Estill and Jackson Counties and a part of Madison County. Most of the competition is in the Republican primary. In 1973 incumbent Sam Brewer of Estill defeated Lloyd McKinney of Jackson, who had represented a district with different boundaries in the late 1960s. In 1975 Charles Muncy of Estill defeated McKinney and another candidate from Jackson, getting 93 percent of his vote from Estill County. In 1977 the Estill County vote was split between Muncy and another candidate from that county. The only candidate from Jackson was McKinney, who won with 86 percent of his vote from Jackson. In 1979 there was one candidate from each of the three counties; McKinney won by three votes, getting 73 percent of all his votes from his county. In 1981 there were two candidates from Jackson, two from Madison, and only one from Estill. Clarence Noland of Estill won, getting 70 percent of his total from his own county. The incumbent McKinney lost votes in Jackson County to Noland and particularly to the other Estill candidate. When McKinney was interviewed after the 1977 election, he was fatalistic about electoral prospects. He apparently did not campaign aggressively or try to build a strong organization. He believed he had won because he was the only candidate from Jackson, and he would probably continue to win unless he faced a serious opponent in Jackson and only one opponent from Estill. He proved to be right.

Two of the incumbent senators who lost primaries represented the 31st district, and their battles reflected deep factional divisions within that district—particularly in Pike county, which has the largest share of votes in the district. In 1979 John Doug Hays defeated Senator Kelsey Friend, the majority whip, by 567 votes after outspending him by by about $63,000 to $24,000. The race foreshadowed a bitter primary contest for county judge executive in 1981. The winner of the judge's race, Paul Patton, who was also serving as state Democratic chairman, supported Friend's successful effort in 1983 to recapture the Senate seat from Hays. Friend outspent Hays by $84,000 to $77,000 in that race. The 1979 and 1983 senatorial primaries in the 31st district were the two most expensive senatorial primary or general election races that had been held in the state.

A different kind of factionalism emerged in the 25th district where veteran Representative Allene Craddock lost the Democratic primary to Chester Gregory in 1984. Gregory had the assistance of many district supporters of Governor Collins, although Craddock denied reports that she had supported Harvey Sloane in the governor's race. There is no reason to believe the governor played any direct role in this or any other Democratic primary in 1983. In the 1950s and 1960s, however, the governor and his local organizations often supported legislative candidates in the Democratic primary occurring in the middle of his term, at least in part to build support for his legislative program in the second half of the term.

A major reason incumbents have become more difficult to defeat is that many of them serve a number of terms and build strong political bases in the district. Fourteen of the 25 representatives defeated in primaries had served only one or two terms, giving them less opportunity to become entrenched. On the other hand, 7 of them were defeated after having served from four to eight terms.

One veteran member of the House, who has repeatedly been renominated and reelected without opposition, told us that he wished he would have at least an occasional opponent. After years without opposition, there was little incentive to maintain the high level of constituent contacts and service that he felt he ought to be doing. Another disadvantage was "You don't keep your contacts or your organization." Moreover, for many years he had had no opportunity to demonstrate his vote-getting ability, and he was concerned that eventually a really strong opponent would recognize that the incumbent was untested and would run a strong race against him.

Four of the seven veteran representatives who lost primaries had faced either no opponents or no serious opposition in the previous three primary elections (and no serious general election challenges). This may have made them unprepared for, and more vulnerable to, a strong challenger. The other three veteran opponents had faced primary opposition more frequently; in one case the incumbent's relatively narrow margin in past primaries may have made him a target for a strong opponent. Perhaps the best experience an incumbent can have is a record of trouncing the occasional opponents who appear on the electoral scene.

Perhaps the most common issue raised by challengers is that incumbents have not been effective: they have not worked hard enough, have failed to represent constituency interests, have not been accessible, or have failed to provide services to constituents. In recent years legislators have become more experienced and professional, more active both in Frankfort and in their districts. These trends have generally helped incumbents become more visible, but they may also have raised the expectations of constituents, thus making some legislators vulnerable to the criticism that they have not been doing enough. This criticism is an easy one for the challenger to make, whether accurate or not, and it is less risky than raising controversial issues.

Most of the incumbents who were beaten in the 1984 primaries were criticized along these lines by challengers. For example, in the 53d district, challenger David Williams claimed that Representative Richard Fryman was not the primary sponsor of any legislation and had not even made a speech in the previous legislative session. Fryman replied that by the time other legislators finish speaking on an issue, "there's nothing left to say unless you want to showboat." Williams also claimed that Fryman, a former professional boxer, lacked the education and qualifications to represent his district effectively.

In the 75th district in Fayette County, Ernesto Scorsone charged that Representative Carolyn Kenton had failed to achieve significant legislative results and had not paid enough attention to her constituents. In the 77th district, challenger Louis Mack charged that Representative David Van Horn "in 12 years has not introduced and passed one single major bill," and had failed to be accessible to constituents. He ridiculed Van Horn for wasting legislative time on his pet legislative project: a bill to designate the coon hound as Kentucky's official dog.

In some cases the personal character and activities of the incumbent become the major issue. The best example of that is the defeat of Elmer Patrick in the 82d district Republican primary. Patrick had been a controversial figure in the district throughout his legislative career. He had attracted a great deal of unfavorable publicity during the 1984 session when he claimed that he had been offered a ten thousand dollar bribe by a banking lobbyist and expressed the view that similar offers had been made to other members. His opponent charged that these accusations, which were never substantiated, had damaged Patrick's effectiveness. The challenger also accused Patrick of using his office to promote his coal and oil business.

In the 1986 Democratic primary in the 32d senatorial district, the challenger, former Representative Nicholas Kafoglis, succeeded in making the political activities of Senator Frank Miller the major issue in the campaign. Two years earlier Miller had run an unsuccessful primary campaign against veteran congressman William Natcher, and Kafoglis was able to capitalize on the resentment felt by Natcher's loyal supporters. Kafoglis criticized Miller, who was chairman of the Banking and Insurance Committee, for actively soliciting campaign contributions from bankers. Kafoglis described "the quality of representation" as the main issue in the campaign and claimed that Senator Miller had a record of high absenteeism in the legislature.

How important have issues been in the defeat of incumbents? It is always difficult to make judgments about campaign issues. Candidates may emphasize issues in their campaign literature and speeches, and issues may be reported or even emphasized by the press. But this does not mean that the voters are paying attention or that these issues are salient to many voters. Legislative races are often overshadowed by other contests and get relatively little attention in the press. There have been virtually no surveys in any state that asked voters their perceptions of legislative candidates and their reasons for votes cast in such races. There have certainly been no such studies in Kentucky. In the absence of hard data, we should be cautious about claiming that issues have been important in specific races.

One issue that attracted considerable press attention in the 1984 race was the so-called "greed bill." In the the 1982 session, the legislature had passed a bill that increased legislative pensions substantially and provided more generous pension plans for members who already had considerable seniority than for those who would serve subsequently. Criticism by newspaper editorials and by one organized group provided challengers with an issue that could be used against those incumbents who had voted for the bill. Because more incumbents than usual lost primaries in 1984, there was speculation that the greed bill had been a contributing factor in some of the races.

The issue appears to have attracted particular attention in Fayette County, and all three of the challengers who defeated incumbents in that county emphasized the issue. The greed bill played a prominent role in Ernesto Scorsone's successful campaign against Carolyn Kenton, and both candidates expressed the view that it had made a significant difference. The race between incumbent Jerry Lundergan and challenger Shirley Cunningham turned into a debate on whether Lundergan had actually voted for the pension increase. Lundergan placed ads in the paper denying that he had voted for the bill as amended to include the legislative pensions. His opponent responded with an ad that included the text of the amendment and the entire roll call vote. Since Cunningham's margin over Lundergan was only twenty-seven votes, it is likely that this issue made the difference. (Of course, with a twenty-seven vote margin, that claim could be made about nearly any issue.) Outside Fayette County there were at least two other districts where successful challengers made an issue of the greed bill, but it is more difficult to prove that the issue had any substantial effect.

The 1984 election followed a legislative session that was devoted largely to education. The legislature enacted a number of educational reforms, but it failed to adopt the governor's plan to make dramatic increases in educational spending and raise taxes to pay for it. Many commentators pointed out that the new election schedule, with primaries being held less than two months after the session, made it difficult for the governor to recruit support for her tax proposals. Across the state a number of candidates talked about the importance of improving education; a number committed themselves to oppose tax increases, and some took both positions. There is little evidence of incumbents being criticized by challengers for their unwillingness to raise taxes for education. The issue may have been less important because the crucial legislative decisions were taken privately in caucus and there were no public votes on taxes. Despite the importance of the education and tax issues, there is no evidence that these played any significant part in the defeat of incumbents in the 1984 primary or general elections.

One other tax issue assumed importance in the coal counties, particularly in eastern Kentucky. Challengers frequently charged that incumbents had failed to prevent their districts from losing revenues from the coal severance tax as a result of changes in the tax formula.

Labor issues frequently assume importance in press accounts of legislative campaigns. They take various forms: collective bargaining for public employees, professional negotiations for teachers, and most recently an effort by business groups to gain passage of a right-to-work bill. In the 82d district, Elmer Patrick, the incumbent Republican who was beaten in the primary, had sponsored right-to-work legislation, and both of his opponents emphasized that issue. Patrick defended his position and charged that his opponents favored collective bargaining for public employees. These issues probably contributed to Patrick's defeat, but they were probably overshadowed by the personal controversies, mentioned earlier, surrounding Patrick.

The Individual Campaign. Every election campaign is different, and there are many factors that help to explain election outcomes. But, if we had to identify a single factor that can make a difference in a campaign, it would be the political skills of the candidates. In primary races and in the more competitive general elections, the winner is usually the candidate who works hardest and has the most experience and skill as a politician. Obviously, there are many districts, particularly rural ones, so dominated by one party that the opposition candidate has little chance. But even in some of these districts, one-party domination is less an established fact than a myth that has not been tested recently by a really strong candidate.

A successful legislative incumbent is one who works at the job year-round, knows the district well, maintains contact with political leaders and organized groups, is accessible to constituents, and handles efficiently their requests for service. Many legislators have told us that their most effective "campaigning" consists of working hard at the job between campaigns. Members often believe that if they are effective enough in these efforts, they are unlikely to have a strong challenger, particularly in the primary.

A successful incumbent takes any challenger seriously and "runs scared" in any campaign. Incumbents obviously have an advantage because they have done it before. They have organized a group of campaign workers and financial contributors, most of whom can be counted on to reenlist when another campaign begins. They have developed a campaign style that has worked before, and they will use it again. Most Kentucky legislators won their first election in large part by going door to door evenings and weekends for many months. When they face an electoral challenge, they start walking the precincts again. One experienced rural legislator, representing three counties, told us that in the course of several campaigns he had been in every home in one county and in a large part of the second, and claimed that he had been bitten by dogs nineteen times while campaigning.

Not every incumbent works so hard at being a legislator or campaigns so intensively when there is a challenger. Being a legislator is a part-time job, and some members are unwilling to sacrifice their business or law practice, for example, to their political career. There is sometimes a conflict between being a legislator and being a politician, particularly now that the legislative session runs into the normal primary campaign season. For whatever reasons, some incumbents do not fully exploit the potential political advantages of incumbency, and it is these who are most likely to attract serious challengers.

The most successful challengers have several characteristics. They have usually had some political experience, working actively in the campaigns of others or running for legislative or other offices themselves. They may have played an active role in voluntary organizations—churches, civic groups, interest groups. From these experiences they have learned how to organize and raise money, and they have developed a large circle of friends and associates who can be mobilized for a campaign. Most important, they are willing to devote substantial amounts of time and money to a campaign.

A good example of a successful challenger is Ernesto Scorsone, who defeated incumbent Carolyn Kenton in the 1984 Democratic primary in Fayette County (75th district) and won the general election. Scorsone, at age thirty-two, had been active in politics since his days as a political activist at the University of Kentucky. He had worked in a number of campaigns, and in 1977 had run unsuccessfully in the primary for another Fayette legislative seat. (In that campaign his his name was spelled phonetically on his bumper sticker.) From his political experience, he had built an extensive network of contacts who could be recruited to his campaign: political activists, university people, lawyers, and other young professionals. He started his campaign organizing and fund raising relatively early and raised over twenty thousand dollars. He campaigned door to door, using precinct lists to reach all the Democrats who vote regularly. He sent out multiple mailings to targeted groups and held many meetings in the district (usually coffees).

Scorsone's original decision to enter the race was based on his judgment that the incumbent had political weaknesses. Carolyn Kenton, the widow of House Speaker Bill Kenton, had won a special election in February 1982 after his death. Because she was a single parent and was attending law school nearly full time, there were limits on the amount of time she could devote to constituency matters. Scorsone perceived that she was vulnerable to the charge of neglecting the district. He also decided that her vote for the legislative pension bill was a vulnerability that could be exploited, and he made the "greed bill" a key issue in his campaign.

In any legislative district there are likely to be at least a few potential candidates who may be waiting for the incumbent to retire. A good example of such a candidate is Bill Lear, who was elected in 1984 from Fayette County to the 79th House seat. Lear is a lawyer who had determined long ago that at some time he would make a legislative race. Because of the heavy demands of his law practice, Lear was in no hurry to make such a move, but when the incumbent, Hank List, decided to retire, Lear felt he could not pass up the opportunity. He faced a strong opponent in the primary and a much better known Republican opponent in the general election.

Once Lear decided to run, he was determined that his initial campaign would not be a losing effort. He had gained political experience and familiarity with the district by helping List with his campaigns, but he was not well known to the public. He ran an unusually sophisticated campaign, using a computer, for example, to send out to each voter letters that were tailored to the particular precinct or area. He had a well-designed brochure and made use of both radio and television. All of these techniques are expensive, and Lear spent nearly $74,000 in the primary and general election campaigns—the largest amount ever spent to win a House seat in Kentucky.

The local political environment affects the campaign tactics that a legislative candidate must use. In some counties, particularly in eastern Kentucky, political factions or alliances are largely determined by family ties. In building a political organization legislative candidates must work through these families; a candidate who belongs to a politically prominent family has a distinct advantage. One legislator from eastern Kentucky told us that he would never have been successful in winning election if his wife had not been a member of a prominent political family.

Factional politics within the majority party, whether based on families or not, has long been a characteristic of many rural counties in Kentucky. Although factional battles may be focused on courthouse jobs, the conflicts may spill over into legislative races. This creates complications particularly for candidates running in legislative districts that include all or parts of several districts. Factional politics may be fading in importance in many counties as counties change and a new generation of political leaders emerges. Moreover, as legislators serve longer terms, they are better able to build personal organizations that are independent of local factions.

In some of the larger cities, notably Louisville, one or both parties have well-established organizations reaching down to the precinct level. Several Louisville legislators have told us that it is important to enlist the active support of precinct captains in order to win primary elections. An incumbent from Jefferson County can normally count on having the support of the party organization in the primary. In recent years, however, some candidates have built their own organizations and have won primaries despite the opposition of party organizational leaders.

In those districts where there are serious contests in the general election, including many urban districts, the local political parties are likely to be strong enough to provide some help to their legislative candidates. This may take the form of voter registration drives, money raising, and the use of headquarters facilities. Usually, however, the local organizations are giving priority to other races at the state or local level, and the legislative campaigns assume lower priority. In the past, legislative races have coincided with statewide and local races; starting in 1984 they have coincided with congressional and presidential races. It will be interesting to see whether the change has much effect on the role played by local party organizations in legislative campaigns.

In 1986 the state Democratic party made a concerted effort to provide assistance to its candidates in 31 Senate and House districts in which the race appeared to be close. The assistance from party headquarters took several forms, with some variation from district to district. The state party assigned college student interns as "campaign coordinators" to work with most of the candidates. It provided electoral targeting at the precinct level, lists of frequent voters, and lists of volunteers and campaign contributors, as well as polling data and research assistance.

The districts targeted by the state Democratic party included all six districts where a Republican incumbent was retiring; seven of the nine districts where there was a Republican incumbent running who had a Democratic opponent; six of the nine districts with a retiring Democratic incumbent, plus one where the Democratic incumbent had lost the primary; and eleven districts with a Democratic incumbent running.

Among the thirteen Republican districts to which it provided assistance, the Democratic party defeated one incumbent senator and captured one open House seat. However, one Republican representative was defeated by a Democrat who had no aid from the state party. Among the eighteen Democratic districts, where the state Democratic party provided aid to its candidates, the party suffered three losses: one by an incumbent, one in an open seat, and one by a candidate who had beaten the incumbent in a primary. These consequences of state Democratic party assistance were obviously not dramatic, but it is impossible to prove whether the results would have been significantly different if the state party had not become involved in legislative races.

However much help legislative candidates get, the successful candidates in competitive races usually are the ones who enlist their own workers, raise their own funds, and run their own campaigns—supplementing their efforts with whatever help they get from the party organization.

Changing the schedule of legislative elections from odd-to even-numbered years has already had an effect on levels of voter turnout, but it is difficult to predict the full consequences of the change. In the past turnout in Kentucky primary elections has been much higher in odd-numbered years (with or without a gubernatorial race) than in even-numbered years—more than twice as high. There is no way of telling whether much of that high turnout has been caused by the presence of legislative races on the ballot. The level of turnout in legislative primaries in particular districts is unstable from year to year, depending in part on the closeness of the competition. But a comparison of Democratic primaries in House races in the years from 1979 to 1986 shows a drop in voter turnout. We examined those districts having a contested Democratic primary in 1979 and/or 1981 and in 1984 and/or 1986 (about 40 percent of all districts). In 1984 three-fourths of these districts had lower turnout than in 1979-81, with the median district having 78 percent as much turnout. In 1986 nearly all of the districts had lower turnout, with the median district having 75 percent as much as in 1979-81.

On the other hand, the shift to even-numbered year elections has resulted in higher turnout for legislative general elections in presidential years and an uneven pattern in congressional election years. We examined levels of turnout in those districts having contested races in at least three of the four general elections from 1979 to 1986 (almost one-third of the total). In every district but one, turnout was higher in 1984 than in the 1979-81 period, and in the median district the increase was 165 percent. In 1986, however, half of the districts had lower turnout than in 1979-81, whereas half had turnout levels at least as high and often much higher; this latter group was concentrated primarily in Jefferson County.

Most legislative candidates face some significant competition in the primary or the general election, but not both. The new election schedule means that, where the primary is the major race, legislative candidates will usually have to face fewer voters; however, where the general election is more closely contested, there will be a larger electorate, particularly in presidential election years. Based on the pattern found in both 1984 and 1986, the largest increases for turnout in legislative general elections will be in Jefferson County.

In a sense, every contested legislative race is unique, but there are some clear patterns that explain the outcome of elections. In the large number of districts dominated by a single party, traditional partisan loyalties are the major explanation, reinforced by the advantages of incumbency. In general elections with closer competition, and in primary races, incumbents have a large head start if they have made good use of the advantages normally available to an incumbent. Differences in campaign spending apparently have less impact on electoral outcomes in Kentucky than in some other states. One reason is the relatively low level and small differentials in spending among those general and primary elections that are competitive; another is the fact that incumbents usually can raise as much as necessary to win. There are a variety of explanations for the occasional defeat of incumbents: redistricting, party factionalism, a few issues, and sometimes the ineffectiveness or laziness of the incumbent. These patterns of electoral outcomes could change if the Republican party makes greater efforts to be competitive, or if the costs of legislative campaigns increases significantly.

3. The New Legislators

The primary purposes of this chapter are to describe the members of the Kentucky legislature, to show how they are different from earlier generations of legislators, and to explain how and why these differences have occurred. We will begin by simply describing the basic characteristics of members, noting where they differ and where they are similar to members in earlier periods. We will then turn our attention to the most dramatic change in legislators over a forty-year period: the drop in turnover and the growing proportion of experienced members. In order to understand why members are serving longer terms in the legislature, we must examine the motivations for seeking legislative office and the process of legislative recruitment. One of the fundamental changes affecting legislative careers is the increasing workload of the legislature, and we will examine how part-time legislators adjust to the conflicting demands of their dual careers. Finally, we will try to provide some individual perspectives on the legislature with a few profiles of a number of current legislators.

THE KENTUCKY LEGISLATOR TODAY AND YESTERDAY

The contemporary Kentucky legislator is, in several ways, similar to a 1960 legislator. Areas of continuity include sex, race, religion, occupation, age, education, and party identification. The typical 1986 legislator is very similar to his earlier counterpart: male, white, Baptist, businessman, in his late forties or early fifties, college educated, and, of course, a Democrat. But there is one important change. The typical legislator in the 1960s and even 1970s was serving his first or second (two-year) term. Today the typical member is serving his fourth term. It is also noteworthy that the average contemporary legislator has had more advanced formal education than was true twenty years ago.

In this chapter we are primarily concerned with comparing current members with those in the 1960s and 1970s, but (where data are available and pertinent) we will also compare Kentucky members with those in the South and those in all the states, in order to determine how typical Kentucky legislators are.

Occupation. In occupational terms Kentucky legislators are rather typical of those in other states, but they are not a very good cross section of state population. As in other states, most Kentucky legislators are businessmen, lawyers or other professional men, and farmers. The business or professional man who is self-employed and perhaps has partners who can carry the load in his absence is obviously more available to spend several months in Frankfort than the wage earner in a factory or a store who is sure to lose money and perhaps even his job if he or she is elected to the legislature. As long as the regular legislative session is from January through early April, the farmer can serve without seriously interfering with planting and harvesting. The lawyer, the insurance agent, and some other businessmen often anticipate that their legislative service will make them well known enough to attract clients, and some of them hope to benefit from contacts with the state or with other companies doing business with the state.

Nationwide, state legislators make up a highly homogeneous group—the vast majority are business and professional people (table 6). The Kentucky legislators are, on the whole, typical of the sample of national legislators and especially of southern legislators in the different occupational groupings. The largest occupational group is that of lawyers, who make up a fifth of all state legislators. The percentage of lawyer-legislators has declined somewhat in the past twenty years; more professional legislatures demand full-time legislators. Only in the South (which includes Kentucky) does the percentage (29 percent) exceed that for the total United States, perhaps in part because southern legislatures generally are less likely to meet for a large proportion of the year.

It is quite striking how few white- and blue-collar workers serve in the legislatures, even in the industrial states with large labor union memberships. It is easy to understand why business and professional people dominate the legislative memberships. They have the personal resources that make it possible for them to pursue political interests and to make the sacrifices that legislative service may involve.

Almost 11 percent of the state legislators are in agricultural occupations, up from 9 percent in 1977 and 1976. The heaviest concentration is in those areas whose economy relies heavily on farming and ranching: 18 percent in the North Central states and 16 percent in the West. Only 9 percent of Kentucky legislators cited agricultural interests as their primary occupation—slightly less than the national average.

Table 7 presents a more detailed occupational profile of Kentucky sena-

Table 6. Occupational Profile of State Legislators

	Nationwide (%)	South (%)	Kentucky (%)
Lawyers	20.0	29.0	28.0
Professionals	21.0	17.0	18.0
Communications/arts	3.0	2.0	3.0
Education	10.0	8.0	9.0
Nonprofit organizations	1.0	1.0	1.0
Other professionals	7.0	6.0	5.0
Business	37.0	40.0	42.0
Insurance	5.0	7.0	4.0
Entrepreneur/ self-employed	15.0	17.0	15.0
Business executive/ managerial	6.0	6.0	7.0
Other business occupations	5.0	2.0	7.0
Real estate/ construction	6.0	8.0	9.0
Agriculture	11.0	8.0	9.0
Government employees	4.0	3.0	1.0
Labor union	*	*	1.0
Homemaker/student	3.0	2.0	1.0
Information not available	4.0	1.0	—
Total number	(7,485)	(2,453)	(138)

Source: Insurance Information Institute (1979: 40,53).
*Less than 1/2 of 1.0%

tors and representatives during two different periods—1952-66 and 1980-86. Some of these figures differ from those in table 6 because in this analysis of Kentucky legislators, in order to get a fuller picture of the range of interests represented in the legislature, we have double counted those legislators who listed two occupations in the 1980-86 period. Typical occupational combinations, for example, include farmer-businessman and lawyer-businessman. In the later period, 1980-86, the figures add up to slightly more than 125 percent; this means that in order to be safe in saying there has actually been an increase in the proportion of an occupation group, there needs to be an increase of more than 25 percent. A good example would be the significant increase of professional and technical individuals, particularly in the Senate, and there has been a notable increase of business owners and managers in the House. There is no real increase among lawyers. Overall, there are no really dramatic changes except the influx of various kinds of professionals in

Table 7. Occupations of Kentucky Legislators

	1952-1966*		1980-1986**	
	Senate (%)	House (%)	Senate (%)	House (%)
Business owners and managers	32.5	36.2	29.9	49.3
Merchants (retail, wholesale)	17.5	18.6	12.3	25.3
Bankers	3.0	0.8	1.8	2.0
Insurance and real estate	5.3	10.6	14.0	12.3
Morticians	2.2	1.4	—	—
Contractors	2.2	2.0	1.8	3.0
Manufacturers	1.8	1.0	—	2.7
Coal mine operators	0.4	0.6	—	2.7
Truckers	—	0.8	—	1.0
Credit managers	—	0.4	—	0.3
Lawyers	32.0	16.0	36.0	21.3
Other professional, technical	10.5	17.6	30.9	24.3
Doctors, dentists, etc.	3.5	1.6	7.9	1.0
Teachers, principals	3.5	7.8	7.9	8.0
Ministers, church workers	—	2.0	5.3	0.7
Social workers	—	0.4	—	—
Newspaper and radio	2.6	1.6	4.4	1.3
Public relations, advertising	0.4	1.8	2.7	2.3
Accountants	0.4	0.8	—	0.3
Engineers	—	1.6	2.7	2.7
Public officials	—	—	—	4.3
Other professionals	—	—	—	3.7
Farmers	16.2	16.2	11.4	21.0
Craftsmen, foremen, operators	1.8	4.4	5.3	4.3
Railroad workers	—	2.6	—	—
Other skilled workers	1.3	1.4	5.3	3.3
Labor union agents	0.4	0.4	—	1.0
Salesmen and clerks	3.1	4.0	—	—
Industrial laborers	—	1.2	—	—
Other, retired, unknown	3.9	3.4	10.5	7.0
Total Number	(228)	(500)	(114)	(300)

*Senate, 1954-66; House, 1952, 1954, 1958, 1962, 1966.
**Senate and House, 1980, 1984, and 1986. The percentages for this period add up to more than 100 percent because some legislators listed two occupations.

the Senate; changes in the occupational profile of House members are minimal.

Lawyers constitute almost twice as large a proportion of senators as of representatives during the two time periods. The large number of businesspersons include a wide variety of retail and wholesale merchants and a large number of insurance and real estate agents. The number of school teachers and administrators in the Kentucky legislature is surprisingly large in view of the conflict between teaching schedules and legislative service. As noted above, the most dramatic occupational increase among senators and representatives is that of professional and technical interests; this fits nicely with a more professional legislature. Those legislators with more technical occupational backgrounds bring added expertise and specialization to their legislative jobs, especially in the committee/subcommittee decision-making stages.

Age. The age distributions of senators and representatives in the 1960 Kentucky General Assembly closely mirror those in the 1980-86 sessions (table 8). In both time periods, more than 60 percent of the senators have been over fifty years old; representatives have been divided into three groups: those under forty years, those in their forties, and those fifty and over, the largest of the three. There has been a modest increase in the age of representatives. It is harder to measure trends in the Senate because the numbers are smaller (for the earlier period), but the proportion who are in their fifties is much higher, those younger is lower, and those older is higher than in 1970 (but lower than in 1960).

The qualifications for election to the Senate and/or House are somewhat different. For the Senate, a candidate must be thirty years of age or older, a state resident for six years, and a district resident for one year. For the House, a candidate must be twenty-four years of age or older, a state resident for two years, and a district resident for one year (*Book of the States* 1984-85).

It is important to point out that age distribution is affected by two factors: how old members are when they enter and how long they stay in. If members are entering the legislature at an earlier age, the age should drop; if they are staying longer, it should increase. If both trends are at work, there might be no dramatic changes in age distribution. In fact, we find in figure 5 that members are entering both the House and the Senate at an earlier age. We will demonstrate later in this chapter that members are serving longer terms, so both factors are at work. But, despite people entering legislative offices earlier, there has been no significant change in age distributions of legislators, as noted in table 8.

At this point we would speculate that members are entering the legislature earlier because more of them have a serious interest in a long-term

Table 8. Demographic Characteristics of Kentucky Legislators

	1960		1970		1980-1986	
	Senate (%)	House (%)	Senate (%)	House (%)	Senate (%)	House (%)
Age						
20-29	—	4.0	—	5.0	—	—
30-39	13.2	20.0	18.4	18.0	5.3	17.7
40-49	23.7	32.0	52.6	41.0	28.1	34.0
50-59	28.9	29.0	21.1	22.0	44.7	33.3
60-69	34.2	11.0	5.3	11.0	18.4	10.0
Over 69	—	4.0	2.6	3.0	3.5	5.0
Education						
High school or less	28.9	40.0	13.2	30.0	10.5	21.3
College	47.4	39.0	36.8	42.0	31.6	43.3
Post-college	23.7	21.0	50.0	28.0	57.9	35.4
Religion						
Roman Catholic	13.2	12.0	7.0	22.0	33.3	26.0
Episcopalian	7.9	—	2.6	1.0	4.4	0.7
Presbyterian	13.2	9.0	10.5	7.0	6.1	5.7
Methodist	18.4	20.0	15.8	15.0	17.5	11.0
Baptist	26.2	36.0	44.7	40.0	29.8	30.7
Christian or Disciples of Christ	13.2	12.0	15.8	13.0	0.1	9.3
Fundamentalist	2.6	4.0	5.3	2.0	2.6	8.0
Nondenomination Protestant	5.3	7.0	—	—	2.6	8.7
Other	—	—	—	—	3.5	—
Sex						
Female	2.6	—	5.3	4.0	5.3	7.7
Male	97.4	100.0	94.7	96.0	94.7	92.3
Race						
White	100.0	100.0	97.4	98.0	97.4	98.3
Black	—	—	2.6	2.0	2.6	1.7
Party Identification						
Democrat	79.0	80.0	73.0	70.0	74.6	76.3
Republican	21.0	20.0	27.0	30.0	25.4	23.7

political career (either staying in the legislature or using it as a launching pad). On the other hand, the type of member who enters the legislature (or used to do so) in his fifties or sixties does this as a sideline, or even as a way of retiring from active participation in a business or profession. Certainly,

Figure 5. Age at Entering Legislature

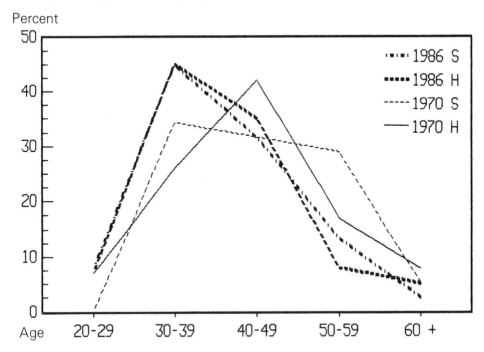

anyone who wanted to use a few terms in the legislature as a basis for running for congressional or statewide office would not wait until their midfifties to run for the legislature.

Education. The relatively high educational level of legislators (table 8) can be accounted for, in part, by their relatively higher class origins. However, within the Kentucky General Assembly, more attended college than other members of the white adult population of the state, regardless of their class origins. Every legislative body in this country contains members who are much better educated than the general public. Since 1960 there has been a tremendous change in the educational backgrounds of the Kentucky senators and representatives. Among the 1960 legislators, about 70 percent of the senators and 60 percent of the representatives had attended or graduated from college, as compared to 88 percent of the senators and 78 percent of the representatives in the 1980-84-86 sessions. The proportions of college-trained legislators and those with postcollege training have been growing dramatically over the last three decades and are likely to continue to grow, both as a result of a new generation of legislators and the increasing representation from urban counties.

Religion. Religion has played a major role in Kentucky's cultural development and continues to be a major influence on the Commonwealth today. The largest Protestant denomination is Baptist, primarily Southern Baptist, closely followed by Catholics, with smaller numbers of Methodists, Christians (Disciples of Christ), Presbyterians, Episcopalians, Lutherans, United Church of Christ, and Jews. Most of these denominations have been represented in the 1960, 1970, and 1980-86 legislative sessions (table 8). The majority of these legislative assemblies are shown to be Baptists, followed by Catholics and Methodists. This religious composition of Kentucky's legislatures over the years is the best example of legislators' mirroring a trait of the population as a whole. The substantial increase in the proportion of Catholic legislators since 1960 is in part a consequence of reapportionment, which gave more seats to Jefferson County and the northern Kentucky metropolitan area, both of which have significant proportions of Catholics in the population.

Sex. In the United States, women have been winning state legislative seats in increasing numbers, especially in the last two decades. In 1951 only 3.3 percent of legislative seats were held by women, compared to 4.5 percent in 1971, 10.3 percent in 1979, and 13.3 percent in 1983 (Nechemias, 1987). The figure rose to 14.7 percent in 1985. Concomitant with this increase in elected female legislators has been an increase in the number of women running for the legislature. For example, in the 1978 elections 1,348 women ran (for 7,482 legislative positions), and 57 percent of them won seats (Rosenthal, 1981b: 30). Following the 1978 election, there were 770 women in state legislatures; a small number of them presumably had been elected to a four-year term two years earlier. If the percentage of women candidates who win were to be consistently close to the 57 percent won in 1978, this would suggest in a crude way that women have roughly the same batting average as men.

In comparison to these significant nationwide increases, Kentucky females have made limited gains in securing elected legislative offices. As shown in table 8, there was only one female legislator in 1960, compared to six in 1970 and nine in the 1980s' legislative sessions (5.3 percent of the Senate, 7.7 percent of the House). Although women constitute 51.3 percent of Kentucky's population, women held only 6.3 percent of the seats in the General Assembly from 1978 through 1986. And most of these female legislators were elected by the more densely populated counties of Jefferson and Fayette.

More women are seeking legislative offices, but fewer offices are won by women in Kentucky (table 9). Despite their valuable contributions as party workers, remarkably few women have won their party's nominations for elective office in Kentucky. Both major political parties have tended to

Table 9. Kentucky Female Legislative Candidates

	House					Senate				
	1973	1979	1981	1984	1986	1973	1979	1981	1983	1986
Number of women running	12	22	28	26	18	2	6	7	3	1
Number of women elected	3	8	7	7	5	1	1	1	1	1
(Number of males running)	279	210	221	236	211	48	47	41	52	44

meet the minimal nominating requirement by nominating female candidates for seats that are unwinnable or for contests in which the opposing candidate is also a woman. Thus, political parties have not functioned as escalators for public office in the state.

Female incumbents remained in office just as frequently as did their male counterparts (table 10). No women lost as incumbents in Senate general election contests, and only one woman lost as an incumbent in a House general election battle. Moreover, only four female incumbents lost House primary battles (and one was against another female incumbent). In most cases in Senate and House general election races, female challengers were pitted against male incumbents, and the women lost the contests. In the later period, so many male incumbents were running that it was hard for women to find open seats to contest. The nonincumbent women only won in open House seat contests. In both periods many women ran in races that they were guaranteed to lose; either they were nominated by their party in districts where that party is generally the loser, or they challenged male incumbents.

In assessing the proportion of women and men who run compared with the proportion that win, during the 1979-81-83/84-86 period, 115 women ran for legislative offices, and 31 of these candidates (27 percent) won the general elections. Of the 1,062 males who ran for legislative seats during these same elections, 445 (42 percent) were victorious in obtaining the offices. Of course, usually female and male incumbents have minimal or no opposition.

As noted in table 10, the number of winning female legislative candidates in the later period more than doubled—31 compared to 8 (in earlier two elections). Also, in the earlier contests all the female victors were from metropolitan Jefferson County, compared with only 13 (42 percent) for the later legislative races. Furthermore, more women are running for legislative seats outside of Jefferson County (e.g., from urbanized Fayette, Kenton, and Campbell counties).

Table 10. Success of Women in Kentucky Legislative Races

	1971 and 1973			1979-81-83/84-86						
	Senate	House	S & H (Jefferson County)	S	Jeff (S)	Other (S)	H	Jeff	Fayette Kenton Campbell (H)	Other
Total won	2	6	8	4	2	2	27	11	5	11
As incumbent	1	6	7	4	2	2	24	11	4	9
As challenger	1	—	1	—	—	—	3	—	—	—
Open seat	—	—	—	—	—	—	—	—	1	2
Total lost	1	16	6	13	8	5	67	24	11	32
Total lost GE	—	6	1	7	5	2	25	11	5	9
As incumbent	—	—	1	—	—	—	1	—	1	—
As challenger	—	4	—	6	4	2	21	10	2	9
Open (other party)	—	2	—	1	1	—	2	1	1	—
Open (competitive)	—	—	—	—	—	—	1	—	1	—
Total lost primary	1	10	5	6	3	3	42	13	6	23
As incumbent	—	—	—	—	—	—	4	1	1	2
As challenger	—	5	4	6	3	3	17	4	2	11
Open	1	4	1	—	—	—	17	6	3	8
In minority, majority incumbents	—	1	—	—	—	—	4	2	—	2
Total	3	22	14	17	10	7	94	35	16	43

Race. Nationwide, membership in the legislatures also has increased in recent years for ethnic and racial minority groups, especially in districts where such groups make up a considerable proportion of the voting population. Nevertheless, the proportions are very small. In 1960 only 0.5 percent of the state legislators were black; by 1966 the figure had grown to 2 percent (Jewell and Patterson 1966). In 1980, 4 percent of the state legislators were black, and this proportion was no greater in Mississippi, where 37 percent of the population is black (Gray, Jacob, and Vines, 1983). In 1986 there were 92 black senators and 304 black representatives—5.3 percent of the state legislators (*Focus*, 1986).

Kentucky's blacks are grossly underrepresented in the legislature, even more than in most states. In Kentucky blacks comprise 7 percent of the population; but in the 1960 legislature there were no black legislators, and in the 1980, 1984, and 1986 sessions, only 2.6 percent of the Senate and 1.7 percent of the House were blacks. Most blacks holding public office in the state are elected from districts serving the predominately white communities of Jefferson and Fayette Counties. The recent black losses in Jefferson County are related to the reapportionment squeezing out districts that are more likely to elect blacks. Black officeholders must continue to appeal to both black and white constituencies.

Party Identification. The Democrats have dominated the Kentucky General Assembly for decades. In 1960 Democrats held 79 percent of the Senate and 80 percent of the House seats, as compared to 63 percent of the Senate and 70 percent of the House in 1970 (table 8). In the mid-1960s the Republicans gained significant strength in Kentucky as a result of not only forced redistricting following the Supreme Court's reapportionment decisions, but also because of the power of Louisville's Republican leaders and the successes of Republican Governor Louie Nunn's administration. These Republican gains in the 1960s were short-lived and soon faded away. During the 1980, 1984, and 1986 Kentucky legislative sessions, Democrats held 74.6 percent of the Senate and 76.3 percent of the House seats. Today, despite what is happening in the Republican party elsewhere in some southern and border states, we do not find a substantial increase of Republicanism in the Kentucky legislature. The Republicans have been quite ineffective in Kentucky compared with their legislative gains in these other states.

TURNOVER

For many years the Kentucky General Assembly was characterized by amateur, inexperienced members. There is much less turnover in the membership of the legislature currently, and, as a result, the members are more

Figure 6. Turnover in Legislature (percentage)

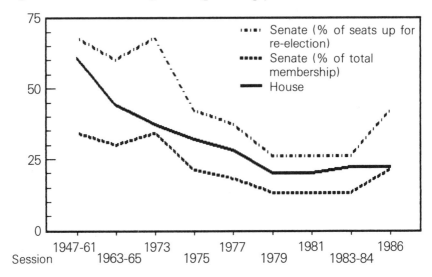

experienced and have more opportunity to become familiar with issues. The decreasing turnover of membership has been one of the most important changes in the Kentucky legislature in recent years. There are fewer freshmen than in the past. In the elections from 1947 through 1965, only one-third of the state senators and about 40 percent of the representatives were reelected (table 1). Over half of the senators and nearly half of the representatives retired (or sought other offices); the rest lost primaries or general elections. The proportion of freshmen in the Kentucky legislature was higher than in most states.

In recent years, as figure 6 shows, two-thirds of the senators and over three-fourths of the representatives have been reelected in each election. Only one-fifth of the senators and one-eighth of the representatives leave the legislature voluntarily in each election. Kentucky is now closer to the national average. The higher retirement rate for senators is understandable because they serve longer terms than do representatives. There are no partisan differences in the Senate, but in the House Republicans are a little more likely to retire or seek other offices.

Shin and Jackson's study (1979) on membership turnover in U.S. state legislatures offers comprehensive data on the turnover of legislators in the fifty states for the period 1931-76. The data show that turnover rates vary substantially among the states over this long period of time; however, in general, turnover has decreased in recent years. The study notes that turnover rates have been declining steadily across most of the different institutional types (e.g., not only the familiar dichotomy between the senates and the houses, but also distinctions between staggered- and nonstaggered-

Table 11. Membership Turnover in State Legislative Chambers (Mean
Values in Percentages)

		National	Southern	Kentucky
1931-1940	Senate	50.7	56.6	40.9
	House	58.7	65.8	72.4
1941-1950	Senate	42.6	48.7	24.3
	House	51.3	59.7	62.2
1951-1960	Senate	40.2	50.4	39.3
	House	44.8	51.9	61.4
1961-1970	Senate	37.3	43.7	37.0
	House	41.1	46.2	51.1
1971-1980	Senate	28.8	30.0	21.5
	House	32.2	33.8	31.0
1981-1985	Senate	24.1	24.7	13.0
	House	28.0	27.1	21.0

Source: Richard G. Niemi and Laura R. Winsky, "Membership Turnover in U.S. State Legislatures," *Legislative Studies Quarterly* 12 (1987): 115-24.

term senates, four-year- and two-year-term senates, and two-year- versus four-year-term houses), but the starting and ending points and the rates of decline vary quite widely, depending on the type of legislative institution examined.

Niemi and Winsky's study (1987) updated Shin and Jackson's work, which ended a decade ago. In examining legislative turnover rates, 1931-85, they found a continued decline in the membership turnover that had been documented by Shin and Jackson. Combining all types of legislatures, average turnover in each chamber is now less than half what it was in the 1930s. Thus the trend toward greater stability of membership still continues, though there are now signs of a leveling off (e.g., the leveling off in senates with staggered terms).

To gain a better perspective of Kentucky's turnover rate, see table 11 for a compilation of membership turnover in state legislative chambers for all the states' legislatures, the southern legislatures, and Kentucky's General Assembly for the period 1931-85 (Niemi and Winsky, 1987). As is shown, the drop in Kentucky's turnover rate has been more dramatic than either the national or southern averages. During the 1981-85 period, Kentucky's turnover rate in House chambers was slightly below the national and southern averages, and in Senate chambers, significantly below the other averages. In the past turnover in the southern states was generally higher than the national average; in the 1980s it has been almost identical. Over the years there has been a fairly dramatic, but gradual, drop in the national and southern averages, with the exception of bigger drops in the 1960s and 1970s; the drop has become smaller in the last few years. It is particularly impressive that the rate of turnover in Kentucky dropped by more than 20 percentage points during the 1970s, and that the gap, in House figures, between Kentucky and the national averages has now closed completely. Since the 1930s Kentucky's turnover rate in House chambers is roughly one-third of what it used to be, whereas the comparable figure for the nation as a whole is less than one-half. As noted above, the trend toward greater stability of membership still continues, although there are now indications of a leveling off in the rate of turnover in our state legislatures.

In order to understand what we mean by turnover and more explicitly how it is manifested in the legislature, we need to look at changes in the distribution of the number of sessions served. A drop in the turnover rate could mean fewer people dropping out after the first term and/or more people serving for longer periods of time. If many legislators drop out after serving only two or three terms, the legislature fails to develop a substantial group of experienced members, such as would emerge if many members have served five or more sessions. Even under the old system in Kentucky, there were a few career legislators. But now in the 1980s, there are considerably more career-oriented members. In the past many legislators used to leave the legislature voluntarily after serving one or two terms; in contrast, today it is rare for a member to drop out after the first or second term because more and more members are oriented toward pursuing a career in the legislature.

There was a dramatic increase in the number of legislative sessions served by Kentucky House and Senate members from 1960 to 1986 (table 12). There has been an extraordinary decline in the number of freshmen, a decline that is comparable to the dramatic decline in the rate of turnover. In 1960 fifty-six representatives were freshmen, compared to just fourteen House members in the 1980-86 legislatures. In 1960 sixteen senators had served only one session compared to three senators for the later period. Moreover, in 1960 only eight representatives served five or more sessions; whereas in the 1980s forty-three representatives served an average of five or more sessions. We find the same significant differences among senators— in 1960 only eight senators served five or more sessions, compared to nineteen senators during the 1980s. There has been a significant increase in the proportion of legislators who have served long enough to be considered career legislators. And this increase in the proportion of senior members shows up more in the differences between the 1970s and 1980s. The growth in the number of senior legislators has been a long-term process; the large proportion of senior legislators in the 1980s has resulted from a culmination of events at work in the legislature for the last two decades.

To explain adequately the reasons why there has been a dramatic drop in turnover would require interviews with all of the legislators, and probably some former legislators would find it difficult to provide a single, clear,

Table 12. Number of Two-Year Legislative Sessions Served

	Representatives in House				Senators in Senate				Senators in Legislature			
	1960	1966	1972-74 (%)	1980-86	1960	1966	1972-74 (%)	1980-86	1960	1966	1972-74 (%)	1980-86
1	56	25	30	14	16	10	14	3	13	10	10	2
2	17	32	25	14	10	10	9	5	8	5	6	3
3	13	18	19	16	2	9	6	5	2	9	6	5
4	6	11	9	13	2	3	5	6	5	4	9	5
5	3	4	7	12	2	—	—	6	3	2	2	5
6	1	5	4	11	2	4	2	3	1	4	3	3
7	1	3	1	8	1	—	1	5	2	1	1	5
8+	3	2	5	12	3	2	1	5	4	3	1	10

accurate explanation of their decision not to run. The most important reason for the drop in turnover is that fewer members leave the legislature voluntarily than used to be the case. This is partly because of the elimination of rotation agreements, following the reapportionment revolution of the 1960s. These agreements (described in chapter 2) required the alternation between counties of legislators in two-county and occasionally three-county districts, and thus prevented the development of member seniority.

One reason members are serving longer legislative terms in Kentucky is that the work of the legislature is growing more important as the body achieves greater independence and acquires more staff, resources, and time to do its job. Legislative service has become more challenging and satisfying. Thirty years ago many of those who entered the legislature seemed to be content to serve a brief term and then return to private life, much as they might serve a term on the hospital board or as president of a local organization. Some members, particularly those in professions like law, insurance, or real estate, hoped that the publicity they attracted and the contacts they made as legislators would help their business. Today the legislature seems to attract more persons with strong political ambitions. Probably not many of them intend to make a career of state legislative service, but they have long-term interests in politics. Often they hope to use the legislature as a stepping stone to higher political office. If such opportunities do not arise, they may stay in the legislature. Some members find legislative service more interesting than they had intended and become committed to long-term careers there.

It is more feasible for members to serve longer terms in the legislature because the monetary rewards for legislators have drastically improved during the past decade. During the 1985-86 biennium, Kentucky legislators received $100 a day throughout the regular biennial session (about sixty days), as well as during the brief organizational session and any special session. They also received $75 a day for each day spent in Frankfort for committee meetings during the interim period. On the average legislators might expect to make a salary of about $13,000 over a two-year period. During the regular session legislators receive a per diem expense allowance of $75; when they attend interim meetings they get actual expenses. During the interim period (about twenty months each biennium), the legislators also receive a monthly expense allowance of $950, which is intended to cover such expenses as secretarial help and mailing; but expense accounts need not be filed, and it is not known exactly how members use these funds. Legislators also receive medical insurance, free office space in Frankfort, and increased staff assistance from the LRC. Those legislators who move into positions of leadership receive additional payments.

Kentucky has a generous retirement system for its legislators. With the passage in 1982 of Senate Bill 102, the so-called "greed bill," legislators voted to raise the assumed average salary on which retirement benefits were based from $18,000 to $27,500. The maximum annual benefit a retired legislator could receive is $27,500, but he or she must have served twenty years or more in the legislature to collect that amount. Although the bill increased the benefits of legislators already in office, it reduced the benefits of those who would be elected in the future (3.5 percent of the annual salary [if one held office for ten years], compared to 2.75 percent for legislators elected after July 1982). The current plan also pays a percentage of premiums for medical and hospitalization insurance based on years of service. Therefore, it has become beneficial to remain in the legislature; seasoned legislators are less likely to have built up a good retirement system in their other jobs. If there were no generous retirement system, many House and Senate members would not be able to afford to remain in their legislative positions.

During the last decade (1977-86) there were 59 voluntary retirements from the House and 20 from the Senate. In examining voluntary retirements, it is important to distinguish three different groups. First, some members leave the legislature in order to pursue another elective or appointive political office. Legislative service may be a steppingstone to some other office, and House members may often leave to run for the state Senate. Second, some legislators leave voluntarily to engage in another profession in the private sector. Some find it necessary to devote more time to their businesses; others decide that they have served long enough to accomplish their main objective of gaining the publicity that will attract clients. Some, who view legislative service as a civic responsibility, decide that they have done their duty. Others find that legislative service is boring, or they become frustrated because they have little sense of accomplishment—perhaps because their party is in the minority. Third, there are those members who die in office during each legislative term or leave because of their advanced age. Of particular interest is the ratio between those members who pursue a different political office and those who return to positions in the private sector.

If we omit the few members who died in office and those who retired at sixty years or older, there were 16 senators and 42 representatives who left voluntarily. Almost half of these senators (7 of 16) ran for another office. Over half of these representatives (23 of 42) sought to remain in politics: 11 ran for the Senate, 9 ran for another office, and 3 were appointed to a job in government.

If we had time series data, we would probably find the proportion of those who leave to run for other political offices, of all those under the age of sixty who retire, has increased significantly. Also, it is possible that we have understated the number of retirees pursuing other political offices because it is not feasible to determine how many other legislators ran for the many local city, county, and judicial offices. During this past decade only nineteen House retirees under sixty have returned voluntarily to private sector positions; whereas in the past almost that many house retirees would leave a legislative session at the same time.

In nine elections, 1947-61 and 1965, only six legislators ran for statewide office (such as attorney general or secretary of state), and thirty-one representatives ran for the Senate. Six other representatives who ran for the Senate were conforming to rotation agreements. It is probable that complete data on legislators who retired to run for other local positions would have increased these numbers only slightly. Except for representatives who ran for the Senate in the elections 1947-61 and 1965, relatively few legislators apparently left in order to seek other elective offices. Among those who retired voluntarily during the period of 1947-65 (except 1963), 70 percent of the senators and 55 percent of the representatives did so without seeking a second term; most of these members returned to their positions in the private sector for many of the reasons cited earlier. Thus, there has been a dramatic increase in the ratio of legislators running for other political offices compared with those returning to their former or new professions since the 1960s.

It is important to keep in mind that the odd-number Kentucky elections created unusual opportunities for legislators to run for other offices without risking anything. Of course, House members must always give up their seat to run for the state Senate. And senators can always run for another office in the middle of the four-year term. But until recently, the legislators could always run for Congress without risking their seat. Now this is impossible, but they can run for statewide races (and for local races) without risk. Under the old system, in theory, there were always seven congressional seats they could seek, but running against an incumbent from either party is a long shot at best. Under the new system, the statewide races never have incumbents running, and so Democrats in particular have a chance to run in those primaries without risk.

Let us look first at some examples of state legislators who ran for Congress during the period 1970-82; then let us see how many legislators ran for the statewide races in 1983 and 1987—the first chance under the new system. From 1970 to 1982, six representatives and nine senators ran for congressional seats; three state senators became House members (Ronald Mazzoli, Carroll Hubbard, and Larry Hopkins) and one, a U.S. Senate member (Walter Huddleston). In 1980 two state senators and two representatives ran unsuccessfully against an incumbent for the Fifth District congressional seat. Probably state senators have had more success than have representatives in their bids for national offices because as senators they represent more than twice as many constituents and, therefore, have more visibility in the district. Under the new system in 1984 and 1986, two representatives and one senator did not seek reelection as state legislators in order to run for congressional offices.

It is too early to tell whether the new election schedule is going to limit the number of state legislators running for Congress or increase the number running for statewide office. In 1983 and 1987, under the new system, several legislators have sought statewide offices. Two representatives, Mary Ann Tobin and David Boswell, were victorious respectively in auditor and commissioner of agriculture races in 1983, whereas State Senator James Bunning lost the gubernatorial contest. Senator Joe Prather entered and then withdrew from the 1987 gubernatorial contest. In 1987 Representative Fred Cowan won the attorney general's race, and Representative Butch Burnette was elected commissioner of agriculture. Representative Roger Noe did not have to jeopardize his chairmanship of the Education Committee in his unsuccessful to run for the office of superintendent of education that same year.

MOTIVATIONS FOR INVOLVEMENT
IN LEGISLATIVE POLITICS

Kentuckians who are interested in pursuing a legislative career must have sufficient interest in politics to seek an office that will require campaigning for the better part of a year, possibly suffering through both a primary and a general election, spending the year and a half after the election involved in some interim committee activities and service for constituents, and then devoting about half of the succeeding year in Frankfort participating in the legislative session—all for about $13,000 in actual salary (for a two-year period) and other financial compensations.

Seekers of General Assembly positions do so for any number of reasons. In terms of Clark and Wilson's broad incentive typology for political activity, individuals may enter legislative life for either material (i.e., tangible rewards), solidary (i.e., fun, excitement), and/or purposive (i.e., civic service, particular issues) motivations (1961). Moreover, Payne, Woshinsky, Veblen, Coogan, and Bigler (1984) delineate five common types of psychological gratifications for political involvement: status or ego gratification (e.g., urge for public recognition and political prestige), program (e.g., substance of issues), conviviality, obligation (e.g., civic duty), and game (e.g., fun and excitement); several of these are incorporated in the Clark-Wilson typology. In our study of Kentucky party activists (Miller, 1986), we find similar kinds of motivational mixes for involvement in gubernatorial politics.

Certain more specific motivations may apply to the legislature because it is a long-term, more demanding commitment than political activity in general. According to Mladenka and Hill (1986), some individuals hope to use their experience in the legislature to seek higher and more lucrative political office. Others frankly hope to use their time in the legislature to make business associations, learn the ins and outs of state government, become acquainted with representatives of the major lobby interests, and then retire from the legislature into an enhanced private career. The latter route can be particularly useful for young professionals in business, law, insurance, and real estate. Moreover, some legislative hopefuls probably get their ambition from family or friendship ties with others seriously involved in political life. Many people reared in a highly political family are socialized to believe that it is natural and even expected of them to enter that life. For example, it was probably inevitable that Senator Mike Moloney and Representative Tom Jones would pursue legislative careers; both their families have been steeped in Kentucky legislative politics for several generations. Finally, some legislative hopefuls are probably like political science professor Frank Smallwood of Vermont (1976), who wanted to find out "what it was like out there in the everyday world of practical politics."

In our survey of Kentucky state legislators in 1983, in assessing first-term legislators' motives for involvement in legislative politics, we find many of the same incentives that Rosenthal documents in *Legislative Life* (1981b: 17-22). For many individuals politics is interesting, and the position of being a legislator is considered by them as worthwhile. For many the prestige of being elected, or of holding office, and of being one of a relative few is appealing. For several the opportunity to serve the public, to accomplish something in the public interest, to do good, is of major importance. Some individuals believe they can do a better job than those already in office. For others there is an overriding issue, a particular philosophy, or a special interest that has to be promoted. For most of them, there is no single reason, but rather a combination that impels them toward legislative office.

It is interesting to examine some of the specific responses of these Kentucky freshman legislators ("What specific reasons led to your decision to run for the legislature in 1981?"). An *opportunity* may exist for several reasons. Often it is a decision of the incumbent not to run. An ambitious young urban lawyer with long-term political aspirations responded, "I wanted to begin a political career. Have been interested in statewide issues. Timing was right and I thought I could win." A well-respected former mayor commented, "There was a vacancy in the office. I had served as a mayor, and had a long-time interest in serving in the General Assembly." A former appointed secretary of state remarked, "I lost the race for secretary of state (full term) and made the decision to remain out of elective office until my family was raised. I took the opportunity to reenter when my friend, Lou Defalaise, accepted the appointment as U.S. Attorney." A Republican building contractor/livestock farmer noted, "I was always interested in governmental process . . . also the former legislator retired."

Sometimes an individual's previous experience or geographic base enables him or her to take advantage of an opportunity. A former county judge, circuit court clerk, and state commerce bureaucrat responded, "Serving in county government gave me the insight of the workings of county and state government. I felt like I could be in a good position to help the people of this district get their fair share." A young lawyer whose family is steeped in Kentucky politics noted, "I was born in Mercer County and now live and work in Anderson County, the two larger counties in the District, and I thought I could win. I believe that it would be a good career move for me and that I could do a good job. I believed it would be interesting work with interesting people."

An individual may be dissatisfied (or feel the public is dissatisfied) with the quality of representation by the incumbent. A bright, young attorney and reformer from a metropolitan area commented, "I thought my district lacked effective representation and that I could do a better job. Many specific issues were involved, including 'annexation' and the lack of understanding of urban issues by my predecessor." A Republican auctioneer/realtor remarked, "I was not satisfied with the way a portion of my district had been represented in recent years and felt that I could bring about some changes in that area. I also felt that a new face and new ideas might be good for our district." A Republican high school principal from a rural county noted, "I wanted to provide representation more consistent with the philosophy of this area." A Republican building materials merchant commented, "I decided to run because the 90th District lacked representation."

A person may feel that certain interests need better representation. A former county judge and attorney/farmer responded, " I had the desire to perform public service and to benefit a constituency of state workers and agriculture, as well as others." A union leader remarked, "I wanted to look out for labor's interests."

Some individuals may feel that certain issues need to be emphasized. A young dentist commented, "I had always wanted to get involved. There were needs in my district that were not being addressed as I would have liked to have seen—specifically roads, economic development, and education. To give people a choice." A health administrator from coal-poor eastern Kentucky remarked, "I became interested mainly because I saw the need for better state health policy."

RECRUITMENT INTO LEGISLATIVE POLITICS

Not only is little known about state legislative recruitment, but also most in-depth studies are confined to one state. But the patterns of recruitment will differ from state to state for a number of reasons—the degree of professionalism, the amount of turnover, the activity of interest groups—and above all, the strength of party organizations and their involvement in recruitment of legislatures. The most valuable study of legislative recruitment, Seligman, King, Kim, and Smith's (1974), provides a thorough analysis and a model that assumes the existence of an active party organization. These scholars in their analysis of the 1966 Oregon legislative elections delineate three phases of the recruitment process: a phase of certification, a selection-process phase, and the role assignment phase. In the certification phase, an acceptable pool of candidates is identified (e.g., occupation, education, reputation). Different types of selection mechanisms are identified in the selection process phase: self-recruitment and various forms of sponsorship (e.g., co-optation, conscription, bureaucratic ascent, or agency ascent). Some individuals outside the political arena (e.g., wealthy businessmen with name identity) are co-opted to run for the legislature. Certain loyal, hard-working party activists are conscripted—asked to run for legislative positions. Some legislative hopefuls rise through the ranks of the party bureaucracy and then are designated the party legislative candidate. This recruitment model assumes a political party organization. When the party is weak, there are likely to be more self-starters; Seligman and his associates found that as many as half the candidates for the Oregon legislature were self-starters (1974: 47). In the absence of party organizations, there might be a plethora of various interest groups, each trying to recruit viable candidates. In the role assignment phase, elected legislators may be expected to be responsive to the demands of the party organization, interest groups, political leaders, or others who had sponsored, endorsed, or recruited them; but it is not clear that the recruiting agents apply a lot of pressure on the elected legislators.

Because the role of party organizations, the degree of legislative professionalism, and the degree of primary and party competition vary among the
states, we can assume that the patterns of recruitment also vary. But we lack
detailed studies to support this assumption. Wahlke and his associates (1962),
in their study of four state legislative systems, find that the party is the major
agency facilitating a legislative career mainly in competitive systems or when
it is especially well organized. In the less competitive systems, their interviews reveal that either interest groups or "friends" or "associates" may
perform the sponsoring function. In a later study of Massachusetts' state
senatorial elections, Mileur and Sulzner (1974) note the very limited role
played by party organizations, with the exception of highly competitive races.
In his campaign for a Vermont state senatorial position, Smallwood (1976)
enlisted the support of actual party political leaders rather than the party
organization. Another study (Kolasa, 1978) reports that where party organization is virtually nonexistent, or where the legislative election is nonpartisan, as in Nebraska, sponsorship of legislative candidates is very likely
to be undertaken by political activists in the private sector, especially businessmen and business groups.

In addition to the effect of party organizational strength in a state on
the extent of party sponsorship of legislative candidates, or self-starting, the
method of nominating candidates can play a part in getting people to run
for the legislature. States with restricted nominating processes, epitomized
by the closed primary or by party organizational endorsement systems, create
conditions that encourage party-sponsored candidacies. States with more
open nominating systems foster self-starting legislative candidacies. Tobin
and Keynes' research (1975) substantiates this general relationship between
candidate sponsorship and the state's nominating system in their research
in two states (Connecticut and Pennsylvania) that have had relatively closed
nominating systems and two states (Minnesota and Washington) with more
open systems. Substantial proportions of candidates in Connecticut and
Pennsylvania received active party encouragement in the form of prenomi-
nation endorsements, compared to well below half the candidates receiving
party endorsements in Minnesota and Washington.

To get involved in Kentucky legislative politics, one must be a self-
starter and probably even a "self-nominator." Political parties and other
formal organizations are not deeply involved in the initial recruitment of
new candidates for the Kentucky General Assembly. The Kentucky Democratic Party, perhaps because of its long-term dominance, makes few efforts
to recruit legislative candidates, leaving this to local political activists. The
role of party factions or other such groupings, both local and statewide, may
well be an important factor accounting for the absence of an official party
front. Many candidates appear to recruit themselves to run for the office.
Lawrence Miller (1977) found, for example, that in a study of individuals

who entered and left the Texas legislature between 1969 and 1976, some 43 percent said they were "self-recruited" to run for office. Only 13 percent said that political party organizations had recruited them.

Proportionately few candidacies are induced or unexpected anymore. James David Barber's (1965) "Spectators" and "Reluctants," the legislator types who comprised a large part of membership in Connecticut about 1958, are now exceptions and no longer the rule in Kentucky. Typically middle aged or elderly, of modest achievement, limited skills, and restricted ambitions, these types were recruited earlier to run for rural, malapportioned, noncompetitive seats. Other types—Barber's "Advertisers" and "Lawmakers"—were younger, more ambitious, and typically sought the nomination for the legislature, rather than waiting for the party or factions leaders to ask them to run. In terms of recruitment, Barber's "Lawmakers" would seem to be the growing, if not the predominant, breed in Kentucky today (1965: 217-33).

A legislative hopeful must be in a personal and professional situation that allows one to run for an office that pays so little and yet demands so much of one's time, even if pursued on a part-time basis. In short, a person must be independently wealthy or have a job that can itself become a second part-time position while he or she is in the legislature. Besides people who are independently wealthy, those who are self-employed are typically better able to meet this requirement.

Lester Seligman and his associates (1974) point out that the part-time nature of the legislature and the possibility for losers to return to their private occupations is very important. It is not necessary to risk either social or occupational status; holding on to an outside career is a cushion against political defeat. Even if one loses, there may be benefits. In their study of Oregon, Seligman and his colleagues found that four out of five losers in both the primary and general elections reported some benefits as a result of their unsuccessful efforts. They gained in social esteem and political influence, enhanced their private occupations, and furthered their political careers (1974: 25, 28, 164).

Rosenthal (1981b), in his comparative analysis of legislative life, notes that in the case of a winner there may be "opportunity costs," those possibilities that are forsaken while the individual serves in legislative office. The loss of time and the depletion of energy that might be otherwise devoted to one's regular occupation constitute costs. Many people are willing to make some sacrifice of their private careers, and perhaps their incomes, as long as they continue to engage in them part time and as long as they have something to return to if they get fed up with politics or are defeated. Part-time legislative service in itself is not a deterrent to individuals engaged in a number of occupations. This is because the costs initially are not prohibitively high (1981: 26-29).

The costs of running for legislative office are not purely occupational ones. Seligman and his associates (1974) point out that in urban districts, business owners, insurance agents, and realtors lose little by the prominence and publicity provided by waging a campaign and serving in office. But in smaller and in rural communities political contests can be disruptive. People know one another and are tied together by interlocking networks of primary social groups. Political combat threatens to jeopardize these relationships, and community norms consequently inhibit many potential candidates. Add to all this the costs to family life, because a political candidate and a legislator who is also engaged in a private occupation will be spending much time away from home (1974: 68-69).

THE PROBLEMS OF HALF-AND-HALF LEGISLATORS

Workload. Because legislators are serving more terms and because legislative work takes more of their time than was the case previously, it is becoming more difficult to combine a legislative career with another profession or occupation. This has become a problem in most states; in only a few, perhaps half a dozen, it has been solved by shifting to full-time legislatures. In most states where the legislature is part-time, an annual session usually lasts from three to six months. During that period members are in session about three and a half days a week, and have constituency responsibilities most of the remaining days; the rest of the year they only have constituency work to do.

In Kentucky the schedule, and thus the time pressure, is somewhat different. For about three and a half months every two years, while the legislature meets, legislators are frantically busy. (This would also apply to any special sessions.) For most of the rest of the two-year period, there are interim committee meetings several times a month; those who are conscientious attend most of them. And there are always constituency chores and some district meetings, with members varying in the amount of time they devote to these. Some also find it necessary to campaign intensively for the primary and/or general election, whereas others have a free ride.

The lengthening of the legislative session and the increase in interim activity have made the job of the member at least a half-time one in Kentucky. And it was obvious from our interviews (1983-87) and surveys (1983) that it has become increasingly difficult for members to serve half time. On the one hand, the pressures of the legislative job push the members to enlarge their commitment of time beyond 50 percent. On the other hand, members learn that it is very difficult to be a 50-percent teacher, or businessman, or lawyer. It is even more difficult to maintain an outside career when you can devote only 30 to 40 percent of your time to it. We believe that this frustration

Table 13. Legislative and Private Workloads of Kentucky Legislators

In Capitol	District Meetings	Casework	Total	Occupation
	House: Quartile Medians			
18	7	11	44	25
15	5	10	30	30
8	4	8	20	48
8	3	4	15	50
	Senate: Top Half and Bottom Half Medians			
10	4	6	22	40
8	3	4	15	40

with part-time careers leads many members to leave the legislature after two or three terms—either to run for an office that is full time or to return to a full-time career outside of politics. Many legislators expressed a need for personal staff because they lack the time to fulfill the demands made on them. But an expanding personal staff will probably lead to more activities by the legislator rather than a decline in the member's work load.

It is important to note that although the time demands have increased, the number of people retiring from the legislature has decreased. In Kentucky a large proportion of individuals who become lawyers, real estate agents, or business persons, for example, enter into a political career with a full realization that they will not have time to become the "best" lawyer, or the "most successful" real estate agent, or business person. The demands of a legislative job attract, to a degree, people with a different set of goals, ambitions, and expectations about their occupational career. Of course, there are those individuals who feel they can do it all. Moreover, some people remain part-time state legislators for a few years and then get elected to Congress as full-time legislators. And there are General Assembly members who do not get elected to Congress but still make the necessary adjustments between their legislative and occupational workloads.

In 1983 we surveyed Kentucky legislators about their legislative and private occupational workloads (table 13). Respondents were asked: "When the legislature is not in session, in an average week, how many total hours do you spend doing your job as a legislator (excluding specific campaigns for reelection) and how many hours a week (on the average) do you spend on your occupation(s)?" After we had recorded for each individual the total number of hours spent on legislative work and how this was divided among their work in Frankfort, district meetings, and constituency services, we rank ordered the legislators in the Senate and House by the total number of hours on legislative work from the lowest to the highest. Among senators there is limited variation in workloads. The median senator in the top half spends about ten hours in the state capitol (committees and other activities), four hours in district meetings (speaking or attending), and six hours in constituency services. In contrast, comparable figures for the median senator in the bottom half include eight hours weekly in Frankfort, three hours weekly in meetings in their districts, and four hours weekly in casework activities for their constituents. In terms of time spent in their private occupations, the median senator from both halves devote about forty hours weekly.

Specific responses from these twenty-one senators reveal a varied picture. One legislator spends forty to fifty hours weekly practicing law and another forty hours weekly doing legislative chores. Another senator spends forty hours as an IBM physician and twenty hours as a part-time legislator. One former professional volunteer spends thirty-five hours weekly as a full-time legislator. Another individual on average farms forty hours and engages in legislative activities thirty hours. A retired banker works thirty-two hours weekly doing legislative activities.

As depicted in table 13, in contrast to Senate members, there is significantly more variation in the legislative and occupational workloads among House members. The median representative in the highest quartile spends each week approximately eighteen hours in Frankfort, seven hours in district meetings, eleven hours in constituency services, and twenty-five hours in occupational activities; whereas the median representative in the lowest quartile spends eight hours in Frankfort, three hours in district meetings, 4 hours in constituency services, and fifty hours in occupational activities. Unlike senators, the more time representatives, in general, spend in legislative work, the less time they spend in their occupational activities.

Specific responses from these forty-seven representatives provide divergent patterns. One seasoned House member spends forty-four hours as a plumbing and real estate contractor and forty-eight hours as a legislator. Another individual devotes fifty hours weekly to his teaching activities and an additional twenty hours to his legislative chores. One woman spends forty to sixty hours as a mother/student and fifteen hours as a part-time legislator. One retired lawyer devotes forty hours weekly to his full-time legislative position. Another House member spends sixty-five to seventy hours weekly at a variety of professions—lawyer, country music writer/promoter, and farmer—and an additional twenty hours devoted to his legislative duties. One first-term member practices general dentistry thirty to forty hours weekly and devotes twenty-five hours to his legislative tasks. Another long-term representative spends forty-five to fifty hours practicing law and twenty hours doing legislative jobs.

In order to understand better the workload pressures of legislators, these interviewees were asked: "Do the time demands of your legislative job seriously interfere with your other occupation or job? If so, how do you cope with this problem?" Most of these senators and representatives reported that legislative time demands did seriously interfere with their other profession. An examination of some of their responses reveals the people who are feeling most pressured.

A seasoned Senate leader (lawyer) responded, "In an effort to continue my occupation or job during the period of time when the General Assembly meets, I find myself coming to the office at 6:00 A.M. during the week, returning after a legislative day and working most all Saturdays and Sundays. In addition, my partners in my law practice assist in handling some of my clients." Another senator (lawyer) commented, "Law partners pick up slack in some instances. In others, I simply neglect timely performance of duties." A long-term senator (banker) noted, "To some extent, but I work as my own boss; I do not have to account for time spent on the legislature." Another long-term senator (minister) remarked, "No, but the legislature is becoming more time consuming."

A full-time House member (retired lawyer) commented, "It would be a problem if I hadn't retired; the legislature now demands full time." A House leader (production control manager) responded, "Yes, it does. I serve the people first. My career at the company for the past thirteen years has been at a standstill." Another House member (farmer) reported, "Yes, I share help with neighbors and often times hire help." One representative (lawyer) remarked, "Yes, I attempt to allocate time in accordance with de- mands of both jobs—cut back on private client representation—cope poorly both in terms of devoting enough time to either job and in income." When the legislature is not in session, one veteran legislator works at a factory from 4:30 A.M. to 3:30 P.M. and then goes home to engage in legislative-related matters. He concedes, "Occasionally pressures develop on me to quit, but it gets worked out." Another House member (realtor) commented, "Nor- mally the real estate business requires sixty or more hours per week. I spend two to three days per week on legislative matters during the interim." One representative (farmer/auctioneer/meatpacker) noted, "I depend on other partners, employees, and let a lot go undone." A first-term House member (lawyer) responded, "Yes. I recently switched law firms—to a smaller firm where I hope to have more flexibility."

Many who leave state legislatures to return to private life do so mainly because of the demands of their regular professions or occupations. Lee Bernick's study (1977) of nonreturning senators from eleven states confirms this. Of those who left the legislature, but not to seek higher office, about two-thirds did so because of business demands and two-fifths because of financial burdens.

Disruption of Family Life. The disruption of family life can also produce great strains for state legislators. According to Rosenthal (1981b), some hus- band-legislators do not see their wives or children for days or weeks at a

time when the legislature is winding up its session. Even when things are
normal, many legislators only manage a few late evening hours together with
their wives, but except for weekends not much time with their children
(1981b: 44-45). During nonsession years, senators and representatives spend
numerous weekly hours in Frankfort, in district meetings, and in casework
services. Legislators must juggle time not only for their occupational and
legislative duties but also for their family activities. Also, some legislators
who live a long way from Frankfort have the added burden of driving time.

Most legislators are willing to tolerate the costs to their families. If there
are no children or if the children are grown, the costs are lower. Women
generally begin their legislative careers at an older age because of the demands of young children at home. Also, Kentucky legislators often mention
family life in explaining why they stay in the state legislature rather than
running for Congress, where they perceive the strains on family to be much
greater. Some legislators pay the price for a disruption of family life: their
marriages end in divorce. Other legislators are unwilling to pay the price;
almost half of the senators surveyed by Bernick (1977), for example, indicated
that interference with personal family life was a principal reason they were
departing the legislature. Moreover, Blair and Henry (1981) found in a study,
based on all legislators who voluntarily left the Arkansas legislature from
1968-80, that family factors explained even more departures than did financial considerations.

According to one Kentucky Senate leader, "The real problem is juggling
time between my family and the legislature, because there are always Rotary,
Lions, or other club meetings every single night. And every weekend. . . . Honestly I would rather not do that. I've got three boys at home.
My wife has to do many of the activities with them without me. This is
becoming more and more a real consideration with me about having this
legislative job."

Psychological Frustrations. As noted by Rosenthal (1981), few individuals
are able to cope with legislative service in a casual, leisurely way. Not everyone can endure the many stresses of legislative life. The normal day is frustrating because of the unpredictability, inconvenient timing, and the
conflicting nature of the various demands on a legislator (1981: 45-46). A
legislator in Oklahoma has described his feelings of frustration (Kirkpatrick,
1978:67):

> During my first term in the legislature, the feeling I had was like
> being a ball in a pinball machine and you don't know what slot the ball
> is going to fall in. That's sort of the way you are when you walk in the
> Capitol. You are like that ball, and you don't know who's going to grab
> you, you don't know what group's going to be there to see you, you

don't know where you are going to be next. . . . It was so bad my first session that when my wife came into the room I got up and shook hands with her.

Shills (1959) has portrayed the frustrations of individual legislators by noting, "The legislator is always confronted with more demands than he can satisfy; he is always in danger of displeasing someone and is never sure of just what it will take to please them . . . ; he is always dependent on someone else's judgment for his equanimity and his security" (1959: 350).

Smallwood (1976), in depicting his frustrations as a Vermont state senator, has asserted, "The pressures are so chaotic and so unpredictable that plain, hard physical stamina becomes of overriding importance, and life is a tiring, grueling, continuous depletion of personal energy reserves" (1976: 223).

Kentucky part-time state senators and representatives must learn to deal with the many frustrations of legislative life. Of course, some decide that the stresses are too great and conclude that being in the legislature is just not worth all the strain.

Kentucky legislators have many of the same characteristics as those in the 1960s. There has been an increase in educational standards and some change in occupational and religious distribution; but there has been surprisingly little growth in the proportion of women members.

The most dramatic change is a growth in the proportion of members who seek and win reelection. One obvious consequence is a decline in the proportion of freshman members and a growth in the proportion serving four sessions or more—and thus an increase in legislative experience. Less obvious but equally important is a change in members' career goals. Members today enter the legislature at an earlier age, and more of them have long-term political ambitions: to rise to positions of power in the legislature and/or to seek higher political office. These men and women are more willing than their predecessors to devote much of their time to legislative service, even though it is difficult to maintain a successful business or profession on a half-time basis. Although few Kentucky legislators are professional in the sense of being full-time, many of them are professional in their skills, their commitment to the legislature, and their goals for a career in politics.

4. Representing the District

American congressmen devote time and attention to their districts. During sessions most of them return nearly every weekend to the district, and between sessions they spend most of their time there. They use the full range of communications devices, from newsletters to radio and television broadcasts, to reach their constituents. They maintain district offices, and a substantial proportion of their staff time is devoted to providing constituency services and gaining benefits from the district.

Increasingly, American state legislators are following the pattern set by congressmen. A recent study (Jewell 1982) of legislators in nine states showed that members are conscious of the need to develop visibility and maintain constituency contacts, and many of them are imaginative in developing techniques to accomplish this. Members differ in the priority they give to constituency service and in the staff resources that can be used for this purpose, but for many of them this is a substantial part of their job. Most legislators are sensitive to the need to gain projects from the state that will help their districts. As legislators become more professional and career minded, they give greater priority to district activity, largely because they recognize the electoral necessity of doing so.

Kentucky legislators are no exception to this pattern. Because the legislative session is so brief, Kentucky legislators may lack the visibility of those in many other states. But the dramatic increase in the tenure of Kentucky legislators, documented in the last two chapters, has made them much more familiar and visible figures in their districts. Kentucky legislators who do not hold leadership posts or chairmanships lack staff assistance that can be useful in providing constituency services, but a hard-working legislator can provide such service personally. Most importantly, it is the growth in the proportion of career-minded legislators in Kentucky that has increased the attention paid to representing the district.

We will begin by looking at variations in types of legislative districts, and by examining legislators' perceptions of their constituencies. Then we will describe the variety of techniques used to communicate with the district. We will look at the problems legislators face in representing the interests of their district. Finally, we will examine the types of services provided to constituents and the member's role in getting benefits for the district.

VARIATIONS IN DISTRICTS

Kentucky uses single-member districts entirely, 38 in the Senate and 100 in the House. The average Senate district has about 100,000 population, whereas the average House district is close to 38,000. The job of representing constituents varies with the geographic size and governmental structure of the district.

The 1963 redistricting of the legislature, passed in response to the new requirements imposed by the U.S. Supreme Court, ended the serious underrepresentation of metropolitan counties. But substantial population inequalities remained because the 1963 law followed the state constitutional requirement that counties not be divided to form districts (except for multidistrict counties). The 1971 redistricting was rejected by a federal court because of population inequalities, and the legislature found it necessary to divide some counties in order to make districts "as nearly equitable as possible.

Because the Supreme Court has somewhat relaxed its requirements for district equality, the districting that took effect in the 1984 election reduced the number of cases in which very small sections of a county were placed in a district. But there remain 19 Senate districts and 45 House districts that extend beyond a single county and that include segments of counties. There are only 10 Senate and 11 House multicounty districts that contain only whole counties and not fragments of counties. In some cases very small slices of a county have been broken off in forming districts. For example (based on the 1984 House elections), 9,812 Whitley County residents voted in the 82d district, while 224 of them voted in the 87th district, along with 11,912 voters from Bell County.

We can distinguish four major types of legislative districts in Kentucky:

1. There are 41 districts that constitute only a part of a larger metropolitan county, 9 in the Senate and 32 in the House. The Senate districts are in Jefferson and Fayette Counties; the House districts are in these counties and in Kenton, Pike, Daviess, Warren, and Hardin Counties. (Small parts of some of these counties are also found in other, multicounty districts.)

2. There are 12 districts, all in the House, that contain only a single county. Only two of these districts exactly coincide with those of a county; in the other cases, fragments of the county are located in other districts.

3. There are 23 multicounty districts (7 in the Senate and 16 in the

House) that are dominated by a single county, but also include a smaller county or parts of another county. (These include districts divided between part of a large county, such as Campbell, Kenton, or Daviess, and part or all of another county.)

4. There are 62 other multicounty districts, 22 in the Senate and 40 in the House. The largest Senate district (in terms of counties) contains nine; the largest House districts are three that contain all or parts of five counties.

We can simplify this somewhat complex pattern in the following terms: 30 percent of the legislators represent a portion (often a small portion) of a metropolitan county; 25 percent represent primarily one county or a substantial part of it; and 45 percent of them represent a cluster of counties or part-counties.

We must keep in mind these variations in the geographical structure as we describe differences in the ways legislators represent their districts. For example, does the legislator representing one district in Fayette County concentrate on the needs of that district or try to represent districts throughout the county? Does a member representing all of one county and one-third of another pay much attention to the needs and interests of that county fragment? How do members cope with the quite different problems of developing communications and gaining visibility in these various settings? How does a Jefferson County legislator compete with twenty-five other members from the county to get coverage in the *Courier-Journal*? How does a member representing four and a half counties make contact with the political and group leaders in all of these counties, and especially those in the half county when the county seat lies outside his or her district?

DEFINING THE DISTRICT

Richard Fenno (1978) in his study of the "home style" of congressmen in their districts, called attention to variations on the way members perceive their constituencies, particularly for reelection purposes. Within the geographic boundaries of the district are a series of concentric circles: the reelection constituency that provides voting support; the primary constituency—the most loyal supporters, who could be relied on in a primary battle; and the personal constituency, made up of the closest political allies. A congressman or legislator may make similar distinctions in determining how to represent the various constituencies in the district. State legislators may not make such subtle or complex distinctions within their districts, largely because these districts are smaller and usually more homogeneous than congressional districts. But it is still important to understand how Kentucky legislators define their districts and perceive their constituencies, and what implications these perceptions have for representation.

In interviews with Kentucky legislators, we have asked many of them how they would define their district. They often defined it first in terms of geographical boundaries: the number of counties or the parts of a county that were included. They often described in some detail the major interest groups that were strong in the district, such as teachers, labor unions, or business groups. Members representing a metropolitan district often talked about specific neighborhood groups, or—in Jefferson County—small incorporated cities.

A minority of legislators described their districts in terms of political philosophy. One Louisville legislator, for example, said, "Philosophywise, I think the majority tends to be conservative—some ultraconservative, some conservative, a few moderates, some liberals, and a few ultraliberals, the whole spectrum—but a majority are conservative."

Kentucky state senators were asked in one study (Griffin, 1985: 93) how they defined their constituency. Two-thirds of them defined it in terms of particular groups, sometimes economic groups, sometimes religious, occasionally racial. The rest either used geographic terms or referred to the philosophical leanings of the district (usually conservative).

Legislators are conscious of the homogeneity or heterogeneity of the district. When asked about the problem of representing several different counties, one member will say it is not difficult because all of the counties are rural and have similar interests. Another member will mention that his district is a microcosm of the state, with both urban and rural interests, and therefore more difficult to represent. One Jefferson County representative expressed concern about the variety of interests in his district, which includes older parts of the city as well as a rural area, with a wide mixture of socioeconomic groups.

Legislators who represent one district in a metropolitan county draw their votes only from that district, but many other aspects of representation involve residents from other parts of the county. Most groups and organizations in the county (except for some neighborhood groups) are not organized at the district level but draw their members from all or most of the county. When a Lexington or Louisville legislator is asked to speak to a group, his audience is likely to be countywide. Similarly, groups such as the Fayette County Teachers Association, the Louisville Chamber of Commerce, or the University of Louisville make requests for legislation or other kinds of assistance to all legislators throughout the county, paying particular attention to those who are on the pertinent committee or who have demonstrated an interest in the issue. When metropolitan legislators do or say something that attracts attention in the press, it is read by voters throughout the county (and even outside the county).

No studies have ever been done on the perceptions that residents of metropolitan counties have of their legislators, but it would not be surprising to find that many are less familiar with their own legislator than with others in the county delegation who are more visible, more experienced, or more active in speaking before organizations. Most citizens are not very conscious of legislative district boundaries (in contrast to the more salient question of school district boundaries). They often move from one house or apartment to the other, oblivious to having changed legislative districts. We know that constituents seek help from a legislator whom they have heard of or met, rather than the one who represents their district. From the viewpoint of anyone living in a metropolitan county, the question, "Which legislator is mine?" becomes pertinent only on election day.

Given these realities, it is not surprising to find that most Kentucky legislators in metropolitan counties try to serve the interests of the whole county as well as give particular attention to their own district. Most of them answer constituency requests from any part of the county. They cooperate with other members from the county in an effort to get benefits for the county, to help the county and city governments with requests for legislation and projects. In Jefferson County, because of its size and diversity, the legislative delegation is sometimes divided over legislation or over county-level projects. Under these conditions, the members pay particular attention to the interests of their district or one section of the county.

Some legislators feel responsive to interests that are broader than their own district but narrower than the metropolitan county. One black legislator from Jefferson County told us that he served the interests of black constituents throughout the county. Some legislators may serve broader interests than a single county. A legislator whose district included parts of both Campbell and Kenton counties said that he represented all of northern Kentucky.

The representational problems faced by legislators in rural, multicounty districts are quite different. Most of them live and work in a single county, where they have become active in local organizations, built their political base, and sometimes run for office. A professional or business person, living and working in the city that is the county seat, finds it easy to stay in contact with the individuals and organizations most active in public affairs and to be accessible to constituents. Developing and maintaining such contacts in other counties requires much more time, effort, and travel.

Legislators differ in the efforts they make to represent the other counties in such districts; but nearly all of them recognize the problem. Constituents living in a county that does not have a resident legislator tend to feel that they are not "really" represented. They see the legislator and read about him less often, and are less likely to send him requests for legislation or services. (This public attitude is a major reason there used to be "rotation agreements" in many multicounty districts, providing that over a period of years the legislator would come first from one county and then from another.)

A Democratic legislator representing two Democratic counties (including his own) and one Republican county finds that he gets relatively few requests and has few contacts from the Republican county. Representatives often find that they get few requests from an outside county if the state senator is a resident of that county.

Legislators often admit that they ought to spend more time in the other counties of the district, but it is time consuming to do so. They sometimes express frustration about the difficulties of establishing contacts with organized groups and with the media located in the fragments of counties included in their district. Some members go out of their way to develop contacts and pay visits in the other counties. A few legislators have an advantage because of family ties or business contacts in other counties of their district. Rarely did we find an example of a legislator choosing to ignore one segment of his district. One former legislator, who represented two rural counties and the Berea section of Madison County, did tell us: "I hardly ever go in Berea. I don't think Berea is very satisfied with being part of the district."

COMMUNICATING WITH THE DISTRICT

To represent the district, it is necessary to gain visibility and develop effective lines of communication. The congressman accomplishes this by flying home to the district nearly every weekend; maintaining district offices; and sending out newsletters, questionnaires, press releases, radio and television feeds, and computer-generated "personal" letters to constituents. To carry out these activities, the congressman has a large staff divided between Washington and the district, free mailing privileges, and access to modern computing equipment.

The Kentucky state legislator has one advantage over the congressman. He or she lives in the district and even during the brief session can spend two or three days each week at home. But most legislators have no staff, and they have no office in the district, no free mailing, and only a limited expense account. The legislator's success in gaining visibility and developing effective communications with constituents depends entirely on his or her skill, energy, and imagination.

The organized groups in a county or city provide the legislator with one of the best opportunities to establish contacts and gain visibility. Groups such as the Rotary Club need speakers for their weekly meetings and are willing to listen to the legislator. Other organizations that have an interest in particular policy issues are even more eager to hear from a legislator.

These groups give the member a chance to express his own point of view as well as to find out about the concerns and interests of constituents. Unfortunately, such invitations are most likely to come during the legislative session, when the member is busiest.

The speech-making opportunities depend, as we have suggested, on the structure of the district. In a large metropolitan county, the better known, more experienced members may have a monopoly on speaking invitations from countywide groups, and the freshman may be limited to neighborhood groups in the district. The legislator representing a multicounty district may have to struggle to gain invitations from groups in other counties.

The imaginative and persistent legislators take advantage of whatever opportunities exist in the district. They attend meetings whether or not they have a speaking invitation. A black legislator from Louisville visits a different church in the district every week. A legislator in northern Kentucky maintains contacts with seven neighborhood organizations through a citizens' advisory council that represents them. In Jefferson County, which has relatively active party organization, some legislators regularly attend party committee meetings.

Legislators attend meetings of school boards, planning and zoning organizations, and city councils to find out what constituents are concerned about, and sometimes to speak out in their behalf. At least a few legislators hold meetings every week or so around the district while the legislature is in session. One rural senator, for example, scheduled nine community meetings in various parts of the four-county district in the month before the regular session, and another fifteen meetings during the first two months of the session. Legislators often find that attendance is poor at such meetings; occasionally, they may hold a joint meeting with the local congressman in an effort to draw more people.

Some legislators make an effort to attend as many civic and social events as possible to stay in touch with constituents. One Jefferson County legislator says, "I work the church picnics and the festivals; you don't just drop out of sight—you never stop working." One rural legislator says that he and his wife go out several times a week, to square dances, fishfries, church picnics, wherever people are meeting. Other rural legislators like to go to country stores or auctions to meet people. There are several reasons for going to events that have nothing directly to do with government or politics. One is simply to be seen and to develop contacts. Beyond that, legislators say that constituents whom they meet will occasionally talk to them about legislative issues or local problems—providing one more way of finding out what people are thinking. Constituents who might never call them up to make a request or voice an opinion will do so when they see legislators in person. Not every legislator makes a point of going to so many nonpolitical activities; some lack the time or do not enjoy it, whereas others consider it unnecessary. But there are many such opportunities available for the legislator who finds it necessary to expand contacts with constituents.

One of the major differences between legislators in metropolitan and in rural counties is access to the media. Because the Jefferson County delegation is so large, it is particularly difficult in that county for a legislator to get frequent attention in the *Courier-Journal* unless he or she plays a major role in the legislature. There are suburban papers with more space available that some legislators have been able to use. Legislators in rural areas have much greater access because (except for a member from the other chamber) they have no legislative competitors for space in the newspapers of their counties. With a minimum of effort they can make enough speeches and generate enough news to get attention. During the session some legislators— particularly in rural areas—write columns that are run regularly by one or more county newspapers. Some legislators are also enterprising enough to make use of local radio stations for interviews.

Since 1977 the Legislative Research Commission has operated a Legislative Information Office (LIO) to assist legislators with media relations. In 1986 the office had six full-time employees, including several professional journalists and a photographer. The LIO sends out press releases on legislative issues and activities to the local newspapers of members at their request, and also provides these papers with pictures of the members at work. When a local newspaper agrees to run a member's weekly column on legislative developments during the session, the LIO will prepare the column— written so as to suggest it was authored by the member. The Information Office also prepares recorded messages by members to be telephoned to local radio stations and writes speeches on legislative issues for members to deliver in their districts.

The newsletter, a standard technique of congressmen, is used by only a minority of Kentucky legislators. Based on a survey, we would estimate that one-third have made some use of a newsletter. The most obvious obstacle is cost; legislators do not get free mailing privileges, and their expense allowance is not sufficient to cover the cost of printing and mailing several thousand newsletters with any frequency. Some of the legislators who use a newsletter have solved the cost problem by having volunteers distribute it door to door, whereas others have persuaded rural newspapers to publish it, very much as they would publish a column. Perhaps one-third of those using a newsletter mail it out; they may be using their expense allowance, campaign funds, or their own resources for this purpose. Other legislators say that they lack the time to prepare a newsletter, or doubt that it serves a useful purpose.

The newsletters that are sent out are often professional in appearance, comparable to those sent out by congressmen. They usually feature pictures of the member and articles on his or her activities and bills introduced. At the end of the 1986 session, one legislator published an eight-page tabloid-style newsletter, including twenty pictures that showed him at work: meeting constituents, working in the legislature, watching the governor sign one of his bills, and so forth. Legislators use the newsletter to announce dates and places for community meetings. The newsletters may describe projects, such as highway improvements, that are under way in the district. One legislator included a detailed description of road improvements along with a district map showing the location of each. The newsletters often describe major issues facing the legislature, or at the end of the session summarize major legislative results. One representative publishes the complete House roll call on a few major issues to show how he has voted.

Most legislators lack the resources and time to send out computer-prepared mailings to members of selected groups on particular issues, as congressmen often do. But some of them do make use of frequent mailings. One legislator said that following the 1986 session he had sent some two thousand letters to members of various interest groups describing pertinent legislative activities. The same legislator sends out a citation to every gradu-ating high school senior. Although this is not typical, it illustrates what a state legislator can do.

Our survey suggests that nearly one-third of the legislators have made some use of questionnaires to measure constituent opinion on issues facing the legislature. Most of these are sent out before the session, and are usually included as part of a newsletter—whether published in the newspaper or mailed or hand-carried to constituents.

Questionnaires can serve at least three purposes. At a minimum, con-stituents are likely to be impressed that the member cares enough about their opinion to send out a survey. If the questions are carefully prepared and a good sample is returned, the survey may provide the member with good information about the salience of various issues and the opinions of constituents on these issues. Finally, some legislators publicize the results of surveys to demonstrate that constituents agree with their position on issues.

A sample of questionnaires used by Kentucky legislators shows that they deal with some of the major issues facing a session, such as proposals to raise taxes, the choice between raising taxes and cutting revenues, a state lottery, mandatory jail sentences for drunken driving, and various proposals for amending the constitution. Respondents are sometimes asked to list other issues that they think the legislature should consider.

The most important question about such surveys is whether they provide legislators with more specific, accurate information about constituent opinion than they can get from other sources. Some legislators who use surveys believe that they are helpful, often by simply reinforcing the impressions that members get from other sources. Occasionally, members are surprised by the results on a particular issue. The surveys may be most useful to provide some balance or perspective on the mail and phone calls generated by pressure groups, and legislators sometimes cite the results to counter the claims made by lobbyists. Most members who use surveys appear to be quite sophisticated and cautious about interpreting the results, and use the surveys only as a supplement to other sources of information. Some members who have tried questionnaires indicated in our survey that they are not particularly helpful. The fact that two-thirds of the legislators have not used surveys suggests widespread doubts about whether they provide enough new data to be worth the cost.

There are several more conventional and less expensive methods of measuring constituent opinion. For several years the legislature has operated a toll-free "hot line" that constituents can use to leave messages for members or talk to them directly. In the 1986 session these toll-free lines received over 250,000 calls. Throughout the session, of course, members receive mail on the issues and sometimes personal visits from constituents in Frankfort.

Back in the district there are many opportunities for face-to-face contacts with constituents, before the session and in the long weekends during the session. Legislators can get the reaction of organized groups to legislative proposals by contacting their leaders or by speaking to groups. They often stay in touch with political leaders, newspaper editors, business leaders, and others who can help them assess public opinion in the district.

REPRESENTING THE INTERESTS OF CONSTITUENTS

A legislator has many sources of information about the views and interests of his constituents. To represent the district well, the legislator must learn how to evaluate this information, to determine what issues are most salient, and to judge whether the letters and phone calls he or she gets are broadly representative of constituent opinion. The legislator must also decide how much weight to give to the demands made by the various organized interests in the district.

During the course of a session, each member must make decisions on a large number of bills. On most of these the legislator hears nothing from the district, because constituents know nothing about the bills and/or because they are not affected by them. On some issues the legislator hears from organized interests in the district. On relatively few issues during a session the legislator may get significant numbers of calls and letters from ordinary citizens.

In reality, most of the input that a legislator gets from the district is organized in one way or another. Most bills are narrow in scope, affecting only a few groups and individuals. Often when the legislator learns about a bill that will affect a particular group or interest, he or she takes the initiative to get a reaction to the bill from members of the group in the district. Constituents who belong to state organizations are urged to contact their legislators about pending legislation. When the legislator returns home for the weekend he will have a call from his local banker on a proposed banking regulation or a visit by a group of teachers to discuss proposed revisions in the teachers' retirement system.

The task of evaluating constituent opinion varies with the nature of the issue. The narrower and more technical the issue, the easier it is for a legislator to determine what constituents want. Relatively few constituents are affected, and there is usually consensus among them about proposed legislation. An example might be a bill to raise the fees charged by county clerks or a change in insurance regulations.

A second category of issues contains major questions, often economic ones, on which important interest groups have taken positions that are usually well known. Examples would be a right-to-work bill, a measure to permit professional negotiations for teachers, or an increase in the severance tax on coal. It is not difficult for legislators to determine the position of organized interests on such issues, and the experienced legislator usually knows how strong these interests are in the district and, at least in a general sense, what is the attitude of the broader constituency.

In a relatively homogeneous district, there are likely to be fewer conflicts among organized groups and more of a consensus of constituent opinion on such issues. The more heterogeneous the district, and the greater the variety of organized interests, the more often constituent opinion will be divided on such issues, creating problems for the legislator. Some legislators, however, believe that such heterogeneity makes their job easier. One rural legislator says, "I am fortunate that the district is varied and that no single group—unions, coal interests, or particular business—can dictate to me. The farmers are a major group in the district, but the farmers often have other business interests, and so they are not tied to a single viewpoint."

The most difficult issues faced by legislators are controversial, emotional issues that generate demands by organized groups but are also salient to the broader constituency. Some of these are "moral issues" such as abortion, capital punishment, gun control, and state regulation of church schools. School busing was such an issue a few years ago. An issue like the lottery has both financial and moral implications. Sometimes major tax proposals stir up both organized and unorganized interests. These issues are difficult for a number of reasons. The moral issues are difficult to compromise; it is hard to find a middle ground on capital punishment or abortion. There are likely to be well-organized interests on both sides of these issues, and they succeed in mobilizing substantial numbers of constituents to send letters and make phone calls. But it is often difficult for the legislator to judge whether the calls and letters that come in are representative of opinion in the constituency as a whole.

Legislators recognize that most of the letters and phone calls they get are organized, and they view these with some caution because of the belief that many of those who contact them have little interest in or understanding of the issues. As one legislator put it, "Almost without exception issues are generated; they are not real." He believes that, except for a few emotional issues or a major tax increase, the general public has little real interest in such issues even when it has been persuaded to write a letter or make a phone call. Legislators are often frustrated because they hear very little from unorganized constituents, and they often find it difficult to judge how the broader constituents feel about issues on which there is considerable organized input.

Political scientists often talk about legislative roles and, specifically, the style of representation. The authors of *The Legislative System* (Wahlke, Eulau, Buchanan, and Ferguson, 1962: 272-80) identified two major approaches that they found legislators taking toward representation. They defined a *trustee* as a legislator who follows his own judgment, based on his knowledge and understanding of the issues and his perception of the needs of the district. A *delegate* is a legislator who follows the instructions of constituents (or of other political actors such as interest groups or party leaders). They also defined a middle category, the *politico*, who may shift from one role orientation to another, depending on the issue or other circumstances.

A number of scholars have sought to place the members of particular legislative bodies into these categories (Jewell and Patterson, 1977: 362), and some have tried—with only limited success—to predict legislative behavior on the basis of these categories of role orientation (Jewell, 1985: 106-7; Kuklinski and Elling, 1977; McCrone and Kuklinski, 1979). We believe that the trustee and delegate roles are neither mutually exclusive nor contradictory. There is some variety among legislators: some rely more heavily on their own judgment, and others pay particular attention to strongly articulated demands of constituents. But most legislators play different representational roles depending on the issue. They follow their own judgment on many issues where they are well informed or have strong opinions, or whether constituents appear to be disinterested or poorly informed. On other issues that are salient to important groups in the constituency, they are responsive to the demands of these groups. We believe it is less useful to stereotype legislators as trustees or delegates than to understand why and under what circumstances legislators choose particular role orientations.

When legislators are asked how they assess constituent opinion, one of their most common responses is that they are typical of the district, meaning that they share the dominant attitudes and viewpoints of the district. A legislator who is really typical can use his own judgment, rather than counting letters and phone calls, and yet be confident that he is not out of step with the constituents. One Kentucky legislator who has lived most of his life in his district said that he knows what people think because he is typical of them and because he has a lot of contacts in the district. As a result, he can judge whether groups that make demands on him are really typical of the district.

An important reason legislators often act like trustees, relying on their own judgment, is their belief that the organized pressures, such as mail and phone calls, are often in conflict with what they perceive to be the views and interests of the constituency as a whole. One veteran legislator told us, "I think I know the district well enough to judge what it wants. I don't ignore the mail, but I have to judge what is right for the district, not just for a few people or groups." A Louisville legislator told us he tried to follow three principles of representation: "Be well informed about bills, which is not easy; keep in touch with your district and know their feelings; and, ultimately, follow your conscience and decide what is best for the district."

Legislators learn to discount many calls and letters because they are often based on misinformation. One legislator says, "When I feel that the voters who contact me are not well informed on an issue, I vote as I wish. People often misunderstand what a bill actually does." Another legislator epitomizes the role of a trustee when he says: "I have a philosophy about this: I have access to certain information that is not generally available to the constituency, and I make a decision on the basis of that information. It may not be to their immediate liking, but I feel like I am voting in their long-run best interests."

Legislators often argue that constituents respect their independence and trust their judgment. According to a veteran rural legislator, "I think the people trust me. They know I will exercise my best judgment. They know my stand and respect it. They may not always agree with me, but they respect my willingness to make my position clear." Some say that most constituents recognize that the legislators know more about the issues. One of the best informed and experienced members of the Kentucky legislature says that when groups in his district meet with him in response to suggestions from their state organizations, they are often apologetic about making requests, telling him, "You know more about this issue than we do."

Legislators often emphasize that during the campaign they made clear their intention to be trustees, and therefore they have a mandate to follow their own judgment. A freshman legislator told us, "I campaigned as a trustee and I said that if they wanted someone to just take polls and vote according to public opinion, they should vote for someone else."

There are some legislators who adopt the role of trustees because of a strong conviction that it is the proper role of a representative. One strongly issue-oriented legislator explained her trustee orientation in these terms:

"Any legislator who simply counts the mail is not a thinking legislator, and is not doing the job. You can't let the district drag you along. If my opinion is different from that of the district because of my background on the issues, it is my duty to vote according to my opinion, and explain it to the district. If they don't like it, they can elect someone else."

It is more difficult to find examples of legislators who articulate primarily a delegate role. But they often specify particular conditions under which they think it is necessary to respond to constituency pressure, such as emotional issues or ones on which there is evidence of an overwhelming district majority in favor of a position.

Terms like *trustee* and *delegate* oversimplify the actual role orientations of many legislators. One Republican legislator described the variety of factors he takes into account in making a decision:

> Basically I am a conservative type of person, and I think I represent the views of a majority of my constituents. When there is little or no input from constituents, then it is my personal tendency to vote conservative. I consider: is it good for Kentucky, according to my political philosophy; is it good for my district, according to my philosophy; is it good for the Republican party? When there is a lot of input from my people, then I try to vote in accord with it. I think it is my responsibility to vote the way a majority would vote if they were in my shoes.

Some issues are controversial enough and some groups feel strongly enough about them so that legislators face real risks in ignoring group demands and following their own judgment. Legislators are very conscious of these risks and have learned to weigh them realistically. One liberal Democratic representative told us that he had antagonized pro-life groups in his district by voting against them on a number of occasions. Early in his term he was worried about the political risks of his stand, and he acknowledges that it has cost him some votes. But he believes that over a period of time voters have come to know him well, to appreciate what he has accomplished, and to overlook those few votes on which they may disagree with him. And a veteran legislator from Louisville says, "In my first term I used to really worry about votes on issues where there was pressure. Now I am more relaxed about it. You get a little more careless, I guess; you are still a representative, but you don't get shaken by threats."

Legislators often emphasize the importance of explaining their votes, particularly the unpopular ones, to constituents. They find that it provides an opportunity to educate constituents—including organized groups—about the complexities of legislation. One member says, "People often don't understand an issue, but when I explain it to them they generally appreciate my vote. Sensible people will listen when you explain your votes, but a few fanatics won't listen at all."

Another legislator says:

> There are a few issues on which I differ with significant groups in the district and on which I have decided to vote against them. I may have to take the heat for a while. You worry about possible opposition even if you haven't had any. If they thought they could beat you, some groups would run someone against you. You don't want to hand an opponent an issue he can eat you with. But it is harder to justify a vote that you don't believe in than one that you do. I think, given a chance to explain my vote, they will buy my explanation and respect me, even if they don't completely agree. But there are some you can't reach.

It is the organized groups in a district, more than individual constituents, who want an explanation of the legislator's voting behavior. It is always important for legislators to stay in touch with the organized groups in the district, and explaining votes is one part of that process. Kentucky legislators, like those in other states, are concerned about the so-called single-issue groups, some of which demand complete support and are unwilling to compromise or listen to explanations from legislators. But these groups would appear to be fewer in number and less aggressive in tactics than in some states.

In his discussion of the "home-style" of congressmen, Fenno (1978: 151) describes the importance of explaining votes in terms that most Kentucky legislators would recognize as valid: "There are at most only a very few policy issues on which representatives are constrained in their voting by the views of the reelection constituencies. . . . On the vast majority of votes, however, representatives can do as they wish—provided only that they can, when they need to, explain their votes to the satisfaction of interested constituents."

PROVIDING SERVICE TO CONSTITUENTS

As the Kentucky legislature has grown more professional and the individual members have become more experienced and more visible, constituency service has become a larger part of the member's job. In a previous study (Jewell, 1982: 141), we asked legislators in nine states about the amount of attention and priority they gave to constituency service and found that Kentucky ranks approximately in the middle. Constituency service is most important in California, Massachusetts, Texas, and Ohio; is of moderate importance in Kentucky, Tennessee, and Indiana; and is relatively unimportant in North Carolina and Colorado.

We believe there are several reasons for the middle position. Providing extensive services for constituents can be a very time-consuming enterprise. Kentucky legislators, other than leaders and committee chairmen, have no personal staff to help in carrying out this work. By contrast, legislators in states like Texas, and particularly California, have personal staffs who handle most of the routine responsibilities of constituency service. Massachusetts legislators did not get a personal staff assistant until 1979, but most of them use that person primarily for constituency service.

Another variable that explains differences among legislatures in constituency service is the political culture of the state. Massachusetts, Ohio, and Indiana are good examples of states that have a long tradition of patronage; citizens have become used to bringing their problems and their requests for jobs to political leaders. Kentucky also appears to fit this pattern. Until the early 1960s, jobs in state government were largely filled on the basis of patronage, and similar patterns remain at the level of county government and school districts. In a state with such traditional practices, it is not surprising that constituents have begun to seek assistance from legislators as they have become more visible and active political figures. And it is not surprising that legislators have been willing to devote time and effort to constituency service, even though they have little or no staff help for such work.

In addition to these state-level variables, there are individual differences in the priority that legislators assign to constituency service. A study of Kentucky senators (Griffin, 1985: 203, 225) showed that nearly all of them considered constituency service important, and most believed that such activity provided significant electoral advantages to members. We found that most Kentucky representatives and senators whom we talked to agreed that constituency service was important, but there were differences in the relative importance they attached to policymaking and constituency services.

Clearly, some legislators are primarily interested in the legislative process. These are likely to include many who have the heaviest leadership and committee responsibilities; some are too busy in Frankfort to devote much time to running errands for constituents, whereas others are simply more interested in their legislative responsibilities.

Some members get particular satisfaction from helping individuals and believe this is the way they can best serve the district. One veteran member says, "I am very people oriented. I get calls from constituents around the clock, and I like being able to serve. I get a real sense of satisfaction out of being able to help people." Some legislators believe that they can have relatively little influence on legislature, but can do more directly for constituents. A former legislator from Louisville said, "Just cutting through the bureaucratic red tape for your people—if you do that you are doing 99 percent of what you were elected to do."

Legislators may emphasize constituency service because they believe it is a prerequisite for winning reelection. A typical comment is: "I value my voting record and I try to make it known to people. But the services you do for people matter a lot more than your voting record, which most of them don't know." A Louisville legislator who said he would rather spend more time on legislative issues explained why he gave more attention to constituents: "The minute than I am not accessible, that's the minute that I am not going to get reelected."

It is clear that some legislators receive many more requests from constituents than others do. Rural legislators and those from lower-income urban districts get more requests than those who represent higher-income urban and suburban districts. Lower-income constituents need more help, and what we have referred to as the norm of patronage may be stronger in rural than in urban areas.

It is also clear that legislators who give high priority to service can generate more requests from constituents by advertising their willingness and ability to provide help. When a legislator is actively involved in helping constituents, the word gets around that district, and more requests are likely to come in. A Louisville legislator says: "I send out newsletters and questionnaires, and I make myself accessible to constituents, listing my phone number on everything I send out. This produces constituency casework because they identify with you and they know who you are. I have instant contact with the people at the factory where I work. When people need something they come to me, no matter what county or district they come from; I'm available to help them out."

The growing visibility of Kentucky legislators has obviously led to an increase in requests from constituents. Legislators often say that they are more likely to get such requests soon after they have sent out a newsletter or gained attention in the press for some form of legislative activity. One active legislator said, "I provided a contrast to my predecessor—he was never around and no one knew what he was doing; but I came along at a time when the legislature became more visible, with more press coverage and the toll-free number in Frankfort." One veteran legislator who has worked steadily to maintain contacts and provide services describes a phone call from a constituent who called to report a break-in at her house. The legislator asked if she had called the police, and the answer was, "Not yet."

There are substantial differences among legislators in the amount of time they devote to casework and the number of requests they receive from constituents. According to our survey of representatives, the median number of hours per week spent on casework was ten to eleven for the top half, eight hours for the third quartile, and four hours for the least active. Senators were both less active and less varied, with a median of about five hours a week on casework. Constituents are less likely to take their requests to senators than to representatives. One reason may be that in rural areas, where senatorial districts often cover four or more counties, constituents may be familiar with and have some contact with a representative who serves in a smaller district.

A good example of a representative who is highly involved in casework is Hank Hancock, whose district involves most of Franklin County, the location of the state capital. He averages about eight letters and twelve telephone calls a day from constituents seeking help, a large proportion of them from state employees. Because of his location and his experience, he gets some requests from state employees all over Kentucky. In an average week when the legislature is not in session, he spends about twenty hours on casework and an equal amount of time on other legislative duties, in addition to running a business. According to Hancock, "I end up working very long hours, working Saturdays and Sundays, and far into the evenings." Several other legislators from districts surrounding Franklin County have large numbers of state employees in their districts and report a high level of casework.

Legislators in rural areas generally report a larger number of requests than those in the cities. In metropolitan areas it is the lower-income districts that are more likely to generate requests for assistance; but one legislator from a central city district believes that many constituents are not well enough informed about the process of government or the role of the legislator to contact him. The lowest proportion of constituent requests comes from the higher-income metropolitan districts. One legislator from a high-income district in Fayette County reports averaging only one or two calls a month, whereas a former legislator from a similar district could recall only one constituent request in a six-month period.

Legislators in Fayette County believe that they are less likely to get requests for help on purely local matters because the urban county government has twelve districts whose representatives handle such matters. One Fayette County representative reports, "When roads didn't get plowed, I didn't get a single call." Legislators in Jefferson County believe they get more local requests because of the size of the county and the perceived distance of the county court house and Louisville city hall. We have found that legislators in the metropolitan areas of other states are less likely to be asked to handle local casework when the major city governments use single-member districting systems.

What kinds of requests do state legislators receive from individuals? They are as diverse as the needs and interests of the state. As we have indicated, constituents often ask state legislators for help in dealing with local government. They may know the state legislator better or perceive local officials to be unhelpful. For similar reasons it is common for constituents to ask state legislators for help in dealing with the national government. Sometimes these requests are misdirected because constituents do not understand the complexities of the federal system, a misunderstanding that is not surprising given the number of programs that are jointly administered. Legislators often serve as a referral service, helping constituents find the particular agency—state, local, or national, public or private—that may be able to help them out.

In a state having many counties with high levels of unemployment, it is not surprising that many of the requests are for jobs. This is, of course, a type of request that is very difficult to fulfill. One legislator estimated that over a two-year term he was able to get about a dozen jobs for constituents, and there were about twenty applicants for each job. For the large proportion of state jobs that are under the merit system, there is little a legislator can do except write a note to the personnel office asking that the constituent be given an exam—an effort that is symbolic rather than substantive. We have already noted that legislators in some districts get many requests for state employees. They may seek to be shifted from part-time to full-time status, to get a review of a request for promotion, or to seek help in dealing with a grievance.

Legislators are also asked to write letters of recommendation for students seeking admission to universities or professional schools, and they usually respond, though they recognize that such requests do not carry any special weight. In counties containing state universities, legislators may get complaints from faculty or staff about how they are treated by the administration, though legislators seem to have relatively little leverage in such cases.

Legislators representing the less affluent districts frequently get requests to help constituents deal with some aspect of the welfare or health bureaucracy. An Ohio legislator once told us that many requests for help come from persons who "fall between the cracks of eligibility" for various welfare programs. Examples would include persons seeking to qualify for workmen's compensation, food stamps, public housing, or various health care programs and facilities. State legislators from coal-mining districts receive large numbers of letters and calls from constituents seeking help in qualifying for black-lung benefits.

Legislators often get requests for help in dealing with state regulatory agencies. A legislator on the health and welfare committee, for example, may be contacted by nursing homes in his or her district seeking relief from state requirements. Legislators from coal-mining districts may be asked to help in getting state agencies to issue permits to operate mines or to be more flexible in enforcing safety standards or requirements for reclamation in strip-mining operations.

Members get requests to intervene in dealing not only with government but with private business: a dispute between a constituent and a merchant or a contractor, a complaint that the utility company has cut off service. One legislator told us that a constituent who had recently been divorced asked her to be on the lookout for someone who might qualify as a new husband! Legislators who are lawyers are often contacted by constituents who really want free legal advice; they differ in their willingness to provide it. One legislator who is not a lawyer explained to one constituent what her rights were under a law providing compensation to victims of crime, and followed the case for a year before it was settled.

Some of the requests from constituents might be considered trivial, such as requests for tickets to basketball games or for assistance in getting a Kentucky colonelcy—but if they are important to constituents, legislators try to oblige.

Most requests, however, are serious. Whether or not constituents are legally entitled to the governmental benefits they are seeking, they deserve help in finding their way through the bureaucratic maze and in getting a prompt answer to their problems. One relatively junior Louisville legislator, describing his experience in calling government agencies, said that he got a much better response when he identified himself as a representative than when he simply gave his name. This led him to conclude that the bureaucracy was not sufficiently responsive to ordinary citizens, and therefore intervention by legislators was frequently justified.

We believe many Kentucky legislators share the views about the importance of providing constituency service that were expressed to us by two representatives in other states:

> The people who come to us don't know what agency or level of government to go to. Or they have been kicked around from one level of government to another. If we have to direct them to another office, we check to see if the problem gets handled.
>
> When people come to our office it is almost the last resort. They have been kicked around. You can't solve all their problems, but you can bring the matter to a conclusion—either solving it or telling them it cannot be done.

GAINING RESOURCES FOR THE DISTRICT

Legislators may differ on the priority given to constituency service, but there is consensus on the importance of bringing state governmental resources into the district. Several years ago, when we were studying the roles of representatives in nine state legislatures, we concluded that, "perhaps because of political norms in Kentucky, legislators appeared to be more heavily involved in getting resources for the district than those in some other states" (Jewell, 1982: 137-38).

In their efforts to gain various kinds of benefits and projects for the district, the legislators' role varies with the type of district. The member who represents a district encompassing several counties shares responsibility with those counties only with the member or members from the other house. In a metropolitan county, however, the members of the county delegation usually work together, in concert with city and county officials, to gain benefits for the county, the major city, and other governmental institutions such as universities. In a metropolitan county, however, an individual member may work on projects of particular concern to his or her district, such as installing a traffic light or completing a specific road project.

In rural Kentucky the highest priority for most legislators is to improve the road system in the district. Good roads need to be repaved, poor roads need to be upgraded, and gravel roads need to be blacktopped. The problems of maintaining and improving roads are particularly serious in the coal-mining counties where heavy coal trucks constantly damage the roads. Throughout the state, but particularly in eastern Kentucky, there is a need to repair and upgrade bridges. When a local bridge deteriorates to the point where it is unsafe for school buses to cross, the consequences for local communities can be devastating. Rural legislators may also work together to gain commitments from the state for major highway projects that will link the more isolated areas to the main interstate roads and turnpikes. The importance that rural legislators attach to highway improvements is often reflected in their newsletters, where they claim credit for what has been accomplished.

Although all legislators are committed to major highway improvements in their district, they may differ on other road priorities. One legislator said that the hardest part of his job was trying to get the roads in the district improved, giving particular priority to requests for blacktopping from his closest political supporters. For sixteen years as a legislator he had been trying to get the roads blacktopped, but there were still a number that remained unpaved. Another legislator said, "I try to facilitate requests for highway improvements made by local officials, but I leave the blacktopping alone; if you get involved in that, you will just antagonize people and get in political trouble."

There are many other kinds of projects that are important to rural districts. Kentucky has an excellent state park system, and legislators whose districts include or adjoin a park try to get improvements in its facilities. Kentucky also has an extensive system of community colleges, and a high priority for legislators is to get building improvements and additions in their local one. There are various ways that the state can provide help to county courthouses, fairgrounds, hospitals, and other facilities. Enterprising legislators will help local officials in gaining information about state and federal grant programs that may be available for their counties and cities. This is a particularly important service in rural areas where the local governments cannot afford to hire specialists in state and federal grantsmanship.

There is nothing a legislator can do for his or her district that is more important than obtaining a major project. It will be remembered much longer than the member's voting record. To gain such projects, the legislator must have a good working relationship with the governor and/or, in recent years, hold an important position in the legislature—such as a leadership post or a seat on the Appropriations and Revenue Committee. We will return in subsequent chapters to the questions of local projects when we discuss the appropriations process and the role of the governor in the legislative process.

In metropolitan counties the role of the individual legislator is less important because most decisions are made collectively. The mayor of Louisville or Lexington will meet with the county delegation to discuss the need for local projects (as well as local legislation) and to enlist their support. Mayors and county judges in major metropolitan areas usually have political influence in Frankfort, but they need as much help as they can get from legislators. Officials of universities located in metropolitan centers are likely to contact the legislators in those areas, asking for their support in getting higher appropriations or particular programs or projects that they need.

The success of local officials in getting projects depends very heavily on consensus in the delegation as well as the political skills of its members. There have been several examples in recent years of serious divisions within the Jefferson County delegation on projects for Louisville and for the county. These divisions result from the socioeconomic diversity of the county and in some cases from splits between the city of Louisville and Jefferson County. In most cases such projects have been stalled until a high degree of consensus was achieved in the delegation.

This emphasis on collective action does not mean that there is no room for initiative by individual legislators in metropolitan centers. An individual legislator may be particularly concerned about the needs of the university or the improvement of health facilities in the county, for example. They also may be concerned with needs in their own district, such as the installation of a traffic light, completion of a sewage project, better drainage to prevent flooding, or local road projects to alleviate congestion.

The task of getting resources for the district is not only an important part of the legislator's job; it is also a difficult part. There are never enough resources to go around, and, increasingly, decisions on resource allocation are based on demonstrated need and not merely on political clout. To be effective in gaining resources, the legislator must work with local officials, and sometimes interest groups, in planning projects, demonstrating their importance, and mobilizing political support for them. In counties represented by more than one member, the skillful legislator must cooperate with his or her colleagues while trying to gain maximum political credit for the project. Because the stakes are high and the political advantages considerable, most legislators recognize that gaining resources for the district deserves high priority.

Kentucky legislators may lack the visibility of the nearly full-time legislators common in some states, and they may lack the personal staff and resources that legislators in many states are able to use for constituency service and communication. But in recent years Kentucky legislators have become more conscious of the importance of the constituency and have begun to use many of the techniques the legislators in other states employ to represent and serve constituents. The problems of representing a constituency varies with the nature of the district. Those in large metropolitan areas face problems of getting media attention, and those representing parts of several counties may have difficulty developing and maintaining contacts throughout the district.

There has been a gradual growth in the members' use of newsletters and questionnaires, despite the shortage of resources for printing and mailing. Constituency service is becoming more important, but the priority attached to it varies by district, depending on both the preferences of the member and the extent of demands made by constituents. Most Kentucky legislators recognize the political value of constituency attention and service; the growing attention that is being given to the members' responsibilities in the district contributes significantly to the growing workload of legislators.

Part Three
The New Legislature

Thirty years ago most American legislatures were relatively weak and ineffective, and some were corrupt. Some legislatures, particularly in southern states, were dominated by governors. Other legislatures were dominated by interest groups, particularly in states with weak party systems or in those where one or two economic interests were predominant. Still others were not necessarily weak, but were controlled by powerful party leaders; as a consequence, the committee systems were weak, and the average member had little influence on decision making.

As legislators began to recognize the need for reform and sought to strengthen legislative institutions, they moved in several directions. The first, and most fundamental, change was to strengthen the committee system. After World War Two, when congressmen sought to reinvigorate Congress so that it could play a stronger role vis-à-vis the president, they focused their attention on the committee system, streamlining the system, clarifying jurisdictions, and providing committee with more and better staff. State legislators followed the same strategy. Most legislative chambers had had twenty-five to fifty committees; the average number was cut to ten to twenty. The jurisdiction of committees was often spelled out more precisely in the rules, so that it was more difficult for leaders to undermine committee authority in making assignments of bills.

In many legislatures the rules were reformed to require that committees provide advance notice on scheduling action of bills, hold more hearings, and conduct deliberations and take votes in public. In many states there was a gradual increase in membership continuity on committees because of less legislative turnover and less committee shifting by those who remained in the legislature (Basehart, 1980). This raised the level of membership expertise on committees. Perhaps the most important trend over the long term was a growth in the number and quality of staff members assigned to committees.

The improvements in committee structure and staffing and in membership expertise, as well as the growth in time allowed for sessions, enabled the legislature to undertake much more thorough reviews of the governor's budget. In the larger states, at least, the legislature developed staffs for budgetary analysis, program review, and revenue study that rivaled those of the executive branch in size and professional competence. The growing size of the budget and the growing complexity of budgetary decisions facing the states made it necessary for the legislatures to accept much greater responsibility for budgetary review.

As the role of state government grew larger and more complex, it was inevitable that state agencies would grow in size and complexity and that many of the important policy decisions would be made by these agencies rather than by the legislature. As legislators became conscious of this trend, they developed new techniques for legislative oversight of the executive, techniques that also relied on the committee system, required more and better staff, and demanded a heavy commitment of time from those members who participated in oversight (Rosenthal, 1981a).

Many legislatures passed so-called sunset laws, requiring that legislative committees periodically review many agencies and commissions to determine whether they should continue to exist or be abolished (Hamm and Robertson, 1981). Most legislatures established committees to review the thousands of administrative regulations adopted annually by executive agencies and to recommend changes in those that appeared to be unfair or improper or conflicted with legislative intent (Ethridge, 1985).

The Kentucky legislature provides an excellent laboratory to study each of these national trends. In the late 1960s and early 1970s, Kentucky committees were streamlined and given clear jurisdictions; the process of providing adequate staffing was initiated. To cope with the rigid constitutional limitations on the length of sessions, an interim committee system was established and gradually strengthened.

The legislative process in Kentucky for reviewing the budget was gradually changed from swift and automatic approval to careful scrutiny and selective revision, largely due to the increasing skills and efforts of members and staff on the Appropriations and Revenue Committee. During the 1970s the legislature established a number of interim committees for legislative oversight, and gradually these committees developed considerable effectiveness.

5. The Remodeled Committee System

MODELS OF LEGISLATIVE COMMITTEES

Committee systems are found in all state legislatures and in Congress, and on paper they look very much alike. In many states the committees have similar names and jurisdictions; most bills are assigned to them for review; they hold hearings and make recommendations to the full senate or house on legislation. Committees usually have authority to kill bills, and in reality this authority is usually final. In recent years most legislative committees have had at least a minimum of staff assistance. Despite these surface similarities, there are many variations among legislative committee systems in the independence, power, and decision-making processes of the committees. These differences can be illustrated most easily by describing several models.

The first model, found in many state legislatures, is one in which legislative party leaders have considerable influence over committee decisions through their power to appoint and remove committee chairmen and members. Under this model the party leaders make their choices of all chairmen and the members of at least the major committees in large part on the basis of their loyalty to the party and its leaders. Moreover, at the start of each new legislature, the leaders can and do remove chairmen and members of committees, to replace them with more loyal members. Because committee seniority has little meaning, members have no great incentive to remain on the same committee even when they have the opportunity to do so. Where party leaders are most powerful, they may give instructions to committee chairmen on bills to be approved and killed, and they may assign the most important bills to the most trusted committees, with little regard for formal committee jurisdictions.

One variation of this strong leadership pattern is found (or used to be found) in states where the governor is able to influence the choice of legislative leaders, and through these leaders can dictate the appointment and removal of chairmen and members of legislative committees.

A second model of legislative committees is one in which interest groups have major influence over committee decisions. In this model neither the party leaders nor the governor would seek to dominate the committees— or at least most of them. To the extent possible, members would be given the committee assignments they requested. There would be high rates of turnover on the committees, however, resulting in part from high turnover in the legislature. Expert knowledge on the committees would come less from experience than from the professional and occupational interests of members. The banking and insurance committees would be dominated by bankers and insurance agents, the education committee by teachers and principals, the judiciary committee by lawyers. Such members would be particularly responsive to the demands of the pertinent interest groups.

The third model—strong, independent committees—is found most obviously in Congress. This independence is based largely on the seniority system and the continuity of membership. The committee chairman is usually the senior member of the majority party and is rarely removed once in office. Normally, members can retain their posts on the committee for as long as they want; members rarely leave a committee once they have accumulated several terms of seniority. The result of this system is that a large proportion of members, and of course the chairman, have served long enough to become experts on the topics over which the committee has jurisdiction. Equally important is the fact that they can make independent judgments on policy matters because, except in rare situations, they cannot be removed by party leaders or anyone else. Congressional committees in recent years have also benefited from generous staff and budgetary resources.

Strong, independent committees are found in a few state legislatures as well. In such states the party leaders appoint the committees but do not try to enforce personal loyalty or party discipline on the members. Few state legislatures have seniority systems comparable to those in Congress, but there are some legislatures where the major committees are run by chairmen and members with extensive experience and specialized knowledge. In recent years some of these committees have also developed strong staff resources. The result is that these committees can make independent judgments, and their views carry weight on the floor of the legislature.

As these descriptions make clear, the most important variable affecting each of these models is the method of selecting and retaining the chairmen and members of committees. Another important variable is the resources available to the committees, including time, funding, and staffs. The dramatic changes that have occurred in the Kentucky committee system have resulted from changes in the selection and retention of committee members, revisions in the Senate and House rules, and the expansion of committee resources.

THE OLD COMMITTEE SYSTEM

For many years prior to the 1968 session, the committee system in the Kentucky General Assembly was organized in such a way as to maximize the control of the governor and legislative leadership over the decision-making process in committees. The governor selected the leaders and worked closely with them in the choice of committee chairmen as well as the members of major committees. This was one of the strongest sources of the governor's power in legislative affairs. Of course, the constitution and the rules of the General Assembly say nothing about such authority. The governor's ability to select his own leaders rested on the legislature's willingness to accept his recommendations.

The legislative rules were designed to insure that those bills of importance to the governor would be sent to committees guaranteed to be loyal to him. Even if the committees had wanted to exercise more independent authority, they lacked the time and resources to study bills carefully or even to hold extensive hearings on them.

During this period the Kentucky legislature had a large number of committees, but power was concentrated in only a few of them. From 1950 through 1966 the number of committees averaged twenty-nine in the Senate and about forty in the House. The most important of the House committees were the Rules Committee and three committees named Kentucky Statutes No. 1, No. 2, and No. 3. In the 1964 session, there were forty-five committees in the House, with very uneven workloads. An examination of referrals of all House and Senate bills in the House shows the Rules Committee got 43 percent, the three Kentucky Statutes committees got 10 percent, seven other committees got 22 percent, and the remaining thirty-four committees got only 25 percent (with five of them receiving no bills). Among the bills that actually became law, two-thirds went to the Rules or one of the Kentucky Statutes committees. In the Senate there was a similar pattern of concentration with Rules getting 41 percent, eight others getting 47 percent, and ten getting only 12 percent. The Senate also made use of small, dependable Kentucky Statutes committees for major bills.

The reason for assigning a disproportionate number of bills to a few committees was that these were the committees on which the leadership had placed the most loyal, dependable legislators. In the 1964 session, for example, the three Kentucky Statutes committees contained twenty Democrats, several of whom were assigned to two of the committees, and nearly all of whom had records of high loyalty to the administration. Although Republicans had a proportionate share of most House committees in 1964, they had no seats on the Kentucky Statutes committees.

The legislative leadership in both houses used the Rules Committee as a further control over the legislative agenda and timetable. The rules provided that during the last fifteen days of the session, all other committees were abolished, and the Rules Committee assumed jurisdiction over all bills that were newly introduced, or came from the other House, or were still awaiting action in other committees. This obviously had the effect of undermining the work of other committees because they had no authority during the crucial closing days of the session. Bills that a committee had buried could be revived in the Rules Committee, and most of the bills passed in one house arrived in the second too late for consideration in a regular committee.

In theory the Rules Committee system guaranteed administration control during the last quarter of the session. In practice this was an inefficient system because the Rules Committee had grown so large. In 1962 and 1964 the House Rules Committee included all nonfreshman members (which discriminated against Republicans, who had growing membership and thus more freshmen). The Senate also used a large Rules Committee, but omitted some antiadministration Democrats and some Republicans.

Nearly every feature of the legislative system contributed to making the committees ineffective and undermining the members' incentives to take their committee work seriously. Because of high turnover and short sessions, most members had little knowledge of or experience with the issues coming before a committee. The most important bills were usually diverted to one of the Kentucky statutes or rules committees. Even if a committee received a bill of some importance and interest, it had little time or resources for a thorough review. The committee functioned for only forty-five legislative days (about seven weeks), and many bills reached the committee late in that period. There was little time (and very little room space) for hearings on bills. There were very few staff resources for research. The leadership often gave the committee instructions on how it should handle a bill. Whether the committee's judgment on a bill was positive or negative, this verdict could easily be reversed by the Rules Committee. When the session ended (fifteen days earlier, in fact), the committee was dead, with no means or power even to study legislation until the next regular session, two years later.

CREATING A NEW COMMITTEE STRUCTURE

The new committee system for the Kentucky General Assembly was conceived in 1967 and born during the 1968 legislative session. For a number of reasons the time was ripe to reform the committee system. There was a national movement under way to reform state legislatures, and in 1967 there were meetings of citizens and legislators in Kentucky to explore ways of improving the legislature. In November 1967 a Republican was elected governor for the first time since 1943. This meant that the Democratic majority in the legislature had an opportunity to choose their own leaders and develop their own programs without pressure from a Democrat in the governor's mansion. It also meant that the Democratic legislators needed to develop alternatives to the governor's program, to lay the groundwork for the next election. There was also a new generation of young legislators, some of whom were impatient to make the General Assembly more effective and powerful.

The father of the new committee system was James Fleming, the able and experienced director of the Legislative Research Commission (LRC). He was encouraged in his efforts by Lieutenant Governor Harry Lee Waterfield, chairman of the LRC, who foresaw in the summer of 1967 that Democratic factionalism might cost the party the governorship.

In July 1967 Fleming presented his proposal to the members of the LRC. In his memorandum Fleming argued that major improvements could be made in the legislature without changing the constitution. "The General Assembly has failed to use all of the powers that it now has." Once it has done all it can to improve the legislative process, the General Assembly "will be in a better position to go to the people and request constitutional reform of the legislative article."

Fleming identified the top priority for reform: "The basic internal weakness of the Kentucky General Assembly is the committee system." Fleming made a number of major recommendations, including the following:

1. The number of committees should be reduced, with parallel committees set up in the two houses.

2. Jurisdictional rules should be adopted to strengthen the committees and balance their workload.

3. The role of the Rules Committee should be reconsidered because it contributes to the logjam of bills at the end of the session; it should no longer replace the committees during the last fifteen days.

4. It would be desirable for the committees to function between sessions, and it should be possible to find a constitutional means of accomplishing this objective.

In 1968 The General Assembly adopted Fleming's proposal for a new committee system, with only a few modifications. It established fourteen substantive committees in each of the houses, with parallel jurisdiction. The jurisdiction of each committee was spelled out in the rules, reducing though not completely eliminating the leadership's discretion in assigning bills. Since that time remarkably few changes have been made. There have been some changes in committee organization and jurisdiction; slight differences in committee structure have developed between the two houses; and the number of committees has increased to fifteen. Except for a few leaders, each member continues to serve on two or usually three committees. The principle was established that each party should have a proportionate number of seats on each committee.

The role of the Rules Committee in the two houses was drastically revised. Each house established much smaller rules committees, dominated by leaders. The committee operates throughout the session and no longer supersedes the standing committees. The extent of the Rules Committee's control over the legislative agenda and timetable has varied from time to time; both the written procedures and the tactics of leaders have shifted, and the most recent trend has been to reduce its functions.

Perhaps the most important change inaugurated by the legislature in 1968 was the establishment of an interim committee system. The legislature initially attempted to establish interim committees and to strengthen the LRC in other ways by passage of legislation, but this was vetoed by the governor (perhaps because of features in the bill other than the interim committees). In May, after the legislature had adjourned, the Legislative Research Commission reorganized each pair of Senate and House standing committees into joint interim committees. Legally, the interim committees were established as subcommittees of the LRC. Because the courts had previously upheld the constitutionality of the Legislative Research Commission, this technique provided a firm constitutional foundation for the interim system.

The interim committees did not become effective institutions overnight. It has taken a number of years for staff resources to be developed, for interim committee activities to be taken seriously by interest groups and the executive, for oversight activities to be initiated, and for legislators to become willing to spend time and effort on interim work.

The interim committee system assumed even more importance because the voters twice—in 1969 and 1973—rejected constitutional amendments that would have permitted annual sessions of the legislature. Consequently, the interim committee system is the only technique (other than special sessions) enabling the legislature to break out of its sixty-day biennial sessions.

The initial goals and resources of the interim committee system were quite modest. James Fleming, who developed the system, expected the interim committees to produce a legislative package, consisting of a modest number of bills, that could be sold to the subsequent legislature. He did not expect the committees to meet regularly or to hold extensive hearings, but only to meet when needed to deal with major issues (Cox, 1975: chap. 3).

The role of interim committees began to expand during the 1971-74 period while Lieutenant Governor Julian Carroll chaired the Legislative Research Commission. Carroll took a more activist approach to the interim committees. He believed that the committees should hold more hearings and actively seek interest group participation in the hearings. He prodded the committees to meet more regularly and develop a larger legislative agenda. Several of the committee chairmen responded to this initiative with increased activity; one of these was Bill Kenton, chairman of the Cities Committee and a future Speaker of the House (Cox, 1975: chap. 3). Carroll's role in encouraging a stronger interim committee system is ironic because as governor (1975-79) he dominated the legislature more persistently and successfully than most of his predecessors or any of those who followed him.

The modest beginning of the interim committee system can be illustrated by looking at the budget. During the five fiscal years from 1969 to 1974, the budget for interim activities increased very gradually from $42,000 to $50,000, but it was raised suddenly to an annual average of $344,000 during the 1974-76 biennium (Cox, 1975: chap. 2).

One of the most serious problems faced by the Legislative Research Commission during its first decade was a lack of continuity. The interim committees were active for about eighteen months from the end of the regular session until the fall election campaign, commissioning staff research, holding hearings, and drafting bills. During this period, however, legislators who had decided to retire had little incentive to play an active role in the interim committee sessions, and those who were defeated in the May primary had even less incentive to participate during the closing months of activity. Cox (1975, chap. 3) found that during the 1972-73 interim, those legislators who were subsequently reallocated were somewhat more active in interim committees than those who were defeated and considerably more active than those who retired.

Moreover, when the new legislature met, the regular House and Senate committees included many legislators who had either not been in the previous legislature or were not serving on the same committees. Consequently, they were often skeptical about the recommendations made and the bills drafted by the interim committees.

Cox (1975: chap. 4) calculated that during the sessions from 1970 to 1974, only half of the committee assignments in the Senate and fewer than half of those in the House were held by members who had been on the same interim committee in the previous session. Over these three sessions half of the Senate committees and two-thirds of the House committees had a majority of members who were unaffiliated with the pertinent interim committee. This lack of continuity resulted both from high turnover in legislative membership and the fact that many of those who returned to the legislature shifted to other committees.

In 1979 voters adopted a constitutional amendment that was designed primarily to strengthen the interim committee system by eliminating this problem of discontinuity. It moved legislative elections from odd- to even-numbered years. The new timetable of elections and sessions permits the newly elected legislature to hold a brief organizational session in January and to devote an entire year to interim committee activities prior to the regular session.

From the outset the interim committee system has fundamentally altered the character of the General Assembly. It has made the legislature, de facto if not de jure, into a continuing body. It has enabled committees to hold lengthy hearings, sometimes at various locations in the state, and to study complex issues in detail. It has given the legislature and its members substantial visibility throughout the biennium. It has made feasible and necessary that the LRC provide each of its committees with full-time, year-round professional staff.

One measure of the growing scope of legislative activities throughout the years is the growth in the legislative budget, which has increased tenfold over a twenty-year period. The following figures show the total appropriations for the legislative branch in a biennium, for selected pairs of fiscal years:

1968-70	$3,028,176
1974-76	$6,366,552
1980-82	$18,303,338
1986-88	$35,102,750

The figures reflect increases in salaries for both legislators and staff; but more importantly they result from the growing size and complexity of the legislative operation: more frequent interim committee meetings, the development of several oversight committees, a larger staff assigned to committees and other activities, more research activities and publications, and the installation of computer facilities.

SELECTION AND TENURE OF
CHAIRMEN AND MEMBERS

To understand how the committee system has operated in recent years, we must know how committee leaders and members are chosen, how long they serve on the committees, and how much opportunity they have to remain on the same committee.

The tradition of gubernatorial selection of leaders and committee chairmen ended, not because the legislators revolted and chose their own leaders, but because Governor John Y. Brown, Jr., gave up that prerogative. After his election in 1979, Brown made it clear that he would make no effort to influence the choice of leadership. When Governor Martha Layne Collins took office in 1983, the leaders for the 1984 session were already in place—chosen in the January 1983 organizational session established by constitutional amendment changing the time of legislative elections. Collins made no direct effort to interfere in the selection of leaders or chairmen that occurred one year after her election, even though at that time there was a major turnover in House leadership.

With the end of gubernatorial influence in the selection of committee chairmen and members, the choices are now made by the legislative party leadership, specifically by the Committee on Committees. In the House that committee consists of the Speaker and Speaker pro tem; the majority floor leader, caucus chairman, and whip; and the minority floor leader. In the Senate the committee includes the president pro tem and assistant president pro tem; the majority floor leader, caucus chairman, and whip; and the minority floor leader and caucus chairman (prior to the 1988 session, the lieutenant governor was also a member). In practice it is the Democratic leaders on these committees who select the chairmen and Democratic members, but—as we will describe later—the Republican leaders usually control Republican assignments.

The legislative leadership now controls the selection of committees, along the lines of the first model described earlier. Leaders may use this authority to maintain maximum control over committee decision, or may seek to accommodate the wishes of members as much as possible. The selection process may lead to considerable stability or turnover in committee membership. How much has the system changed with the removal of the governor from the process? What has been the actual pattern of committee selection in recent years? How are chairmen and members chosen, how long do they serve? What effect has the lower turnover in the legislature had on the legislative committee system?

To answer such questions we will examine the pattern of committee membership for six legislative sessions: 1976, 1978, 1980, 1982, 1985-86, and 1987-88. Only during the first two of these sessions was the governor involved in the selection process. (The 1984 session is omitted because, during the transition to a new election schedule, there were very few changes in chairmanships or membership between the 1982 and 1983-84 legislatures.)

Committee Chairmen. We begin by looking at change and continuity in committee chairmanships during these six biennial sessions. If committee chairmen enjoyed the same kind of security that those in Congress have, they would never leave a chairmanship except to accept a more powerful or attractive chairmanship or to take a leadership position. On the other hand, if a new governor took office and/or there was a turnover in top leadership positions, we might expect to find turnover in a large proportion of committee chairmanships. In reality the pattern of continuity and turnover of committee chairmanships in Kentucky lies between these two extremes.

There is a practical reason why turnover of chairmanships is limited in the Kentucky Senate. Normally, members do not receive chairmanships

Table 14. Changes and Experience of Committee Chairmen for 1976,
1978, 1980, 1982, 1986, and 1988 Sessions

	Senate	House
Gained chairmanship	31	34
On committee, previous session	12	26
On committee, an earlier session	6	4
Never on committee	13	4
Shifted chairmanships	12	6
On new committee, previous session	4	1
On new committee, an earlier session	3	3
Never on new committee	5	2
Shifted from chairmanship to leadership	4	5
Lost chairmanship	8	9
Stayed on committee	3	7
No longer on committee	5	2

during their first two years in the Senate. During the 1976-88 period, the number of Democrats with at least two years of senatorial experience averaged twenty-four, and nineteen of these could expect to receive one of the fifteen chairmanships and four leadership positions to be filled. Consequently, a new governor and/or party leaders might be expected to move a few of their most loyal allies into the most important chairmanships and deprive a few opponents of any chairmanship. But it would not be feasible to bring about a wholesale change in chairmanships.

Over the period of six sessions there were twelve chairmen in the Senate who lost their posts and did not gain another chairmanship, but four of these moved to leadership positions. Of the remaining eight, only three remained on the committee they had previously chaired. There were twelve other senators who moved from one committee chairmanship to another (table 14).

Let us look more closely at the changes that occurred in the Senate during the 1976-88 period. During Wendell Ford's governorship, a factional rivalry between Ford and Lieutenant Governor Julian Carroll persisted. Ford had selected legislative leaders loyal to him for the 1972 and 1974 sessions. Carroll became governor in 1975, when Wendell Ford entered the Senate, and—as was to be expected—he played a role in choosing a group of leaders who would be loyal to him in the 1976 session. In that session only two senators were deprived of a chairmanship (not including one who became a leader), but four others shifted committee chairmanships. The most important change affected Mike Moloney, an ally of Ford who had chaired the powerful Appropriations and Revenue Committee in the two previous sessions. Moloney lost his chairmanship and membership on that committee and was moved to the chairmanship of one of the judiciary committees. Two years later, in the middle of Carroll's term, there were only three changes, including appointment of another chairman of the Appropriations and Revenue Committee and the removal from a chairmanship of Tom Easterly, who had the reputation of being too independent.

In 1980, when John Y. Brown, Jr., became governor, he made no effort to influence the choice of leaders or chairmen. But control of the Senate passed to a group of senators who had developed a reputation for independence during the Carroll administration: the so-called "Black Sheep Squadron." The new leadership made a few important changes in committee chairmanships. Two senators lost chairmanships: Mike Moloney regained the chairmanship of the Appropriations and Revenue Committee, and two other chairmen shifted committees. In the middle of Brown's term there was only one change.

There was continuity of Senate leadership between 1980 and the 1985-86 session, and only four changes in that session. Of the two senators losing a chairmanship, one change was for reasons of health. Two chairmen exchanged committees, apparently in order to give the more important post (the State Government Committee) to a senator with close ties to the leadership and the governor. In the 1987 organizational session, one committee chairman moved to a leadership position, one chairman shifted committees, and four senators gained chairmanships as a result of vacancies when members left the Senate.

During the 1976-88 period in the House, the average number of nonfreshman Democrats was sixty, and in most sessions there were only fifteen committees. Consequently, it would have been possible for a new group of House leaders to find replacements for all the committee chairmen if they wished to do so. In fact, however, turnover in committee chairmanships was about as frequent in the House as in the Senate. During this period the total number of House members losing chairmanship (without becoming leaders) or shifting chairmanships was fifteen, compared to twenty in the Senate. Nine House chairmen lost their posts without gaining another chairmanship (plus five others who moved from chairmanships to leadership positions); seven of the nine remained on the committee. Six representatives moved from one chairmanship to another.

In the 1976 session, the first under Governor Carroll, a new set of House leaders took office, headed by William Kenton as Speaker. Ten representatives gained chairmanships and three chairmen shifted committees; three chairmen moved up to leadership positions, and only one chairman was demoted. (The other new chairmen replaced legislators who had left the House.) The only chairman to be demoted was Joseph McBride of the Banking Committee, a strong Ford supporter; he was replaced by James Bruce, who had chaired the committee in 1970. It is noteworthy that one of the new chairmen was Norbert Blume, who had been ousted as Speaker by William Kenton. Two years later there were only minor shifts in chairmanships.

In the 1980 session, Governor Brown made no effort to influence the choice of chairmen. William Kenton was reelected as Speaker of the House, after defeating a challenger, Donald Blandford. The House leadership removed three committee chairmen, each of whom had supported Blandford in the race for Speaker. However, they reappointed Blandford as chairman of a somewhat restructured Agriculture Committee. (One other chairman moved up to a leadership position.) In the 1982 session, after Kenton's death, Bobby Richardson moved up from majority leader to Speaker and James LeMaster, a committee chairman, became majority leader. Only one chairman lost his post, and there was one shift of a chairman to replace him.

Under the new schedule of elections and sessions, an organizational session was held in 1983 for the 1983-84 legislature. Richardson was reelected as Speaker, easily defeating Mark Farrow; shortly thereafter Farrow lost his committee chairmanship. The only other change in chairmanship came when Donald Blandford gave up his post on the Agriculture Committee after defeating the incumbent Speaker Pro Tem.

The most important recent change in House leadership occurred at the start of the 1985-86 legislature when Donald Blandford defeated Richardson as Speaker and Greg Stumbo defeated the incumbent majority leader. The new leadership named six new committee chairmen, and in the process removed four chairmen who had supported the losing candidate in the battle for the speakership. (Two former chairmen had left the House.) Of the nine chairmen who retained their posts, several apparently had supported Blandford in the contest, but several others had remained loyal to Richardson. The most prominent committee chairman who kept his position despite his support for Richardson was Joe Clarke, of the Appropriations and Revenue Committee. Apparently, some of Blandford's supporters insisted that Clarke be reappointed, and Blandford recognized that he was nearly indispensable as chairman of that committee.

Two years later, in the 1987 organizational session, only four new chairmen were chosen, all replacing members who had left the House. In a move apparently designed to heal factionalism in the House, the leaders selected Bobby Richardson as chairman of the Energy Committee and restored Adrian Arnold (a Richardson supporter) as chairman of the Counties Committee. The other two new chairmen held chairmanships at earlier periods (prior to the 1982 session).

In Congress many years of service on a committee is a prerequisite to becoming a chairman; but that is not the pattern in most state legislatures or in Kentucky. Among the eighteen senators and representatives who shifted from one chairmanship to another, only five had been serving on the second committee in the previous session, though six others had served on it in some previous session. There were thirty-one senators and thirty-four representatives gaining a chairmanship who had not held such a post in the previous session. Only thirty-eight of these (twelve senators and twenty-six representatives) had served on that committee in the previous session, although ten others had been on the committee in some earlier session.

The committee on rules and procedures appointed in 1985 by the House Democratic caucus proposed that committee chairmanships be limited to persons who had served two previous terms in the legislature and who had served on the committee they were to chair in the previous session. This proposal was not adopted by the caucus; the opponents argued that the House leaders needed more freedom in restructuring committees when they took office.

Although we have described a number of changes that have occurred in chairmanships, often as a result of changes in leadership, it is important to emphasize that continuity of committee leadership has been increasing in recent years, and both houses include some chairmen with long experience. Table 15 lists the legislators who were serving at least their fourth consecutive term as chairmen of their committees during the 1986 session. (Both Senator Moloney and Representative Bruce had served one additional term as chairman prior to their period of continuous service.) The most striking example of continuity evident in table 15 is Joe Clarke, who had chaired the powerful Appropriations and Revenue Committee under four governors and four Speakers.

Committee Members. The Senate rules provide that majority and minority party committee members shall be appointed "on nomination of the members of said party on the Committee on Committees." In practice this means that the Republican floor leader can choose Republican members of committees.

There is no such rule in the House, but for a number of years there has been an informal agreement that the House Democratic leadership will normally accept the committee assignments for Republicans made by the minority leaders. This agreement occasionally breaks down if the Republican leaders nominate for membership on an important committee (like Appropriations and Revenue) someone whom the Democratic leaders believe would be an obstructionist or "trouble-maker." Under these conditions the party leaders negotiate, but in the last analysis the Democrats have an effective veto over committee appointments. In similar fashion the Democratic leaders may occasionally ask the Republican leaders to nominate a particular

Table 15. Legislators Who Served Four or More Consecutive Terms as Chairman of Same Committee

	Terms	Committee
		Senate
Kenneth Gibson	7	Agriculture and Natural Resources
Gus Sheehan	7	Elections and Constitutional Amendments
Nelson Allen	6	Education
Michael Moloney	4	Appropriations and Revenue
Daniel Meyer	4	Cities
Georgia Powers	4	Labor and Industry
A.D. Yocum	4	Business Organizations and Professions
		House
Joe Clarke	8	Appropriations and Revenue
James Bruce	6	Banking and Insurance
Sam Thomas	4	Business Organizations and Professions
Terry Mann	4	Energy
Herbie Deskins	4	Natural Resources and Environment

person for a major committee. The ultimate control of Democratic leaders over committee appointments has the potential for seriously undermining Republican leadership. It is not unknown for Republican legislators to bypass their own leaders and go directly to the House Democratic leader in an effort to get choice committee assignments by promising to support the Democratic legislative program. In recent years, at least, the Democratic leadership has resisted the temptation to make such bargains.

The leadership gets rank-ordered requests for committee assignments from new legislators as well as requests for changing committees from continuing legislators. The general pattern followed by the party leadership in both houses has been to accept members' requests for committee assignments as much as possible, except for a few of the major committees. These include, most importantly, Appropriations and Revenue, and also State Government and (especially in recent years) Education. The leadership chooses members to these key committees more carefully, for several reasons. There is usually more demand for these committees than there are available seats, and thus some choices have to be made. If there has been a contest for the leadership, some commitments may have been made for seats on these committees. Moreover, the major committees deal with issues of great importance to the leadership (and the governor).

In Kentucky, as in most state legislatures, there is much less continuity of committee membership than is found in Congress, where the seniority system assures stability. The congressional norm of seniority gives members the right to remain on a committee if they want to (except in unusual situations). The seniority system also provides members with an incentive to remain on the same committee in order to become eligible eventually for committee and subcommittee chairmanships (or, in the case of a minority member, to become the ranking member). Consequently, although members sometimes seek a move to a more powerful or politically useful committee, they rarely give up a committee once they have accumulated several terms of seniority on it.

In the Kentucky legislature, however, there is no seniority system. The leadership may move members from one committee to another (with one exception, noted below). Members have less incentive to stay on the same committee because long service does not guarantee a chairmanship. Members may want to change committees if they get a chance to serve on a more important one, or if their interests or the concerns of their constituency should change.

The rules of the House provide that the "Committee on Committees shall appoint a member with service in the immediately preceding regular session to at least one committee on which the member served in such previous regular session. Such appointment to the one committee shall be at the preference of the member, and the Committee on Committees shall be bound by the member's preference for that one committee." A chairman who wishes to be considered for another term as chairman must select that committee as the one he wishes to retain.

This rule, which was implemented in 1980, obviously strengthens the position of individual members and particularly their ability to hold onto their seats on major committees. One consequence of this rule is that new leadership may have only limited opportunities to add members to the most important committees, such as Appropriations, State Government, and Education. In 1985 the new House leadership increased the size of the Appropriations and Revenue Committee by two and the Education Committee by four members to accommodate legislators it wished to add. A significant difference between the two houses is that the Senate does not have such a rule protecting one committee assignment for each senator.

In table 16 we see what proportion of members returning to the legislature in each of six sessions made changes in their committee assignments. The table is divided into two periods (1976-78 and 1980-88, omitting 1984) to emphasize that there has been a recent trend toward somewhat greater stability of committee membership.

All senators, except the president pro tem and majority leader, have three committee assignments. The proportion of returning senators making no change increased from one-third to one-half during the period; more than one-third made a single change; the proportion of senators making two (or very rarely, three) changes dropped from over one-fourth to just over one-tenth.

Table 16. Change and Continuity of Committee Memberships for 1976, 1978, 1980, 1982, 1986, and 1988 Sessions

	1976-1978		1980-1988	
	(N)	(%)	(N)	(%)
Senate				
No change	21	34.3	65	51.6
One change	23	37.7	47	37.3
Two (or three) changes	17	27.9	14	11.1
Total	61	100.0	126	100.0
House				
No changes	45	31.9	134	42.6
Drop one	10	7.1	23	7.3
Add one (or two)	26	18.4	28	8.9
Change one	42	29.8	87	27.7
Change two (or three)	18	12.8	42	13.4
Total	141	100.0	314	100.0

In the House the normal assignment is three committee memberships, but there are a number of exceptions. The Speaker and majority leader normally do not serve on committees. Some other leaders in both parties and committee chairman serve on two committees. Freshmen Republicans (and some other Republicans) also serve on only two. Consequently, in the House members may add or drop committees, as well as change them. The proportion of representatives making no change rose from 32 to 43 percent over the period; the proportion adding or dropping a committee fell from one-fourth to one-sixth; the proportion who changed one or more committees dropped slightly but remained over 40 percent.

There are probably several reasons for these modest increases in committee stability. There has been relatively stable membership in leadership positions in both houses; since 1980 the House has had the rule allowing members to protect their seats on one committee; as more members serve longer terms they may be less inclined to initiate changes in committee membership.

To what extent do members get the committee assignments they request, and to what extent are changes in assignments initiated by the members rather than the leadership? To answer such questions in a comprehensive fashion, we would need access to the lists of assignment requests submitted by legislators at the start of a new term. In the absence of such data, we rely on a questionnaire to which about half of the members of each house responded in 1983. They were asked about their assignments in the

1982 session, as well as whether they would seek a change of committees in the 1985-86 session.

About two-thirds of the new members (nine of fourteen) said that they got all of the assignments they requested; each of the others got most of the committees they sought. In several cases the missed assignment was on the Appropriations and Revenue Committee, although several freshman did get assigned to that committee.

Of the twenty-eight continuing members who did not change any committees in 1982, only two said they had tried to make a change. Six of the seven senators who made some change in assignments in 1982 or 1983 said they had initiated these themselves. Fourteen of twenty representatives making a change said they had initiated the change, four said that leaders had done so, and two others said they had made one change and leadership another change. In only two cases was it clear that leaders had forced changes on unwilling members. One Republican said that he was the victim of factional politics, and one Democrat said he had been dropped from a committee because of policy differences with the leadership.

All legislators were asked whether they expected to seek any changes in committees in the 1985-86 legislature. Of the twenty-one senators, only seven planned to make a change, thirteen did not, and one was unsure. Of the forty-eight representatives, ten planned on seeking a change, twenty-five did not, and two were unsure; eleven others were not counted because they were not reelected in 1984. There were fifteen legislators who planned to seek a change and specified what they wanted; seven of these gained their objective, and several made unanticipated gains instead, such as committee chairmanships or leadership posts. Several of those who did not anticipate changing committees did so, in most cases gaining better assignments as a result of unanticipated opportunities.

In recent years committees have assumed more importance in the Kentucky legislature, committee activity has taken more of the legislator's time, and members have begun to serve longer terms on committees. These trends have enhanced the importance of the legislator's choice of a committee. Studies at the congressional level (Fenno 1973) have defined several predominant motivations for selecting committees. Congressmen may seek committees that are most powerful, those that will best serve the interests of their constituents, or those most pertinent to their own interests and experience.

We find the same motivations most frequently mentioned by Kentucky legislators. In our mail survey of legislators (with responses from twenty-one senators and forty-eight representatives), we asked members about their reasons for serving on specific committees. New members were asked the reasons for their committee requests; continuing members were asked why

Table 17. Legislators' Motivations for Seeking Committee Membership

Committee	To Serve District Interests	My Interest, Knowledge, or Experience	Committee Power or Importance	My Profession or Business
Appropriations and Revenue	12	5	12	0
State Government	4	2	9	0
Education	9	7	6	4
Agriculture and/or Natural Resources	13	3	1	2
Cities, Counties	16	9	1	0
Transportation	8	2	1	0
Energy	5	0	0	1
Health and Welfare	6	5	0	1
Labor and Industry	5	3	0	0
Banking and Insurance	1	3	0	4
Business Orgs. and Professions	1	4	0	2
Judiciary committees	1	3	1	7
Total number	81	46	31	21

they wanted to continue serving on the same committees or why they requested specific changes. These were open-ended questions, but in addition they were asked whether membership on any of their committees was "particularly helpful for their district." (Because this specific question was asked, the responses may exaggerate the relative importance of district interests in committee assignments.) We compiled all of the answers that referred to particular committees; on those few occasions when a member listed two reasons for being on a committee, both were coded (table 17).

In describing why they sought certain assignments, legislators said that a committee dealt with issues of particular concern to their district. This was most often the reason for seeking membership on committees dealing with agriculture and/or natural resources; the Cities and Counties committees; and the Transportation and Energy committees. It was frequently mentioned with regard to the Appropriations and Revenue and the Education committees. Members were often quite specific in describing the issues pertinent to their districts, such as coal mining, highway projects, and school problems.

In forty-six cases members said that they had particular interest, knowledge, or experience regarding an issue. This is the motivation that was most evenly distributed among the committees; there were several members with interests or experience pertinent to almost every committee. For example, several legislators who had previously served in local elective office were experienced in issues coming before the Cities or Counties committees.

Several expressed a strong interest in education, or had family members who were teachers.

There were thirty-one legislators who sought assignments because of the power or prestige of specific committees or the importance of issues under their jurisdiction. Only a few committees were in this category; most of these responses concerned the Appropriations and Revenue (12), State Government (9), and Education (6) committees—the three that are generally recognized today as the most important committees. (Included among the nine references to the State Government Committee are three persons who said they wanted to be on that committee because it would deal with redistricting in the 1982 session.)

Kentucky legislators mentioned one motivation that is not common to congressmen, but that probably influences legislators in other states. In twenty-one cases a legislator said that he wanted to serve on a committee because of his business or profession. This included seven lawyers who mentioned one of the judiciary committees, four educators, and four who were in banking or insurance. These responses are in addition to members who talked about previous experience in elective office or interests that might have derived from professional or occupational experience.

COMMITTEE CHAIRMEN

Committee chairmen, like other legislative leaders, have both formal and informal sources of power. The formal powers are based on the rules of the legislature and the specific committee. The informal rules depend on the skill and experience of the chairman. Some of the committee chairmen in Kentucky are much more effective than others, and the differences result almost entirely from variations in skill and experience. This is not a new phenomenon. In the past some chairmen were much more skillful than others in carrying out the decisions of the governor—and perhaps in having some input into these decisions. But the variations in the influence of chairmen have assumed greater importance than in the past. Strong, skillful chairmen have great opportunities to shape the decisions of their committees and ultimately those of the legislature. Weak, ineffective chairmen may lose the initiative to other committee members or perhaps to interest groups.

The rules of the House and Senate define a few of the formal powers of the chairman. The rules provide for regularly scheduled meetings during the session; in addition, the House rules provide that the chairman or a majority of the committee may call additional meetings. The rules do not spell out the procedural details for conducting committee business but require that the rules of the respective chamber be followed. In practice, a chairman has some leeway in recognizing members, calling for a vote, adjourning the committee, and so forth. The chairman also has considerable flexibility in scheduling full-scale hearings for bills. There is a difference between the two houses in the authority of the chairman to schedule bills for action in committee. The House rules provide that the chairman, or a majority of the committee members in a meeting, shall post a bill for consideration by the committee at least three days prior to a committee meeting. In the Senate there is no such requirement for advance posting of bills; this means that a committee chairman may wait until the meeting itself to announce which bills are to be considered by the committee. Some senators believe that the Senate can operate more informally without formal notice of posting bills because of the smaller size of its committees.

The chairman's authority to post bills is an important source of power. One committee chair told us, "It is the only real power that a chairman has." Because the pressure of time is so great in a sixty-day session and because committees usually meet only once a week, a chairman's decision to delay posting a bill for several weeks may have the effect of killing it. In theory, a majority of the committee can post a bill; in practice, the chairman's authority is rarely challenged. There are differences, however, in the tactics employed by chairmen in the use of this authority. Some chairmen are reluctant to use this authority to block bills and will almost always post a bill if requested by a member of the committee. At the other extreme are chairmen who will refuse to post any bill that they are personally opposed to.

More commonly, the committee chairman will take into consideration the views of the committee members in posting a bill. As one chairman described it, the chairman must maintain authority and keep demagogues on a committee under control, but success in accomplishing this depends on keeping the support and confidence of committee members. A chairman may occasionally refuse to post a bill that has committee support, but is unlikely to do this with any frequency because this would jeopardize his relationship with the members and might make it more difficult to mobilize support for those bills that the chairman wants to pass. Moreover, there is always the risk, however remote, that the committee will overrule the chairman, thereby seriously eroding his influence on the committee.

There are a number of reasons a chairman will delay or prevent consideration of a bill. Often there are bills that a majority of the committee believes ought to be defeated but the members "might be unable to muster the fortitude to vote against it" (as one chairmen put it). If the chairman understands that this is the sentiment of the committee, he may refuse to post the bill. One example was a bill to outlaw pornography in Louisville. A majority of the Judiciary Committee believed it was unconstitutional, but they did not want to be put in a position of "voting for pornography," and they wanted to keep the bill buried in committee. Another example of difficult legislation is bills to restrict abortion. Members of the Health and Welfare Committee will privately urge the chairman not to post abortion bills because members cannot afford to vote against them even when they consider such bills to be unconstitutional or poor public policy.

A chairman may decide to block a bill after concluding that it has no chance. This may be obvious because the same bill has failed in previous sessions, or because the chairman has sounded out committee members. Particularly in the closing weeks of the session, the committee is reluctant to waste time on bills that are going nowhere.

Politics obviously plays a part in a chairman's decisions on committee priorities. A chairman is likely to give priority in posting to bills introduced by Democratic members. Republican bills may be posted later in the session if the committee has enough time, though obviously bills that are posted late in the session have less chance of making it through the legislative labyrinth. Bicameral politics may also affect posting decisions. A House committee chairman, for example, may delay posting a Senate bill if the sponsor of the bill is holding House bills hostage in a Senate committee.

Friendship plays an important part in all aspects of legislative decision making. Committee chairmen often find it difficult to resist requests to post legislation that are made by colleagues who are close personal friends or political allies. Similarly, they may occasionally block posting of bills at the request of a friend or to punish a legislator or an interest group that has created problems for a friend or ally.

A chairman may delay or block posting of a bill at the request of the party leadership, although in recent years the leaders have been less likely to intervene in committee business than they were in the past. In the Senate the Democratic caucus may occasionally express concern about a bill pending in committee and ask the chairman not to post the bill.

The criticism most often heard of committee chairmen is that they permit too many "bad bills" to be reported by their committees. This term may, of course, have a variety of meanings. It may refer to bills that are poorly drafted or unnecessary, that represent the views of one narrow interest, or that present the legislators with particularly painful choices if they come to a vote on the floor. The chairman's best opportunity to prevent a bill from being reported, of course, is to refuse to post it in the committee. Consequently, there is strong support in the legislature for the principle that chairmen should exercise their power to prevent the posting of bills, provided they do not act arbitrarily and do take into account the wishes of the committee majority.

A committee chairman is judged not only by the willingness to block bad legislation, but by the priorities he or she establishes and skill in fashioning the compromises necessary to get bills passed in committee and to maximize the chances that such bills will be supported on the floor of the

House or Senate. In other words, one of the major skills required of a committee chairman is the ability to build coalitions behind those bills that he or she considers important. When Gertl Bendl was chairman of the House Health and welfare Committee, she gave priority to bills that she considered important: nursing home reform and other issues of concern to the elderly. When Tom Burch became chairman in 1986, he emphasized another set of concerns: organ procurement, a living will, and spouse abuse, for example.

In order to build a majority in committee to support any bill, a chairman must show sensitivity to the interests and wishes of members and demonstrate skill in negotiating compromises—particularly with the various interest groups concerned with the issue. The chairman must also be alert to problems that may arise when the legislation gets to the floor, especially if certain interests or viewpoints are underrepresented on the committee.

Among the most successful and powerful committee chairmen are those who have acquired detailed knowledge about the issues with which their committee deals. Some of them have chaired, or at least served on, their committee for a long period of time. Some can draw on their business or profession for such knowledge. Most of the best informed chairmen have attended hearings faithfully, made good use of staff work, and done their homework well over a sustained period of time. The best examples of chairmen who have combined long terms of service with detailed study of the issues are Michael Moloney and Joe Clarke, chairmen of the Senate and House Appropriations and Revenue committees. James Bruce has become an expert on banking and insurance through many years on that committee. The chairmen of the Senate and House Education committees have professional experience—Senator Nelson Allen as a school principal and Representative Roger Noe as a college professor.

Despite examples such as these, it is also true, as we have already shown (table 14), that legislators—particularly senators—are frequently appointed as chairmen of committees on which they have never served, or at least are not currently serving. This suggests that legislative leaders are less concerned about having chairmen with detailed knowledge about issues facing the committee than about having ones with adequate political skills and loyalty to the leadership.

COMMITTEE HEARINGS

There was a time when a committee hearing was an unusual event in the Kentucky legislature. Before the interim committee system was developed, when committee meetings had to be crowded into eight or nine weeks, there was simply no time available for committees to hold hearings on most bills. Most committee meetings were squeezed into small rooms where it was impossible for the interested public to participate in, or observe, hearings. A few times during a session, when a committee decided to hold a hearing on a very controversial issue, it usually took over the House or Senate chamber. Lobbyists who wanted to express their views sought out committee members individually rather than trying to make public statements. They tolerated this situation probably because it was more important, in passing or blocking legislation, to persuade the governor and his staff than the legislative committee.

It was the establishment of the interim committee system that made extensive hearings possible because committees could meet nearly every month between sessions, devoting extensive studies to those issues that were most controversial or complex, and therefore most likely to require an organized system of input from interest groups, experts, and officials from the executive branch. They could also hold hearings in other parts of the state and visit state facilities during the interim. In addition the 1979 amendment modifying the legislative schedule gave the committee members several more weeks during the regular session for hearings.

The legislature also took steps to provide adequate space for hearings. The legislature took over a substantial amount of space in the capital annex. In addition to gaining office space for leaders and very modest space for members, the legislature created a number of rooms that have ample space for committee hearings, including space for witnesses, the media, and large numbers of spectators. When a hearing is in progress on an important issue, particularly during the session, there may be several television cameras covering the hearing and fifty to a hundred lobbyists, state officials, and spectators packed into the room. An observer who was out of touch with the changes in the Kentucky legislature might believe that he or she had stumbled into a hearing in Washington rather than in Frankfort.

Committee hearings serve several purposes. They provide representatives from executive agencies a formal, structured setting in which to explain their views on issues. Similarly, they give lobbyists for interest groups, as well as individual citizens, a chance to express their support or opposition, or propose modifications and amendments, to proposed legislation. These formal presentations do not take the place of informal lobbying, but they supplement it. It may be more efficient for lobbyists to present their viewpoints at some length directly to the committee members, perhaps supplemented with a written statement, than to try to catch the attention of these members privately one by one long enough to explain their view on a bill. Attendance by members at committee hearings tends to be much better than is true in Congress. The lobbyists may bring a number of supporters to the hearings to demonstrate the breadth of support for their position. Moreover, the media may cover some of the hearings, giving lobbyists a chance to publicize their point of view and perhaps win broader support.

Hearings serve several important purposes for committee members as well. They provide an important opportunity to gather information, particularly on more complex or technical issues. More significantly, the hearings alert committee members to the viewpoints of organized interests regarding legislation. Legislators are very sensitive to these viewpoints. If county attorneys are concerned about a proposed change in the penal code, or the Kentucky Education Association wants to modify a bill affecting teacher retirement, or coal interests believe that a measure designed to clean up the state's rivers will be excessively costly, the legislators want to know about it. The committee may not be able to accommodate the wishes of all those who testify before it, but it often tries to achieve compromise. Whenever possible legislators want to legislate by consensus. The members of a committee will often postpone action on a bill to give the sponsor and the interests supporting a bill time to negotiate with those who are opposing it.

The committee members will be particularly sensitive to the views of executive officials on legislation. They respect the expert knowledge that these officials often have. Moreover, they want to know whether the agency is supporting or opposing the bill, or remaining neutral, and whether the agency's position is also supported by the governor. The committee will not necessarily bend to the wishes of the governor or an agency head, but— before reporting a bill to the floor—it wants to knows whether to anticipate executive support or opposition.

The hearing serves other purposes for some legislators. The sponsors of a bill are often members of the committee, and they may use the hearing to generate support for it. They will invite individuals to testify who will be effective advocates for the bill, and during the hearing they will ask questions of these witnesses designed to strengthen their case. The hearing may be the best way of generating publicity in the media or attracting the attention of legislators not on the committee. This may be particularly true during interim committee hearings when there is enough time before the next session to build public support for the legislation. Sometimes when a legislator is promoting legislation that is so controversial, innovative, or expensive that it is unlikely to be adopted during the session, the main purpose of introducing the bill is to gain a hearing on it, as a way of planting the seed that may grow into legislation in a subsequent session.

COMMITTEE DECISION MAKING

Any analysis of changes in the Kentucky legislative committee system must eventually confront the question of what difference it makes. If the committees have become more independent of gubernatorial and party leadership, with more time and staff resources, have they acted any differently?

If the committees are actually making a more independent and better informed judgment about legislation, we would expect to find the following changes in the pattern of committee decision making (based on Rosenthal 1947):

1. The committees should scrutinize bills more carefully than in the past, and consequently should report favorably a smaller proportion of bills than they used to do.

2. When the committees report bills favorably, they should more frequently modify and improve the bills by adopting amendments.

3. Assuming the committees are more selective in screening bills and report more of them with amendments, these bills ought to be more often adopted by the legislative chamber. In other words, the products of the committee ought to be better bills, or at least bills that are more acceptable to other legislators.

There have been two stages in the reform of legislative committees. We have described the radical modification on the structure of committees and the adoption of interim committees that occurred in 1968. That reform made the committee structure more rational, and it gradually made more time and staff resources available, but it did not necessarily increase legislative independence. Beginning with the 1980 session, the changing tactics of the governor and (particularly in the House) the legislative leadership has given the committees greater opportunity for independence. Given this time sequence, we ought to examine committee decision making both before and after the 1968 reform and also during the more recent period.

Fortunately, data are available from previous research on House committee decisions immediately before and after the 1968 reforms (Moncrief 1977; Hamm and Moncrief, 1982). We have carried out similar calculations for both the Senate and House in the 1986 session. The results for the three time periods are displayed in table 18, covering committee and floor action only on bills originating in each chamber.

Reporting of Bills. We find that there has been no significant change in the proportion of bills that have been reported favorably by committees; it has remained at slightly more than half during the three periods. It appears that the committees are not being more selective in reporting bills, but are simply making their selective decisions in a different fashion. The old committee system may have been weak, but it did not automatically report out bills at the request of sponsors, as has been done in some states. Under the old system, the governor's staff and the Senate and House leaders kept a close watch over legislation in committees and notified the chairmen about which bills they wanted passed, amended, or defeated.

At the present time, bills are being reported favorably or unfavorably, based, not on the governor's wishes or even the leaders' wishes, but on the

Table 18. Senate and House Committee Action on Bills Originating in
          Same Chamber

	1962/1966 House (%)	1972-74 House (%)	1986 Senate House	
			(%)	(%)
Proportion of bills reported favorably by committee	56.3	55.7	58.0	54.4
Proportion of such bills amended by committee	13.2	35.4	34.3	42.7
Proportion of favorably reported bills adopted by chamber	75.9	80.0	89.4	84.8

decision of the committee. And the somewhat longer session (and the interim) provides a little more time for sponsors to generate support for bills.
We have not tried to measure how responsive committees are to interest
groups; to do so would require a much more detailed study of committee
operations. But the conventional wisdom among legislators is that those
committees that vote out too many bills are responding too much to interest
group pressure.

There is some variation in the proportion of bills reported favorably by
each committee. In the 1986 session, four Senate committees and three in
the House reported favorably over 70 percent of the bills; there were three
committees in the Senate and four in the House endorsing fewer than half.
(These figures pertain only to bills originating in chamber of the committee.)
In both chambers the Appropriations and Revenue Committee was particularly reluctant to report bills favorably because of its concern with maintaining limits on spending. The Counties committees in both chambers
reported a high proportion of bills, presumably because few of these local
bills were controversial. For the most part, however, the parallel committees
in the two chambers did not have similar records of reporting bills. This
suggests that most of the variation in reporting patterns results from the
preferences and priorities of various committee chairmen and members
rather than from differences in the types of subject matter handled by the
committees.

Amendment of Bills. After the 1968 reforms, there was a major change in
the proportion of bills that were amended by House committees (table 18).
In the 1986 session the proportion of amendments was somewhat higher in
the House than in the 1972-74 period, but the proportion of amendments
in the 1986 Senate was comparable to that in the House in 1972-74. This

trend suggests that the legislative committees have more time and take their jobs more seriously than did the old committees in the pre-1968 period.

Not all of the amendments made in committee are very important. If we exclude from our calculations those amendments that are described in the Legislative Record as being "technical" or being simply title amendments, the proportion of bills amended in 1986 by House committees drops from 42.7 percent to 39.9 percent and those amended by Senate committees drops further—from 34.3 percent to 26.3 percent.

Do closer committee scrutiny of bills and more frequent amendments have the effect of improving legislation? This is obviously difficult to answer without making normative judgments about every bill that is amended in committee. But it is probably accurate to conclude that closer committee scrutiny and more amendments improve the chances of passing legislation. A major purpose of committee scrutiny is to determine whether there is opposition to a bill and whether the criticisms raised by opponents can be cleared up by amendments. If the legislative process is largely a process of compromise, the bargains are usually struck in committee, and they usually take the form of amendments. When the sponsor is defending a bill on the floor of the House or Senate, he is often asked whether a particular interest group is agreeable to the bill; frequently the sponsor replies that the bill has been amended in committee to take care of concerns raised by the interest group.

Support for Committee Action on the Floor. If the amending process is now being used more effectively to deflect criticism and achieve compromise, then a larger proportion of bills reported favorably by committee should be passed. There has been a modest and very gradual increase in the proportion of bills that are passed in the first chamber after being reported favorably by committee (table 18). This suggests that the decisions of the committee carry somewhat more weight than they used to in the rules committee and on the floor.

We can get a clearer impression of how the committees have been operating recently by examining in more detail the 1986 session of the legislature (table 19). Note that the committees in both chambers, and particularly the Senate, are more likely to report a bill favorably that originated in the other chamber. The reason is that by the time bills reach the committee in the second chamber, the poorest bills and the redundant ones have already been screened out. If a Senate committee must choose between a House bill that has already passed the House and a Senate bill that is similar or identical in content, it will usually report the House bill to simplify and speed up the process. Moreover, bills that have already passed one chamber have developed momentum; those legislators and lobbyists supporting the

Table 19. Senate and House Committee Action on Bills Originating in
Both Chambers, 1986 Session

	Senate		House	
	Bills Orginating:		Bills Originating:	
	Senate (%)	House (%)	House (%)	Senate (%)
Proportion of bills reported favorably by committee	58.0	72.0	54.4	81.9
Proportion of such bills amended by committee	34.3	—	42.7	—
Proportion of favorably reported bills adopted by chamber	89.4	89.0	84.8	89.8

bills will work harder because the bills have some chance of passing. It is noteworthy, however, that once a bill has been reported by committee in the second chamber, it has approximately the same chance of being passed as one that originated in that chamber.

There are variations among the committees in their rate of success in getting bills passed by their chamber (including bills that originated in either chamber). These variations are not large because nearly 90 percent of all favorably reported bills are adopted by the chamber (table 19). There are several plausible reasons for such variations that occur. Some committees may be more likely than others to report "bad bills" or to ignore the necessity of fashioning compromises before reporting the bills. Some committees deal with issues that are more likely to be controversial (such as Health and Welfare), and some may include members who are not representative of the chamber membership as a whole (such as a Labor and Industry Committee packed with members sympathetic to labor unions).

Bills that have been favorably reported by a committee but fail to get passed in that chamber may be a victim of the Rules Committee or may get defeated on the floor. During the 1986 session, 8.8 percent of all bills favorably reported by House committees failed to survive recommital by the House Rules Committee and another 5.2 percent were defeated on the floor. In the Senate 7.6 percent percent of bills endorsed by Senate committees died after recommital by the Rules Committee and only 3 percent were defeated on the floor. In both chambers bills were more likely to be defeated on the floor if they had originated in the other chamber.

The Rules Committee is basically an arm of the leadership, and in chapter 7 we will describe the different strategies used in the Rules Committee by various leaders. During the 1986 session the Senate Rules Committee was deliberately used by the leadership on some occasions to kill or delay bills. Some of the bills that were recommitted by the Rules Committee eventually emerged in revised form and were passed, but (as noted above) 7.6 percent of bills favorably reported by Senate committee died as a result of such recommital. The House leadership in 1986 rarely used the Rules Committee to kill bills that it opposed. However, House bills with fiscal implications were routinely recommitted by the Rules Committee to Appropriations and Revenue, where they often languished because they were perceived to be too expensive. Consequently, the proportion of bills killed in the House (8.8 percent) by recommital was higher than in the Senate.

The Record of Interim Committees. One way of assessing the work of interim committees is to examine what happens to bills produced by those committees. Very often, after studying an issue, the interim committee will give a favorable recommendation to a bill that is prefiled in the legislature. Although the studies of an interim committee may lead to the development of other bills, its most direct impact on the legislative session is through these prefiled, recommended bills.

In the three sessions in 1986, 1984, and 1982, interim committees prefiled a total of 275 bills. This included those prefiled by oversight and special ad hoc committees. There was great variety among the committees in the quantity of bills prefiled. Those interim committees with the largest number were Education, Transportation, Agriculture and Natural Resources, and Counties—each of whom filed more than twenty. At the other extreme, during the three sessions, Labor and Industry prefiled none, and Banking and Insurance and Appropriations and Revenue had only six each.

In table 20 we have summarized the fate of all bills recommended by interim committees during the 1982, 1984, and 1986 regular sessions. We also included data reported by Cox (1975) on the 1974 and (more briefly) 1972 sessions. The first conclusion to be drawn is that a high proportion of bills recommended by the interim committees pass: 60 percent during the 1982-86 period, compared to only 32 percent of all bills during those sessions. During the early years of the interim committee system (1972-74), the proportion of interim committee bills that passed was smaller (43 percent), but was still higher than the proportion for all bills in those sessions (31 percent).

Table 20 also provides some explanations for the defeat of bills endorsed by interim committees. During the 1982-86 sessions, 70 percent of these unsuccessful bills failed in the chamber where they were first introduced. Over two-thirds were defeated in committee, and another one-fifth failed as a result of action by the Rules Committee; only a few were defeated on the floor.

Perhaps the most interesting data in the table is that nearly 40 percent of all bills that failed died in a committee having the same jurisdiction and membership as the interim committee that had recommended it. There may

Table 20. Outcome of Bills Prefiled by Interim Committees

	1972 (%)	1974 (%)	1982-86 (%)
Status of all bills introduced			
Bills passed into law	42.4	42.7	60.0
Bills not passed	57.6	57.3	40.0
Number	(32)	(82)	(275)
Chamber where bills defeated		1974	1982-86
Same chamber		80.8	70.0
Other chamber		14.9	28.2
Other		4.2	1.8
Number		(47)	(110)
Where bills defeated—either chamber		1974	1982-86
Committee		59.6	68.2
Parallel to interim committee		—	(39.1)
Different from interim committee		—	(29.1)
Rules committee		29.8	20.0
Floor of chamber		6.4	10.0
Conference committee		2.1	1.8
Vetoed		2.1	0.0
Number		(47)	(110)

be several reasons why this should happen. Within the interim committee the members from one chamber may support a bill, whereas those from the other may be divided. Once the regular legislative session begins, a change in circumstances may adversely affect the bill. Budgetary problems may make the costs of the bill too high. A different or better bill on the same topic may be introduced by an individual legislator and passed. Interest groups that had paid little attention to a bill during the interim may mobilize against a bill during the session. It is also possible that interim committees sometimes report a bill to satisfy the wishes of its sponsor, without intending to push it any further.

Nearly one-third of the bills that are defeated die in a committee that is unrelated to the interim committee that recommended it, in addition to the 20 percent that fail in the Rules Committee. It is not always clear why a bill gets assigned to another committee during the session, although the scope of some bills is broad enough so that more than one committee can claim jurisdiction. Some bills originating in another interim committee are referred to Appropriations and Revenue, usually in the House, where they face substantial scrutiny. More than half of the bills that die in a different committee are ones originating either in interim oversight committee or in ad hoc special committees. Obviously, such bills must be referred to a standing committee that has authority to report legislation, but its membership will be different and the legislators may not fully share the views of those on the oversight or special committees.

The effectiveness of the interim committee system ought to be judged not only by the number of bills that are prefiled and the proportion that pass but by the importance of this legislation. In theory, the interim committees are the ideal places for detailed study of complex issues and the development of major legislation. In practice, the bills reported by interim committees range from some of the most important to bills that are trivial or narrow in scope.

At the start of the 1986 session, the prefiled interim committee bills included the following important ones: the highly controversial and unsuccessful seat belt bill, a successful bill to reinstate the presidential primary, bills that passed revising the election code and the campaign finance act, a state constitutional amendment to let city mayors serve more than one term (passed and adopted by the voters), a state constitutional amendment to make the state superintendent appointive (though a different version actually passed the legislature), and a major revision of the uniform commercial code.

There were also interim committee bills of considerably lesser significance: a bill to raise the deduction on the inheritance tax allowed for burial expenses, an exemption of disabled veterans from hunting and fishing license requirements, a legislative redistricting bill moving two precincts, a revision of the laws regulating bee keeping, and a new requirement that local school boards excuse students who attend the North American International Livestock Exposition.

Perhaps the best example of an interim committee being used to develop a package of legislative proposals on a major issue occurred in the Education Committee during the period leading up to the 1982 session. After an extensive study of problems in the public schools, that committee introduced a package of twenty-five bills dealing with various aspects of educational reform; twenty of them were passed and signed into law.

A Quantitative Assessment. We have reached several conclusions about quantitative change in committee performance: There have been no significant changes in the proportion of bills favorably reported, but bills are more likely to be amended by committee. There has been a modest and gradual increase in the proportion of reported bills that are adopted by the chamber, and that proportion is now very high. It seems reasonable to conclude that the more careful review of bills by committee often results in amendments that remove most objections to bills and result in their approval in the chamber. The detailed study of legislative proposals that is possible in interim committees leads to a particularly high rate of passage for bills that are prefiled by committee. In short, legislative committees have become more important and powerful decision-making bodies.

Despite these conclusions we believe that the quantitative analysis provides an incomplete record of change, one that fails to capture some of the more important qualitative changes that have occurred in the committee system.

Some of these limitations result from using Rosenthal's (1974) criteria to measure committee effectiveness. Though most of these criteria are useful, Rosenthal defines an ineffective committee system as one that fails to be selective in reporting bills. In fact, during the earlier period, the Kentucky committees were quite selective about reporting bills—in response to the requests of the governor and the majority leadership.

It is also difficult to measure quantitative changes in Kentucky because the committee system has changed gradually over twenty years. Following the 1968 reorganization of committees, the growth of staffing and the development of the interim committee system took many years. Similarly, there was a gradual increase in membership continuity on committees. These structural membership changes produced only modest enhancement of committee independence prior to Governor Brown's decision in 1979 not to dictate the selection of leaders and his failure to play an active role in the legislative process.

A Qualitative Assessment. Anyone who observes the Kentucky committee system carefully must be impressed by the extent to which its operation depends on the tactics and the strengths and weaknesses of individuals, particularly party leaders and committee chairmen. In reality, the independence of committees in each chamber has varied from session to session with the tactics and skill of legislative leaders. Intercommittee variations in effectiveness result in large measure from variations in the effectiveness of the chairmen. The structural changes in committees have made the personal variable more important.

Have the changes resulted in committees that are dominated by the organized groups most affected by each committee—the second model that we referred to at the beginning of the chapter? Alternatively, have the changes given an advantage to particular types of organized groups? In practice, there is considerable variation among the committees. There are a few (like Labor and Industry) most of whose members are perceived as being supporters of one group or another (probusiness or prolabor). In the new committee system, with more time devoted to hearings, the decision-making process is more open, with all pertinent interest groups having input. Moreover, there is a strong norm in the committees that—whenever possible—

the concerns of all significant groups will be accommodated by compromises and amendments.

The growing strength and independence of the committees have made it more difficult for the governor to pass or defeat legislation. On important issues the committees have often taken the initiative to reshape the governor's program to their liking. One good illustration of this was the role of the Education committees in the Senate and particularly in the House in developing and passing the 1985 educational reforms. During the interim prior to the 1984 session, the House Education Committee studied the problems of the educational system and developed a number of proposals for reform. These proposals were one of the sources of the educational package that Governor Collins introduced during the 1984 session. When the legislature refused to raise taxes, only a few of the less costly reforms were adopted.

During the first six months of 1985, the House Education Committee developed a new package of educational reforms. The new chairman, Roger Noe, and several of the other "Young Turks" assumed most of the responsibility for drafting the new program, with the blessing of Speaker Blandford. In order to win support from the Kentucky Education Association (KEA), they incorporated several measures that the KEA considered important, notably a provision for longevity pay for experienced teachers. They held several meetings with the governor and her education advisers to explain their proposals and reach consensus on the package of education reforms. The program that was endorsed by the governor and passed by the House was essentially the program that was developed by the House Education Committee.

The Senate Education Committee, which had been kept informed about the program being developed by its counterpart in the House, succeeded in making some changes in the bill when it reached the Senate. For example, it gave higher priority to the reduction of class size in the first three grades, and it gained approval of an annual $300 pay increase based on merit. But for the most part, the Senate Education Committee played a supportive role and steered the bill successfully through the upper chamber.

There were several reasons the educational reform program was largely written by the Education Committee and not by the governor's office or others in the executive branch. The members of the committee were committed to the goal of educational reform; they became experts on the subject; and they succeeded in negotiating with the KEA and building political support for their legislative package. The governor, on the other hand, was less interested in the substantive details of the legislation than in getting educational reforms accomplished during her term.

Not every important issue, of course, receives such thorough study in committee, nor are the members of every committee willing to devote the time to becoming experts on complicated issues. In many cases committees review quickly, even superficially, bills drafted by interest groups, executive agencies, or the governor's office. But the committees have adequate staff and sufficient time between sessions to study issues in depth and develop their own legislative initiatives if they choose to do so.

The 1985 special session did not provide a test of strength between the governor and the Education Committee. The committee did not achieve its goals by defeating the governor, but by providing her with a detailed package of reforms that she could endorse and that could be passed. When a committee decides to make a major change in one of the governor's legislative proposals or to initiate or support a bill that is opposed by the governor, there is no certainty that the committee will prevail. The outcome depends on the political strength and skill of both the governor and the committee members and the role played by party leaders, interest groups, and others. A strong, skillful governor still has many political tools that can be employed in legislative battles. But the governor's office no longer has a monopoly on expertise or legislative initiatives. Legislative committees have the capability, and often the will, to develop alternatives to the governor's proposals. In dealing with committees, or with the legislature as a whole, the governor often must be prepared to negotiate and compromise.

6. Legislative Budgetary Review

In addition to passing legislation, the General Assembly can influence the policies and programs of government in two major ways: through reviewing and amending the the governor's budget and through overseeing administrative decisions of the executive branch. In the early 1960s, budgetary review consisted almost literally of rubber stamping the executive budget; there were no committees actively engaged in oversight of the executive. In recent years the legislature has played a much more active and powerful role in both budgetary review and administrative oversight. In both cases the legislature's role has grown because of revitalization of the committee system. In both cases this development has occurred gradually over the last twenty years. In this chapter we examine budgetary review; in chapter 7 we analyze various methods of legislative oversight of the executive.

TRENDS IN STATE LEGISLATIVE BUDGET MAKING

One of the most consistent and most important trends over the last twenty years in American state legislatures has been the growing scrutiny of the executive budget and increasing influence over budgetary decisions. The budget is usually developed by an agency subordinate to the governor, although in a very few states legislators play some role in this process. A committee on appropriations, or appropriations and revenue, plays the major role in reviewing the budget. Increasingly, the committee operates through subcommittees, making possible more extensive hearings and greater specialization by committee members. As budgetary review has assumed greater importance, there has been pressure in many legislatures to increase the size of the committee or in some other fashion to involve more members in budgetary review (Rosenthal, 1981b: chap. 13).

As legislatures have devoted more careful attention to budgetary review, they have inevitably developed larger, more expert staffs and have come to rely very heavily on them. In some states these staffs are assigned directly to the house and senate appropriations committee (or jointly to both). Other legislatures have established a separate staff agency, which might be called a fiscal or budgetary office, to analyze the governor's budget and carry out other budgetary studies. Some of the larger states have as many as fifty professional staff members engaged in budgetary analysis. Many legislatures now require that the legislative budget staff receive copies of each agency's annual or biennial budget request at the same time that it is submitted to the executive budget office. Legislatures are making increasing use of computers to analyze the budget, to study the impact of proposed amendments, and to track the implementation of state budgets. One trend in the last decade in many states has been an effort by legislatures to oversee the acceptance and use of federal grants in the states, an effort that has raised some complex legal and practical problems.

Extensive review of the executive budget by the appropriations committee and its staff does not, of course, guarantee that there will be major changes in the budget passed by the legislature and enacted into law. The governor has extensive political resources that can be used to defend his budget, including promises and threats regarding projects in particular districts. In most states the governor also has the item veto over appropriations. But in all states the final budget is now a product of careful scrutiny and joint decision making by both branches of government and not merely by the executive.

CONTRASTS IN THE KENTUCKY BUDGET-MAKING PROCESS

On Tuesday, January 4, the opening day of the 1966 session, Governor Edward Breathitt's biennial budget was introduced in the House and referred to committee. Early Wednesday morning the House Appropriations Committee met and approved the bill. On Wednesday and Thursday mornings the two appropriations committees held joint "hearings," at which the commissioners of finance and of revenue and the budget director explained the budget and answered questions from legislators; none of the committee members asked questions. Meanwhile, on those days the bill was receiving its first and second readings on the House floor.

On the following Wednesday, January 12, when the House took up the budget, the Democratic leadership successfully moved the "previous question" to prevent adoption of any amendments, and the budget was passed 99-0. Later that day, when it received the bill, the Senate recessed for five minutes, the Appropriations Committee met and approved the bill, and it received its first reading. On Friday, January 14, the Senate took up the budget bill, the previous question was moved and adopted, and the bill was passed 31-5. Later that day Governor Breathitt signed the bill, which was identical to the budget proposal he had submitted ten days earlier.

Governor Breathitt explained that the legislature's quick action reflected confidence that the administration's revenue and budget staff "will prepare a sound budget within the context of the governor's program and campaign." He added: "Budget-making is a complex process, which requires experts. Most efforts I have seen to open up budgets have been for the purpose of harassment or for political purposes." House majority leader John Y. Brown, Sr., echoed these sentiments: "Over years of experience, I've found that an inexperienced legislator who tampers with one part of the budget upsets all of it."

Eighteen years later, in 1984, the budgetary review process was very different. In May 1983 the state budget office held several meetings with members of the Interim Appropriations and Revenue Committee to discuss instructions to be sent to state agencies; these instructions were sent in June. The agencies submitted their requests to the budget office, with copies sent to the committee. Soon after Governor Collins's election, her staff began to prepare the biennial budget, working on the assumption that no new taxes would be sought. In mid-January, however, when the governor was notified that a serious revenue shortfall was anticipated, she ordered a revision in the budget to include a tax increase. Because the legislature had mandated a budget submission by the fifteenth legislative day, the budget and revenue staffs rushed to revise the budget and develop a package of tax proposals.

On January 25 Governor Collins proposed new taxes that would produce $324 million in new revenue during the biennium to support increased spending for primary and secondary education. The tax package went through several changes before being introduced late in the session. The chairman of the House Appropriations and Revenue Committee announced that he would not seek committee approval for a tax increase unless it could pass the House. On March 19 the governor's tax program was rejected by the House Democratic caucus, and two days later the governor abandoned her effort to raise taxes.

The collapse of the tax program undermined the governor's budget, and the House and Senate Appropriations committees assumed responsibility for writing a new one. For two months they had been holding hearings to review the spending requests of each executive agency. Now they each drafted versions of the budget, which were approved by the two chambers. The committees made cuts in other areas of proposed spending in order to make possible a limited amount of new funding for several educational programs. The final version of the state budget was hammered out by the conference committee behind closed doors. In part because the chairman of the Senate Committee was suddenly hospitalized, the final version largely reflected the recommendations of the House Appropriations and Revenue Committee.

TRANSFORMING THE BUDGETARY PROCESS

In eighteen years the appropriations committees had been transformed from rubber-stamping machines to hard-working, well-informed institutions that were capable of establishing budgetary priorities when they were called upon to fill the vacuum created by the collapse of the governor's budget. To understand how this transformation occurred, we must trace the gradual, often tentative, steps by which the legislature—and particularly its Appropriations and Revenue (A & R) committees—acquired knowledge and power over the budget-making process.

In the previous chapter we described the reform of the committee system and the establishment of an interim committee system in 1968. These changes provided committees with staff assistance and time for research and hearings during the interim—two prerequisites for developing the capabilities of the A & R committees. But, in order to influence budgetary decision making, the committees also needed political power; this was slow in developing.

During the 1968 and 1970 sessions, the legislature had an unusual opportunity to exercise political power because the governor, Louie Nunn, was a Republican who had played no role in selecting the majority leadership or committee chairmen. Nevertheless, in 1968 the governor had the loyal support of a large Republican minority and used his control over the executive budget and the threat of item vetoes to enlist the support of enough Democratic votes to pass his budget and his proposed increase in the sales tax from three to five cents. Most Democrats agreed with Governor Nunn's budgetary priorities and, although many opposed a flat increase in the sales tax, they were deeply divided over alternative taxes.

During the 1968 session, the A & R committees labored under several handicaps. The new committee system had been organized, but the interim committee system had not yet taken effect. The budget bill was introduced late in the session, and the committees held only three days of joint hearings—more than in the past but not enough time to provide the members with detailed information about proposed expenditures. The House A & R Committee approved both the budget and the tax increase, largely because of Republican votes. The Senate A & R Committee, after another day of hearings on tax proposals, recommended an alternative tax plan and several cuts in the budget (particularly for education), but the Senate voted for the governor's budget and tax package.

It was during the 1970 session that the A & R committees began to play a more significant role in the budget-making process. The interim A & R Committee had met several times between sessions under the leadership of Senator Gibson Downing and Representative William Curlin (the latter a new chairman). The two chairmen worked particularly closely with the six-member Legislative Audit Commission and the Legislative Auditor appointed by that group. The commission had been established in 1966, and by 1970 had gained enough expertise to be useful to the A & R committees.

The new House A & R Committee appointed in 1970 included several freshman and sophomore members who were committed to strengthening the role of the committee and who were searching for ways to accomplish this. A first step was to make greater use of committee hearings. The A & R committees held joint budgetary hearings for nearly a month during the first half of the session, even meeting sometimes on Saturdays. Because some members held leadership positions or chairmanships of other committees, the bulk of the work in hearings was done by about one-third of the members. All of the agencies appeared at the hearings, some of them reluctantly. The extended hearings served at least two important purposes: they educated the legislators about the operations and costs of state government, and they demonstrated to the agencies that they should be prepared for more careful scrutiny in the years ahead.

The hearings did not lead directly to dramatic changes in the governor's budget. It was estimated at the time that at least $1 million and perhaps almost $3 million in cuts made by the committee came from information gained at the hearings, but most of the changes in the budget came from investigations and negotiations by the committee chairmen and party leadership that took place outside the committee hearings.

In his budget message, Governor Nunn left a "surplus" of $18 million and invited the legislature to allocate these funds as it wished. At the same time, he provided no increase in teachers' pay and minimum funding to facilitate entry of the University of Louisville into the state system. The Democratic plan, developed by the chairmen of the A & R committees, used the $18 million and reallocated another $16 million, giving priority to a modest increase in teachers' pay and more funding for the University of Louisville. The Democratic plan passed the both houses virtually unanimously, with only limited criticism from Republican legislators.

In the 1970 session the A & R committees had forced the executive agencies to justify their spending requests and had demonstrated that they had both the willingness and the ability to make changes, however modest, in the governor's budget. The election of Wendell Ford in 1971, however, raised the question of whether the committees would be willing and able to review thoroughly and revise, even modestly, the budget of a Democratic governor. Ford restored the practice of gubernatorial control over the selection of majority party leaders and committee chairman.

The new chairman of the House A & R Committee was Joe Clarke, who was beginning his second term in the House. Gibson Downing continued for another session as chairman of the Senate A & R Committee and, when he retired, was replaced by Michael Moloney. Under these leaders the committees continued to develop their capabilities and expand their activities; but they avoided direct confrontation with the governor. During the Ford administration the staff available to the A & R committees increased in both numbers and experience.

The two A & R committees continued the practice of holding joint hearings on the budget for several weeks, but they made only very minor changes in the governor's budget. In 1972 the legislature approved Ford's proposal to add a coal severance tax and to remove the sales tax from food and medicine. The most serious challenge to Governor Ford's budget came in 1974, not from one of the A & R committees but from the House floor. A mountain caucus of representatives from eastern Kentucky succeeded in passing an amendment to Ford's budget to permit the sharing of severance tax revenues with local governments; after a recess the House leadership persuaded enough members to change their votes to force reconsideration and defeat of the amendment. Subsequently, Ford developed his own version of severance tax revenue sharing, which the legislature adopted.

As the A & R committees gained experience, skill, and staff resources, there was growing potential for conflict between more assertive committees and governors who expected prompt and complete support for their budgets. This conflict came to a head during the Julian Carroll administration. Carroll, who had served as Speaker of the House and lieutenant governor, knew the legislative process and used that knowledge to dominate the legislature as skillfully as Wendell Ford had done.

At the start of 1976 session, Michael Moloney was replaced as chairman of the Senate A & R Committee because he was closely identified with former Governor Ford. His successors as chairmen during the 1976 and 1978 sessions, Delbert Murphy and Woodrow Stamper, were men who could be counted on to cooperate fully with the Carroll administration. During these years the struggle for greater legislative influence over budgetary policy was centered on the House A & R Committee. Joe Clarke, who continued to serve as chairman of that committee, was developing both a reputation for independence and widespread recognition as an expert on budgetary matters. Clarke presumably was not Governor Carroll's ideal choice for chairman, but he made no effort to replace him. At one point Carroll told Clarke that the A & R Committee should be divided into subcommittees on appropriations and on revenue. Clarke, who perceived this as an effort to undermine his authority, refused to make the change and threatened a public resignation. Carroll retreated, and Clarke's position was strengthened. Although Clarke remained as chairman during the Carroll years, the House leadership made sure that a solid majority of the A & R Committee members were loyal to the administration.

The conflicts between the A & R Committee and the governor began at the start of the Carroll administration. The Legislative Research Commission (LRC) had provided a new staff of fiscal analysts to the A & R interim committee, and it established a special budgetary review subcommittee of A & R members chaired by Clarke, which held extensive hearings on agency requests during the fall of 1985. (The legislature had previously adopted a law requiring that by November 15 of each year preceding a legislative session each state agency must send a copy of its budget request to the Legislative Research Commission, in order to give the A & R Interim Committee more time to become familiar with budgetary issues.)

Early in January 1976, before the governor's budget message, the subcommittee made its own recommendations on spending, which were labeled in the press as an "alternative budget." During the 1976 session, however, Clarke discovered the limits of his influence over the committee. When he tried to get his "alternative budget" printed, the staff director of the LRC (under pressure from the governor) decided that the LRC could not afford to do so. Within the House A & R Committee, Clarke was defeated on many of his proposed budget revisions, sometimes by a vote of 10 to 1. The director of the LRC also reassigned the staff that had been assigned to the A & R Committee, and Clarke had to rebuild his staff resources.

In 1978 the A & R committees made no attempt to prepare an "alternative budget," but they held what the governor described as "the most thorough hearings on the Executive Budget in the history of the commonwealth." Following the hearings, the governor recommended adding $73.5 million to the budget, most of it to deal with issues that had been raised by various groups during the legislative budget hearings. One notable change involved the state auditor, who had frequently criticized the Carroll administration. The governor had originally eliminated almost all of the auditor's budget and proposed that he collect fees from agencies that were audited. The governor recommended restoring the appropriation of nearly $3 million, as recommended by a subcommittee of the House A & R Committee.

The election of John Y. Brown, Jr., in 1979 marked the end of gubernatorial interference in the selection of party leaders and committee chairman. In 1980 Joe Clarke started his fifth term as chairman of the House A & R Committee, and in the Senate Michael Moloney regained the chairmanship of the Senate A & R Committee. Moloney was determined to enhance his committee's influence on the budget-making process and its reputation for independence. As a first step, he started holding separate hearings on the budget, and he ran those hearings with a firm hand.

When the interim A & R Committee began its review of state agencies in the summer of 1979, there was discussion in the press about the committee developing an alternative budget. But in the 1980 session, the initiative for such a budget came from the Senate and House Democratic leadership. Faced with a serious revenue shortage, Governor Brown had suggested that some form of tax increase should not be ruled out as one way of balancing the budget. But early in February Democratic leaders called Senate and House caucuses that instructed the A & R committees to develop their own revenue estimates and to produce a balanced budget in accord with those estimates by reducing or eliminating existing programs, delaying unfunded proposals, and including only those new programs deemed essential by the legislature. In early March a set of budget recommendations prepared by House and Senate A & R subcommittees were presented to the House A & R Committee several days before Governor Brown presented the budget message to the legislature. The governor was displeased at being upstaged by the A & R committees; legislators were displeased that the governor had delayed presenting his budget until only three weeks were left in the session. The House A & R Committee made a number of significant changes in Brown's budget, including cuts in social services and increases for education. The Senate A & R Committee passed a budget that was a compromise between Brown's budget and the House version. The final compromises were worked out by the conference committee. Governor Brown also won passage, by narrow margins in both houses, of a bill to establish a gasoline tax based on a percentage of the wholesale price rather than nine cents a gallon. This was designed to provide more tax revenue as the price of gas rose, but it proved to be a disappointment when prices stopped rising.

Unfortunately, state revenue during the 1980-82 biennium fell far short of estimates because of the impact of the national recession on Kentucky. Twice during 1981 Governor Brown found it necessary to make major cutbacks in state spending, with a total of nearly $450 million being cut. The governor refused to consider raising taxes to make up for the lost revenue, and he refused to call a special session of the legislature at the start of the 1981-82 fiscal year to share in decision making on budget cuts. Although some legislators criticized Brown's unwillingness to share responsibility, others were happy to avoid that burden.

In 1982 Brown delivered an austere budget proposal to the legislature during the first week of the session. The A & R committees reviewing the budget faced more uncertainties and problems than usual. There continued to be uncertainties about the revenue projections for the biennium. There were more uncertainties about the impact on the budgets of cutbacks in federal spending being proposed by the Reagan administration. A number of groups testifying before the committees insisted that spending for social services and education needed to be increased to make up for the cutbacks in the last biennium and reductions in federal programs, even if it meant increasing taxes.

The chairmen of the Senate and House A & R committees, Michael Moloney and Joe Clarke, warned their colleagues and the governor that additional revenues were necessary to deal with these uncertainties and support seriously underfunded programs. There was considerable support in the legislature for increasing funding for education if the funds could be found. In early March the governor proposed a series of new revenue measures, including a truck tax, various increases in fees, and changes in administering the liquor tax, to make possible some additional spending, primarily for education. With much difficulty the governor succeeded in getting most of his revenue measures passed in somewhat different form. The role of the A & R committees in this session had been to publicize the programs that were most in need of added funding.

During the administration of Governor Martha Layne Collins, Michael Moloney and Joe Clarke continued to chair the Senate and House Appropriations and Revenue committees. And they continued to be prophets of gloom and doom about the growing gap between the needs of state government and the revenue available from existing taxes and from federal grants. Although their warnings seem to have fallen on deaf ears much of the time, both governors and legislators have been forced intermittently to grapple with fiscal realities.

At the beginning of this chapter we described Governor Collins's late and reluctant decision to ask the 1984 session of the General Assembly for tax increases. The governor was defeated in this effort, but in 1985 she called a special session that adopted an increase in business taxes to finance much of the cost of increased spending for education. In the 1986 session the Speaker of the House led a successful drive for a higher gasoline tax to overcome deficiencies in the road fund.

Throughout the Collins administration, the House and Senate A & R committees continued the practice of holding extensive hearings and then revising gubernatorial budgets to fit their own priorities. We have described how the committees eventually wrote the budget in 1984 after the governor's plan for a tax increase failed. In 1986 the House A & R Committee made more changes in the budget than did the Senate, and the final bill represented a compromise between the two. In the field of higher education, for example, the legislature cut back and delayed the governor's proposals for "centers of excellence" in order to put more funding into faculty salary increases.

LEGAL FOUNDATIONS OF THE LEGISLATURE'S
BUDGETARY AUTHORITY

In 1982 the General Assembly passed legislation designed to strengthen its oversight of the entire budgetary process, from the preparation of spending estimates by agencies to the implementation of the budget during the interim. For several years the LRC and the A & R committees had been receiving copies of agency requests at the same time these were sent to the governor's budget office. The new law also gave the A & R committees (through the LRC) the authority to prescribe the instructions that were sent to governmental agencies to guide their preparation of budget estimates.

During Governor Brown's first session, and in some previous sessions, the legislature had been frustrated by delays in submission of the governor's budget. Consequently, the 1982 law provided that the governor must submit a budget no later than the fifteenth legislative day in his or her first session and the tenth legislative day in the second session.

The law spelled out in considerable detail the provisions that must be contained in budget bills to deal with either revenue surpluses or revenue shortfalls, provisions designed to limit the governor's freedom to make budgetary decisions between legislative sessions. During Julian Carroll's administration, the governor had considerable flexibility in spending the surplus funds that accumulated, and during the 1980-82 biennium Governor Brown had assumed responsibility for making major cuts in the budget necessitated by revenue shortfalls.

The law required that each budget include a budget reduction plan to be implemented in the event of revenue shortfalls. Each branch of government was required to provide a plan, subject to revision by the legislature before its enactment into law, for reducing expenditures in case of a revenue shortfall of between 2.5 percent and 5 percent. The law required that the LRC and/or the Interim A & R committees be regularly kept informed about the financial and revenue situation of the state, spending reallocations and reductions undertaken by agencies to implement the plan for revenue shortfalls, and any interpretations of state budget items made by government agencies. The purpose of these detailed provisions was obviously to permit the Interim A & R Committee to monitor very closely the implementation of the budget—particularly during periods of cutbacks—and to force the executive budget office to explain the decisions it was making.

When various provisions of this law were challenged by the Brown administration, the Supreme Court issued a decision (*LRC v. Brown*) largely upholding it. The court asserted that the budget "is fundamentally a legislative matter," and "the final action on the enactment or adoption of the budget is a legislative matter." The court discussed each of the provisions in some detail and decided that none of them constituted a legislative veto or interference by the General Assembly in the executive function of implementing the budget. The LRC and A & R committees retained broad powers to oversee the implementation of the budget.

Faced with the necessity of cutting spending programs in 1984, the legislature passed a bill providing that a budget bill may suspend or modify a statute for the duration of the budget bill; and it passed a budget bill that suspended several laws mandating particular expenditures. For example, the budget bill modified existing legislation guaranteeing state employees an annual salary increase of 5 percent, cutting the increases to 2 percent and 3 percent for the two years of the biennium. The budget law also transferred a number of agency funds generated by fees to the general fund. Attorney General David Armstrong challenged the constitutionality of these provisions. But the Supreme Court (in *Armstrong* v. *Collins*, Ky., 709 S.W.2d 437) upheld the power of the General Assembly to modify or suspend laws through the budget process. It also permitted budgetary requirements for the transfer of public money from agency funds to the general fund, but excluded from such transfers privately contributed money, such as pension funds.

THE BUDGET-MAKING PROCESS TODAY

One reason for the strength of the Appropriations and Revenue committees today is the knowledge and experience of their members. In the 1987-88 legislature, Michael Moloney was serving his sixth term as chairman of the Senate A & R Committee, and Joe Clarke was serving his ninth term as chairman of the House A & R Committee—making him the most senior chairman of such a legislative committee in the country.

In the 1987-88 session, three of the nine members of the Senate A & R Committee were serving in their fifth or sixth term on the committee, and one other was serving his seventh term on either the Senate or House committee. In the House A & R Committee, Clarke was serving his tenth term and six others were in their fifth through eighth term; five had served three or four terms; but nine were in their second term and two in their first term. The House rule that members can protect a seat on one of their committees has helped preserve the continuity of this committee. In the five sessions since that rule went into effect, only seven continuing members of the House have left the A & R Committee, and four of the five Democrats doing so were becoming chairman of another committee.

Moreover, the A & R committees now have a staff of about a dozen analysts, most of whom have extensive budgetary experience and have spent a number of years specializing in the work of one subcommittee. Don Judy, the director of the staff (and assistant director of the LRC) since 1978 has brought both stability and a high level of professionalism to the staff. The comments of members of the A & R committees reflect a high level of satisfaction with the quality of staff work.

During the interim period the House and Senate committees operate as a single committee: the Joint Interim Committee on Appropriations and Revenue. The interim committee is organized into six subcommittees: General Government, Finance and Public Protection; Education; Human Resources; Commerce, Energy and Natural Resources; Justice, Corrections and Judiciary; and Transportation. Throughout the interim the subcommittees hold regular meetings, and the full committee seldom meets, except on questions involving taxation. Each of the subcommittees has particular staff members assigned to it.

Preparing the Budget. Under the 1982 law on the budgetary process, the Interim Appropriations and Revenue Committee drafts the budget instructions to be sent to all agencies of government. Although these instructions are highly technical, they include the financial parameters that agencies must follow in preparing their funding requests. In recent years, for example, the instructions have limited aggregate spending increases to 3 percent. In practice, these instructions are initially drafted by budgetary officials in the Office of Planning and Management, but the leadership of the A & R Committee is closely consulted on the preparation of instructions, and the committee has the ultimate authority to determine their content.

When the agencies of government submit their spending requests in October prior to the legislative session, a copy of these requests goes to the Interim A & R Committee. The A & R subcommittees have the opportunity to collect information on these requests and evaluate them at the same time that a parallel review and evaluation is being conducted by the Office of Planning and Management and by the governor. The factual groundwork is laid for members of the A & R subcommittees to establish somewhat different spending priorities from those developed by the executive branch.

In theory, this system works well. In practice, both the legislative and executive branches operate under serious time restraints when a new governor takes office. The initial budget requests are prepared by members of the outgoing administration; a new governor and new agency heads have relatively little time to become familiar with factual details and budgetary realities. Under these circumstances it is possible that the members of the Interim A & R Committee will have a better understanding of budgetary problems and choices than either the incoming governor or many of the agency heads. This experience, of course, enhances the influence of the A & R committees during the session.

The Budget Process during the Session. When the legislature meets in regular sessions, the two A & R committees operate very differently. The House A & R Committee maintains the organization by subcommittees, which hold hearings and eventually recommend changes in their segments of the budget to the full committee. The Senate A & R Committee, on the other hand, makes no use of subcommittees; it meets as a whole for hearings and decision making.

In fact, the decision-making process is quite different in the two committees: more decentralized in the House and more concentrated in the Senate. The House A & R Committee has been operating through subcommittees since the late 1970s. In 1980 the House started the practice of assigning liaison members from other committees to the A & R subcommittees. Each of these subcommittees includes four members (one serving as chairman) from the Appropriations and Revenue Committee and three liaison members from pertinent committees. The Education subcommittee of A & R, for example, includes members of the Education Committee, and the Human Services subcommittee includes two from Health and Welfare and one from the Labor and Industry Committee. The liaison members serve on the interim committees; during the session they participate fully in hearings and have voting rights in the subcommittee, but decisions of the subcommittee can be overruled by the full A & R committee, on which they play no role.

An executive committee, consisting of the chairmen of the subcommittees, along with the chairman of A & R, plays a major role in the budget-making process. The committee chairman sets the original spending targets for each of the substantive areas. After completing budgetary hearings, the subcommittees submit their recommendations directly to the executive committee. Frequently, the recommendations of individual subcommittees exceed these targets. Most of the competing demands of state agencies and functions are reconciled by the executive committee. When the full membership of the A & R Committee meets to make final budgetary decisions, the members of the executive committee are the best informed legislators and their recommendations carry a deal of weight.

In 1985 the House Democratic caucus took a further step to broaden participation by members of substantive committees in the budgetary process. It required all members of pertinent committees to be notified of presession budget review subcommittee meetings and budgetary hearings during the session. And it required the A & R subcommittees to hold briefings for members of the substantive committees on their proposed budget recommendations. In practice, during the 1986 session the members of those committees showed little interest in attending the briefings and raising questions about the recommendations; the practice may be discontinued for lack of interest.

The subcommittee chairmen and members of the House A & R sub-committees are chosen by the chairman of the committee. The new House leadership that took office in 1985 had promised subcommittee chairmanships to some legislators, and Chairman Clarke cooperated with the leadership in making these selections. As the A & R subcommittee system has developed, these positions have become comparable in importance to the chairmanships of many other committees. The chairmen of the subcommittees have gained more expertise and power, and they have become more independent of the committee chairman. They have become the acknowledged budgetary specialists on the areas under their subcommittee's jurisdiction; and they have a powerful voice in setting priorities, negotiating compromises, and drafting budgetary recommendations within their area. This gives them the chance to include in the budget programs of particular concern to them or their constituents.

The are several reasons for this decentralization of power in the House A & R Committee. Chairman Joe Clarke encouraged the use of subcommittees because he was being criticized for exercising too much power, he felt the need to share major responsibility for the budget with more committee members, and he did not have time to manage the detailed review of each area that he considered essential. The House A & R Committee is large enough that it can operate through subcommittees, particularly when the membership is increased by the liaison members. Some of the pressure for broader participation in the budgetary process has also come from members of the substantive committees, who recognize the crucial importance of budgetary decisions to the areas of their jurisdiction, such as health and welfare, education, and transportation. Clarke believes that the present system maximizes participation in the budgetary process: "We've got about as many people involved in the process as are willing to be involved."

Some observers in Frankfort believe that the budgetary process has become too decentralized, and the House subcommittees and their chairmen have become too independent. One indication of the Education subcommittee's power is that two-thirds of the state's budget—both education and higher education—falls under its jurisdiction. It must be remembered, however, that the recommendations of each subcommittee are reviewed, and sometimes altered, by both the executive committee and the full membership of the House A & R Committee.

The Senate Appropriations and Revenue Committee works very differently. Its members serve on interim A & R subcommittees, and may informally specialize in these areas during the session, but the committee meets as a whole for hearings and decision making. There are no liaison members from other committees involved in the budgetary process. The committee avoids subcommittees because of its small size and because this is the way Chairman Mike Moloney prefers to operate.

Moloney runs the Senate A & R Committee with a firm hand. He often dominates committee hearings with his questions. He devotes nearly all of his time in the Senate to the work of that committee, and he is recognized by his colleagues as the senatorial expert on budgets. His domination of the committee is partly a matter of his personality and his expertise. It also reflects the fact that most other members of the A & R Committee are preoccupied with other responsibilities; in recent sessions the other six Democrats have included the majority leader and three or four committee chairmen.

In the past, when the legislature used to approve the governor's budget without change, there was no need to have a conference committee. Now that both the House and Senate Appropriations and Revenue Committees consistently revise the budget in line with their own priorities, conference committees are regularly held to work out the final version of the budget.

The chairmen of the two A & R committees play powerful roles in the conference committee because of their detailed knowledge of the budget and their close working relationship. The compromises worked out by the conference committee are usually based heavily on preliminary negotiations between the two chairmen. In 1984, when Senator Moloney was hospitalized just before the conference committee met, the Senate members were seriously handicapped in their negotiations because they lacked detailed knowledge about the budget.

In 1986 the conference committee included five representatives: Chairman Clarke and the four party leaders (three of them Democrats) on the House A & R Committee. The party leaders were not experts on budgetary matters because they had had less time than most members to attend committee meetings. The three Senate members were Chairman Moloney, President Pro Tem Prather, and Majority Leader Wright. Normally, the Republicans have had only one senator and one representative on the eight- to ten-member conference committee, but in 1986 Republican senators were denied any representation on the committee.

In 1986 the chairmen of the House A & R subcommittees, who had tried unsuccessfully to gain representation on the conference committee, persuaded Speaker Blandford that each of them should be permitted to participate in the conference while it was dealing with the budget items pertaining to his subcommittee. When this plan was implemented, it enhanced the power of subcommittee chairmen. The negotiations in the conference committee consisted largely of a dialogue between Senator Moloney and the chairman of the subcommittee, the two individuals most responsible for the two versions of the budget. Before the conference met, some of the subcommittee chairmen had negotiated privately with Moloney, supplementing his discussions with Chairman Clarke. If this practice of participation by subcommittee chairmen in the conference committee is continued, it will further institutionalize decentralization of the House A & R Committee.

It is a measure of the Appropriations and Revenue committees' expertise and power that their budgetary recommendations in recent years have been approved on the floor of the House and Senate without change. Similarly the recommendations of the A & R conference committee are routinely approved by both houses.

In the years when the legislature routinely approved the governor's budget without any change, there was no reason to veto any appropriations. Recently, however, the governor has made use sparingly of the item veto. In 1984 the governor vetoed items totaling $5.5 million, most of it for proposed buildings at two community colleges—an item that had been added in the conference committee. The vetoes were sustained by the House. These were believed to be the first budgetary item vetoes since 1946 (when there was a Republican governor). There were no appropriations vetoes in 1986.

Overseeing Implementation of the Budget. The work of the Appropriations and Revenue Committees on the biennial budget does not end when the General Assembly adjourns. The Interim A & R Committee keeps a watchful eye on implementation of the budget, a responsibility that has become more important as revenue shortfalls have become more common. The two chairmen and their staff maintain informal contacts with budgetary officials in the governor's Office of Policy and Management (OPM), discussing how to interpret the intent of the legislature and how to implement the details of the budget.

As we have noted, in recent years the legislature has required that the budget document specify how shortfalls will be met and requires the executive budget office to provide specific information on how such steps are implemented. In recent years the legislature has required that the budget contain specific provisions for handling revenues shortfalls that range from 2.5 percent to 5 percent of the budget. But implementing this system has proven to be difficult, partly because a series of spending cutbacks may be required during a year and partly because it is difficult to specify in advance how best to make such cuts. In practice, the interim A & R Committee has provided advice to OPM officials on budgetary revisions and has given its blessings to changes that it considered reasonable. During the 1986-87 fiscal year, for example, the A & R Committee agreed that, instead of making cuts in new programs as called for by the budget reduction plan, the administration could make use of unexpended funds from other areas as much as possible. The committee and the administration also discussed how best to use the $100 million reserve built into the budget for the biennium.

During the interim period, the subcommittees of the Interim A & R Committee hold regular hearings to gather information about the operation of state agencies and programs and to explore a variety of budgetary problems. Perhaps the best way to show the range and complexity of these issues is to summarize a few of these hearings during a one-month period early in 1987. The Subcommittee on Commerce, Energy and Natural Resources discussed the economic development bond program and the problem of interpreting the intent of the legislature in adopting the program. It then discussed the technicalities of financing a gas pipeline to the new Toyota factory, under the state's agreement to provide $125 million in assistance to the Toyota company. The Subcommittee on Transportation discussed the implementation of a plan to reduce the cost of debt service for Kentucky highway bonds by retiring some of the bonds more quickly, and it gathered information on a major new highway project that was under way. The Subcommittee on General Government, Finance, and Public Protection reviewed plans for budget reductions during the current fiscal year. The Subcommittee on Human Resources discussed an ongoing program to provide day-care centers for low-income families, and heard briefings on the problems of teenage suicide and teenage pregnancy.

EVALUATING THE LEGISLATURE'S ROLE IN THE BUDGETARY PROCESS

The most obvious conclusion to draw about the legislature's impact on the budget is that it is infinitely greater than was the case in the 1960s. The legislature's role has grown gradually for a number of reasons, most of which are related to the greater capability and independence of the Appropriations and Revenue committees. The committees have more and better staff; they make effective use of time available during the interim; their membership has greater stability and thus more experience; they have outstanding leaders; and these committees have gained political independence from the governor. The A & R committees have the experience and skill necessary to understand the technicalities of the budget. They have gained enough understanding of the details of state agencies and programs to make their own decisions on priorities. And they command so much respect in the General Assembly that their budgetary recommendations are regularly adopted on the floor almost automatically.

When the legislature demonstrated its unwillingness to adopt the tax increases proposed by the governor in 1984, the Appropriations and Revenue committees demonstrated their ability to set priorities and write a new budget based on lower revenues. The legislature has developed a mechanism

giving the Interim A & R Committee authority to oversee budget adjustments necessitated by revenue shortfalls, though rigid requirements seem
to work less well than informal consultation. Perhaps the most important
role the A & R committees play is the careful, persistent scrutiny of budget
requests from the executive agencies. Because members of these committees
are well-informed enough to ask tough questions, the agency heads who
appear before them must be prepared to defend their programs and justify
their requests for increased spending. As the demands on state government
continue to grow faster than the available resources, such careful scrutiny
becomes increasingly important.

Legislative review of the budget has seldom resulted in major changes
in spending priorities. Often this means that executive agencies are successful in making a strong case for their programs. It may also reflect fundamental agreement between the governor and a majority of legislators on
spending priorities. In some cases both the governor and the legislature are
responding in similar fashion to demands from interest groups, such as teachers. On some issues the governor's budget has closely reflected the priorities
of legislators. That was largely the case in 1986, when the executive budget
was designed to implement education programs passed by the 1985 special
session of the legislature, programs that had largely been crafted by the
education committees of the legislature.

Another reason why the legislature has seldom made major changes in
the governor's budget is that recent governors have had substantial political
support in the legislature even though they have not dominated that body
like their predecessors. In several recent sessions the Senate has been less
willing than the House to make significant changes in the governor's budget,
and the final document has naturally represented a compromise between
the two houses.

The legislature has also demonstrated considerable independence of the
governor on the question of taxes, most dramatically in 1984 when it rejected
Governor Collins's tax package. In 1986, on the other hand, the legislature
adopted an increase in the gasoline tax that was proposed by the Speaker
of the House with little encouragement from the governor's office.

We must conclude that the Senate and House A & R committees—and
particularly their leaders—have had less influence on tax policy than they
have had on the budget. In recent years the two chairmen, Michael Moloney
and Joe Clarke, have repeatedly warned that revenues are not keeping up
with spending commitments made for the next few years, and that the legislature must be willing to provide more revenue. Although their views
command respect, legislators have been reluctant to enlist in the cause of
increased taxation. The adoption of major changes in taxation to produce
more revenue normally requires the active support of the governor. Only
the governor can provide the leadership of public opinion that is usually

required to bring about such changes; and such leadership must be skillful and well planned. It is probably asking too much of legislative leaders, or of the Appropriations and Revenue committees, to expect them to carry most of the responsibility for initiating and gaining adoption of major tax increases.

7. Legislative Oversight

OVERSIGHT ACTIVITIES IN STATE LEGISLATURES

In the last decade, Congress and the state legislatures have dramatically increased their efforts to oversee executive agencies, not always successfully and some times half-heartedly. Legislative oversight of executive agencies is highly decentralized and takes place in many different locations in the legislative organization. In Kentucky legislative oversight may be performed in a variety of ways and to varying degrees, ranging from mere monitoring of activity to actual control of what agencies do. Hamm and Robertson (1981) delineate seven different types of oversight activities: casework, budget review, investigative hearings, review of administrative rules and regulations, program evaluations and sunset laws, advise and consent of executive appointments and impeachments, and review of organization and reorganization plans. We can understand the development and limits of oversight in Kentucky better by briefly reviewing general patterns of oversight in state legislatures.

Motivations for Involvement in Oversight Activities. To the individual legislator, time invested in overseeing executive agencies may not always seem well spent. Legislators may not think it is valuable to engage in oversight work unless there is some patent connection to the interests of their constituencies, or some linkage to their prospects for reelection. But in recent years, public demands for watchfulness on the part of legislators have made oversight work appear more politically rewarding to legislators. Moreover, many legislators are interested in helping to create good, effective, feasible, economy-minded public policies.

The general orientation toward oversight that a legislator brings to the committee determines his or her commitment to the process of oversight and the extent of active participation in the committee's business (Ogul,

1976; Rosenthal, 1981a, 1981b; Scher, 1963; Fenno, 1978; Fiorina, 1977). As the literature on legislative oversight suggests, a legislator is only marginally oriented toward performing oversight responsibility. Four explanations generally account for this marginal interest: (1) legislators are concerned with oversight only when they feel they can establish a political record or when they differ in policy orientation from the bureaucrat involved (Ogul, 1976); (2) legislators seek to maximize credit, but oversight confers little credit in comparison with other legislative activities (Rosenthal, 1981a; Scher, 1963); (3) legislators attempt to achieve concrete results, but oversight seldom leads to reducing government programs or generating budget cuts (Rosenthal, 1981a); and (4) legislators seek appointments to prestigious committees, but oversight committees are seen as unattractive which, in turn, produces little interest in such committee's work (Bibby, 1966). Some legislators, though, are oriented toward oversight activities. These "oversight-oriented legislators" (1) "want to learn more about the functions of state government, its policies and programs in order to enhance their own expertise;" (2) seek to improve state government; and (3) possess a commitment to the legislature and legislative process and recognize oversight as a means of ensuring legislative integrity (Rosenthal, 1981a: 126).

Legislative influence over administrative agencies is also important to the legislature as an institution. Legislative investigations, reviews, and even involvement in administrative policymaking provide the legislature with a basis for evaluating and assessing legislative policies. Legislative innovation and responses to executive agencies are highly fragmented, or atomized. Although oversight of executive agencies flows mainly through the work of committees and subcommittees, contacts between legislators and administrators constitute a very important form of legislative oversight. Contacts with agency people are very likely to be motivated by constituency demands. Members of Congress enjoy both very substantial resources for the provision of constituency services and opportunities for a wide range of contacts with agency personnel. In the states the resources available to legislators for purposes of casework-based oversight are variable.

In general, state legislators are less likely than congresspersons to make use of constituency service work as a vehicle for oversight of executive agencies (see Rosenthal, 1981b: 314-39). State legislators, less visible to their constituents than congressmen, often find it difficult to claim full credit for their oversight efforts. The staff resources available to legislators in most states are paltry enough to preclude very intense oversight activity on the part of individual members. And many state legislators fear that ad hoc oversight efforts stir up more trouble than they are worth (Rosenthal, 1981a). One detailed study of two states—Minnesota and Kentucky—found only a modicum of oversight activity present, but demonstrated substantially more oversight in Minnesota than in Kentucky. This difference occurs largely because of the more professionalized status of the Minnesota legislature, with its greater resources in members' time and staff expertise, compared to the legislature in Kentucky (Elling, 1979).

From the viewpoint of their reelection value, one observer has said that congressional "bureaucratic fixit services" are "all profit" (Fiorina 1977: 47). For state legislators the potential political value of oversight activities is no less substantial, but generally speaking it is less realizable given the much less visible public image of state legislators. Moreover, smaller resources for oversight in the state legislatures probably mean that when their members find bureaucratic deficiencies in the course of constituency service work, they are not equipped to sustain thorough investigation and persistent watchfulness in regard to them.

Legislators must make a variety of strategic political calculations as to whether to engage in oversight activities; many legislators see opportunities for greater rewards in developing new legislation, or in constituency service activity, than they do from engaging in oversight of executive agencies. Legislators may maintain "cozy" relationships with agency people in order to serve their constituency or interest group needs, and find these jeopardized by staff or committee oversight investigations. Certainly, legislators' strategic calculations may include the concerns of political interest groups, especially those that are important in members' districts. Accordingly, members of legislative committees may wish to avoid agency review if they expect it will provoke costly reprisals from important interests, economic or environmental, regulated by the agencies. Moreover, legislators who calculate that their political fortunes are intimately tied to the fate of the governor may, out of loyalty, wish to avoid close examination of the performance of agency officials appointed by the governor.

Legislative oversight of executive agencies may be affected by tension between the generalist, politically sensitive knowledge of the legislator and the specialist, technical knowledge of the administrator. To the citizen-legislator of the state legislatures, withdrawal from oversight as a resolution of generalist-specialist tension may be more common than among members of Congress. A student of state legislatures has said, "To legislators, oversight seems an unfathomable business, and not at all convenient to pursue. They do not want to engage in a long study; they do not want to spend inordinate time on an issue; they do not want elegance or preciseness in the solutions they adopt. They want simple, straightforward options" (Rosenthal, 1981a: 121).

An Overview of Oversight Activities. In the 1970s legislative oversight "came of age" in the states (Rosenthal, 1981b: 314). Many states established oversight committees, provided oversight staffing, adopted legislation providing for review of agency rule making, and provided for sweeping evaluations of agency worth. Basically, the states' plunge into oversight involved wresting control of postauditing from executive hands (traditionally, auditing offices have engaged in investigations intended to ensure that administrative agencies spent public funds in accord with what had been authorized by law). Once in legislative control, many states enlarged the purview of postauditing so that audits included a wide range of agency activities, not just financial management. Many such offices came to be involved in general program and policy review, most effectively in Hawaii, California, Illinois, Colorado, Montana, and Kansas (Rosenthal, 1981b: 316). In addition, legislative fiscal bureaus and staff service agencies began to move more fully into oversight work.

Program evaluation has been used effectively by many legislatures, which adopted several ways of integrating program evaluation into the legislative process. Connecticut, Mississippi, New York, and Virginia have separate staff agencies for program evaluation. Other states have placed this function in an existing legislative audit agency, fiscal or research staff. Program evaluation seems to be most effective when closely tied to the budget process or standing committee review (Pound, 1984: 82).

"Sunset laws" that require full-scale reviews by legislative committees or staff offices of executive agencies and their programs have been adopted by thirty-five states, not including Kentucky. These reviews are supposed to determine whether the executive agencies are performing in accord with the intent of the legislature, whether they are doing their job or providing their services efficiently, and whether they should continue to exist in the future—or go off "into the sunset" (Hamm and Robertson, 1981: 138-40). The best general assessment of the state sunset laws after several years of experience with them seems to be that, although they did require the legislatures to take on oversight responsibilities, the time needed to conduct sunset reviews and the costs incurred have not been well justified in terms of financial savings, elimination of unneeded programs, or termination of agencies (Pound, 1982: 183-84).

More persistent efforts to strengthen oversight in the states have been laws endowing legislative committees (or the whole house) with jurisdiction permitting review of all rules and regulations emanating from executive agencies. Some kind of administrative rules review now exists in forty-one states, and the legislature in twenty-nine states has the power to veto, suspend, or modify proposed administrative rules (Pound, 1982: 184). The rules review processes vary widely in their procedures and authority: rules review may be done through a special committee or regular standing committees; it may be advisory or binding; suspension or veto of proposed rules may be by resolution or may require a bill; and such power may be vested in a committee or exercised only by the full legislature.

The Role of Staff in Oversight Activities. Much of the day-to-day oversight work that is accomplished by Congress and by the state legislatures, and particularly by their committees, is done by the staff. Indeed, the rising tide of oversight activity on the part of legislatures that has taken place since 1970 accounts for a very large part of the dramatic growth in the numbers of legislative staff people in Congress and in the state legislatures. The recent dramatic growth in professional staffing for the state legislatures has demonstrated, in many states, that "there is a lot more involved in having a good education or natural resources program than just having a good law" (Rosenthal, 1981b: 337). But effective follow-up by the legislature that can win the respect of the executive agencies requires the legislature to have information sufficient to give its members an understanding of policies and programs, and the difficulties of their implementation. This is the task of the staff. But it is the effective working relationship between staff professionals and legislators that makes for effective oversight, not staff work alone.

The presence of full- or part-time staff determines how rules oversight functions. Full-time staff are capable of handling a high volume of proposed regulations and performing a thorough review of these rules (National Conference of State Legislatures, 1979: 21). Part-time staff or staff drawn from a central agency may lack these capabilities. Staff are also influential when (1) the issue is specific and technical, (2) a "zone of indifference" surrounds the issue, and (3) the issue is new and unrelated to the ongoing legislative concerns (Rosenthal, 1981b: 229). Staff also affect the balance among policy, discretionary, and procedural review by controlling the information passed to or kept from committee members. Also, staff management decisions regarding how broadly or narrowly to construct provisions of the state's administrative procedure act and to which of these provisions to give emphasis also affect this balance. How staff make these decisions is a function of the dominant philosophy or attitude toward rules oversight found among staff, and particularly staff management.

Because of these wide-ranging means for staff to influence rules oversight, it is possible that the process may become staff dependent and possibly staff dominated. The occurrence of this phenomenon may be heightened in those situations where rules oversight is conducted by a joint committee. A legislator's service on a joint committee is usually in addition to his or her existing committee assignments. This structural deterrent to participation, coupled with the general low saliency of the oversight responsibility among legislators, further encourages staff dominance by the direct abdication of responsibility by committee members to the staff or by the latter's awareness of the limited interest and capacity of the members to fulfill the oversight responsibility. But, as Ogul (1976: 14) reports, "Professional staff members will usually mirror the policy and process orientation of the congressmen who hire them and direct their behavior." But rules oversight presents a unique opportunity for staff dependency or dominance. This is particularly true when the committee members' orientation toward oversight is low and when the process of rules oversight is channeled through a joint committee whose members are already over-burdened by their regular legislative responsibilities.

USE OF OVERSIGHT COMMITTEES IN KENTUCKY

The Kentucky General Assembly has greatly expanded its role in executive oversight in recent years through the establishment of permanent legislative oversight committees. This trend began in 1972 with the naming of the Administrative Regulations Review Subcommittee of the Legislative Research Commission; it was followed by the creation of the Personal Services Contract Review Subcommittee (1978), the Legislative Program Review and Investigations Committee (1978), and the Capital Construction and Equipment Purchase Oversight Subcommittee (1979). All of these function as subcommittees of the Legislative Research Commission. The members select the chairman of each of the committees.

The establishing of the permanent committees and subcommittees reflects the desire of Kentucky legislators to take a more active role in all aspects of governmental operations. Because the legislature meets only biennially for less than four months, the governor and the executive agencies have the opportunity to make many decisions in the long interim. Executive decision-making flexibility has been reduced as a result of the oversight committee initiatives discussed here.

In 1982 the legislature passed a number of laws intended to strengthen its authority in several areas of oversight. For example, the Legislative Research Commission (LRC) was given authority to block implementation of administrative regulations unless the governor declared that an emergency existed. The LRC was also given a veto power over federal block grant applications and over reorganizations of government agencies proposed by the administration. In 1984 these laws were overruled by the Kentucky Supreme Court, however, in *Legislative Research Commission* v. *Brown*, which held that the LRC could not exercise "legislative powers" between legislative sessions, but the court left standing the legislative oversight authority that had existed before 1982.

LEGISLATIVE PROGRAM REVIEW AND
INVESTIGATIONS COMMITTEE

The Legislative Program Review and Investigations Committee (PRIC), established in 1978, conducts performance reviews of state agency operations to gauge program effectiveness and expenditure appropriateness. Establishment of this committee signaled a direct legislative interest in reviewing executive agency operations in an organized manner with statutory support. For example, the committee has the power to subpoena witnesses and records and to require testimony under oath.

This sixteen-member committee, consisting of eight senators and eight representatives, has staff and support services provided by the LRC. This committee studies the agencies, programs, and activities of state government as to their effectiveness, efficiency, cost, and compliance with legislative intent. It reports its findings and recommendations as a result of such studies to the agencies involved, the governor, and the General Assembly. The committee's reports may relate to whether an agency is carrying out activities and programs as directed or authorized by the General Assembly, whether it is doing so efficiently and effectively, and whether any change or reorganization is necessary to accomplish legislative intent in establishing a particular program.

The success of the Program Review and Investigations Committee depends on the effectiveness of its staff, the level of participation of its members, and the commitment and skill of its chairman. According to a veteran cochairman of the committee: "Legislators don't have lots of time. You let the staff independently make recommendations—and that puts some pressure on them. And if staff reports that things are running well, the legislator who wanted action may get impatient. The staff report to the chairmen initially but ultimately to the committee." A senator who has been on the committee since its inception is frustrated with the staff: "Some staffers are not aggressive enough. Some of the junior people who do research are good. There is too much potential for the examiners to simply take the word of administrators that they are doing things well. This ought to be the best and most aggressive staff."

One problem that has plagued this committee (and many others) is poor attendance; one senator remarked: "The committee does suffer from members being unwilling to put interim time on it. Some six to eight members are the nucleus and spend the most time on it. Sometimes it is hard to get a quorum."

At one time the members of the PRIC elected a chairman from either house for a two-year term; now they select a chairman for only one year, with the chairmanship alternating between the Senate and the House. Leadership on the committee has been weakened by this lack of continuity and by the lack of active interest by some of the recent Senate chairmen.

When asked about the major accomplishments of PRIC, the House co-chairman answered:

> They include such things as insurance and bank deposits during the Brown administration. Brown took credit—but the committee really did the significant work. We made some real progress on transportation. And some progress on state printing. The study of personnel, done with a subcommittee of the State Government Committee, has led to savings to avoid repetition of what happened under Gov. Brown. It took a long time to work out the details of legislation, to incorporate the rules of personnel department on lay-offs—to avoid all the suits by laid off employees that cost the state so much. The coal pact study was useful on a smaller scale—got some funds reimbursed. Sometimes, when we start studying an issue, the agency will change its practices—so it is not so obvious what we have accomplished.

One Senate member praised the work of committee in dealing with the exorbitant costs of insurance: "Our report cut the insurance costs for state buildings from $2.5 million to $0.5 million. They eliminated parceling out of insurance to friends of the administration, competitively bidding insurance, and doing some self-insurance. Our recommendations were immediately adopted by John Y. Brown." Another Senate committeeman felt, "The best thing the PRIC ever did was its study of state investments; it all came from our committee—as much as $30 to $50 million the state was losing—and then eventually the Brown administration picked up on it."

The PRIC members sometimes get frustrated with their investigations; one representative stated: "In the last interim we got tied up in Senate Resolution #30 on higher education. That was a very time consuming thing, and a lot of people lost interest in it. Therefore, nothing significant came out. I was surprised at its failure. The Education people were taking the initiative and they never really dug into the issues. Many of us grew impatient."

One representative who has served on the committee since its creation thinks the PRIC is "potentially the most important oversight committee. It is most effective as a watchdog committee. It has jurisdiction to investigate anything that is considered necessary to study." But there are differences of opinion about whether the committee has lived up to this potential. The chairman of the House A & R Committee believes that the PRIC ought to be "an adjunct to the budget process, able to make an in-depth study of a particular topic, which the A & R Committee lacks the time to do." One member of the PRIC offers this prescription for strengthening the Committee:

> The subpoena power makes our committee potentially powerful. But we have to make the rest of the legislature appreciate what this committee can accomplish—improve our public relations with the legislature, so other members will trust us more—perhaps let members of other committees sit in on our meetings when pertinent to their topic, the way we do with Appropriations and Revenue liaison members. I hope we can begin to do more things with more impact on executive policy.

PERSONAL SERVICES CONTRACT REVIEW SUBCOMMITTEE

The Personal Services Contract Review Subcommittee (PSCRS), established in 1978, receives proposed state agency contracts with firms and individuals outside state government. The committee reviews proposed contracts from three perspectives: Does the need for the proposed service exist? Can the service be performed by state personnel? Are the cost and duration of the proposed contract appropriate? The PSCRS consists of seven members: four representatives and three senators.

State agencies proposing to negotiate personal service contracts are required to transmit copies of such contracts and documentation in support thereof to the Personal Services Contract Review Subcommittee. The subcommittee reviews such contracts and may lodge its objections to any of them with the negotiating agency. The agency may comply with the objection or may propose no such complying action. If the agency chooses not to comply, the particular contract is referred by the director to the standing or interim committee on appropriations and revenue. If the contracting agency persists over objections raised by such committee, the matter is referred to the subsequent session of the General Assembly for its action.

A representative who served on the committee for its first six years evaluated its accomplishments during this earlier period:

> When it was set up, there was an enormous volume of personal service contracts, in terms of dollar totals. After we got set up as a committee, and began to ask questions, the volume of such contracts went down drastically. The volume is reduced, and the procedures have changed. We have got them to cut drastically what is charged for auditing, for example. Our involvement has led to consolidation of such contracts, and great savings. A continuing problem is the hourly fees

charged by consultants and particularly lawyers—where they claim that unless we hire high priced talent, we will lose the lawsuits. I think the committee has been extremely effective. There are still abuses—we are limited in time and power. But if we find something wrong, it embarrasses the agency. The fact that we are there means that lots of these abuses don't occur—agencies will bargain better in the future—and they will search for different vendors sometimes. Often we feel that the contracts for legal services can be done in-house—and we haven't fully solved that problem yet.

According to a PSCRS staffer, the major problem of excessive fees has been greatly reduced by the establishment of strict maximum fee guidelines for contracting professional services such as attorneys, doctors, engineers, architects, real estate auctioneers, and so on. These guidelines were originally set in 1980, and once a year they are revamped if necessary. For example, instead of some attorneys being paid as much as $150 per hour, now a lawyer practicing alone receives a maximum of $40 per hour and a law firm receives a maximum of $75 per hour. Some other guidelines include: $55 per hour maximum for engineers, $60 hourly for psychiatrists, $50 hourly for pediatricians, $50 hourly for institutional doctors, and fees for real estate appraisers based on $250 per diem for eight hours. Before these guidelines were adopted, each personal service contract was the result of "what they would take." Although these are just guidelines, they are strictly adhered to by the PSCRS in its recommendations.

When asked about an example of a recent contract with fees outside the guidelines, one representative remarked: "We agreed to uphold paying $60 per hour to a sole attorney to review the activities of other attorneys—disciplinary actions. There was a demonstrated need for his specialization and so the Committee decided to allow the demanded fee which was in excess of the guidelines for lawyers working alone."

Sometimes committee members who have particular expertise in their field of private livelihood will question the conditions of specific contracts. For example, a representative with real estate interests and a senator with auctioneer experience noted a problem with a contract between the University of Louisville and an auctioneer regarding the selling of a particular piece of property. By overseeing the original contract, PSCRS members pressured the parties to revise the contract's conditions concerning the auctioneer's advertising promotional fees. In the end the committee saved the University of Louisville $8,000.

PSCRS staffers feel that after Governor Collins took office in 1983, the administration became very supportive of adherence to these fee guidelines. Early in her first year of office, she issued a policy statement that prescribed that the "rate guidelines shall be the rates." Before her public stance, personal service contracts *may be* exempt from competitive bidding. Under Collins *all* contracts would be bid competitively—all exposed to public scrutiny. The PSCRS is a good example of legislative oversight bringing about a significant change in how the state does business.

According to one House committee member, every administration will get a few department heads who test the guidelines. For example, Alice McDonald, superintendent of public instruction under Governor Collins, issued auditing and legal contracts to political friends in Louisville. These contracts did not adhere to PSCRS's guidelines; lawyers were paid $1000 each to attend some meetings. The PSCRS chairman called McDonald and gave her the opportunity to withdraw the controversial contracts, but she refused. Consequently, McDonald and her department faced tough questioning by PSCRS members and a "raking over the coals" by the media.

The PSCRS staffers have good working relationships with the different state executive agencies. According to one staffer:

> If I see a problem with a contract, I will contact the agency and go over the controversial areas and give them every opportunity to revise, change, or dissolve the contract. In most cases the agencies and the universities will talk among themselves about the contracts, and they *know* the oversight committee's position on the fee guidelines and other things. They don't want to be embarrassed in public. The Department of Education has come around now; they know we are here, and they do not want further embarrassment; they have become more cautious.

The PSCRS chairman, who works very closely and effectively with his staffers, also maintains regular contacts with the various departments. If he sees a potential politically embarrassing problem, he, too, will call the particular department and tell them he thinks they have a problem involving a specific contract.

Some committee members and staffers perceive the PSCRS as a "fall guy" for the administration. One staffer noted that "this committee keeps the administration from being boxed in. The governor and her staff can say that the Committee will raise the hell about a particular contract and it won't let us pay more for personal services." In agreeing with the staffer's comments, a long-term member said, "The PSCRS gives the governor a good out—someone else to blame. Those S.O.B.s over there have the tough questions and your name will appear in the newspaper. Therefore, the administration does not have to hand out the formerly expected patronage contracts to supportive campaign workers and financial contributors."

The PSCRS has not always enjoyed good relationships with the finance department. In the early years, the committee's recommendations were frequently overruled. Under Governor Brown, George Atkins gave serious consideration to the personal service contracts. Under Governor Collins, Gordon Duke very rarely overruled the committee's recommendations— only on one or two occasions.

Many of the contracts that fall under the committee's oversight are routine and necessary. Because of legislation passed in 1986, all contracts— even those under $1000—are to be reviewed. A long-time staffer commented that he is very familiar with the usual recipients of the innumerable contracts; therefore, he continually looks for patterns of giving to the same individuals or political friends and any irregularities among all the contracts—routine and nonroutine. PSCRS members look at all contracts on the nonroutine list—anything that does not meet the prescribed guidelines.

The volume of personal service contracts is affected by whatever is going on in state government affairs—any new activities. Therefore, some recent state endeavors have increased the need for more contracts, for example, group homes, abandoned mine programs, the AA Highway in northern Kentucky, and so on. The PSCRS is careful to look at any new categories such as federal auditing contracts for the Department of Human Resources and federal mine reclamations. The committee is concerned that Kentucky people are hired for any new contract activities.

One senator who has been a PSCRS committee member since its creation summarized its effectiveness as follows:

> The PSCRS is one of the most effective ones—perhaps the most effective committee having no real power. Its only power is to air things publicly. As a direct result of the committee, the administration has cleaned up its act—as soon as the committee began to operate. At the start it reviewed all sorts of terrible contracts—wasteful, ineffective. The administration has simply stopped negotiating such contracts because of committee objections. The fees were too high, work wasn't specific enough, etc.

When asked for his evaluation of PSCRS, the chairman who has held this position since the committee's creation responded:

> PSCRS has saved the Commonwealth between $12 to $14 million. In the beginning, 1978, over 300 people would attend meetings which would take on average 2 to 2 1/2 days to look at each contract. There was so much wasted time and effort. Now we have very effective proceedings which usually last only 1/2 day. We have a lot fewer contracts to review because most are on the routine list which the staff oversees

ahead of time. I am very pleased with what's been happening on the committee. We established strict guidelines, and we tightened up what we can and cannot do. We ask the tough questions, and we let the chips fall where they may. Even the minority members, past and present, have praised the committee's accomplishments and its fairness; Republicans have opportunity to have their say. Although we are just a *review* committee and do not have a final say, the Director of Finance rarely overrules our objections. And another *good sign* of our effectiveness is that not one of the 1987 gubernatorial candidates mentioned *bad* personal service contracts in their campaign rhetoric. Personal service contracts used to be a very volatile political issue in Kentucky gubernatorial campaign politics. PSCRS is definitely not a rubber stamping body!

CAPITAL CONSTRUCTION AND EQUIPMENT PURCHASE OVERSIGHT COMMITTEE

The Capital Construction and Equipment Purchase Oversight Committee (CCEPOC), established in the 1979 special session, reviews records of the amounts expended and transferred for capital construction projects and equipment acquisitions and monitors the costs of such projects and acquisitions. During the Carroll administration, some legislators had been concerned about the governor's use of surplus funds to initiate capital construction projects not authorized by the legislature. The committee was created in part to establish some control over the spending of surplus funds, but since its establishment the state budget has been characterized by frequent revenue shortfalls rather than by surpluses.

This permanent subcommittee of the LRC is charged with reviewing proposed fund transfers from the capital construction and equipment contingency fund to the allotment account of a capital construction project or major equipment purchase. Prior to any such proposed transfer the Department of Finance must submit to the committee the specification of the amount proposed for transfer, documentation of the necessity therefor, and, regarding capital construction projects, documentation of amounts already expended and alterations to the project since its consideration by the General Assembly at its most recent regular session. Within thirty days of such submission the committee is required to determine the necessity for the proposed transfer, whether its amount is reasonable and whether any alterations made or planned materially change the project as such was considered and authorized by the General Assembly.

The CCEPOC consists of seven members—four representatives and three senators—appointed by the LRC with minority representation as nearly proportional to their members in the General Assembly as possible.

Although monthly committee meetings usually last only two hours, the members generally receive in advance from staffers detailed paperwork to wade through, and therefore this is a very time-consuming legislative oversight assignment.

According to one representative:

> The committee gets the first shot at all capital projects and then they go on to Appropriations and Revenue and the General Assembly. The threat of the sword hanging there gives us leeway. The committee has built enough credibility with A & R, and they know that we're not going to send them a lemon.

> A senate member commented on the committee's effectiveness: Formerly the highway department spent moneys for nontransportation uses, and now they are not allowed to. Formerly universities were not watched; all they did was consult with the Department of Finance. Now all their capital expenditures are reported to our committee. Formerly there was no record of state leases; as of 1985, all state leases must be reported, and the costs of state leases have been substantially reduced.

The CCEPOC's most recent chairman (since February 1987) has strong, positive feelings about the operation and effectiveness of the committee: "It is the most interesting committee I've served on; it is not repetitious. I feel like our job is to be a *watchdog* for state government. We act as a weather vane and a lightning rod; we raise a *red flag* if we note irregularities and excessive spending. We do not rubber stamp; we have helped make state building projects more professional, accountable, and efficient."

When questioned about cases where the committee has made a major impact, members cited several examples. One representative commented about the controversy surrounding increased expenditures for the fairgrounds in Louisville. Another mentioned the committee's effectiveness in turning down the state police request for more helicopters. One senator remarked about the committee's role in turning the management of the ski lift at General Butler Park over to private hands so it could be run more efficiently. Another area of major impact has concerned prison issues; one representative noted: "The committee has held a number of hearings about the controversy over the prison in Boyle County. Committee members were worried that it was not maximum security. The committee was instrumental in getting the administration interested in building more maximum security prisons."

According to one staffer, the committee has brought forth major changes in the way state government makes major capital construction expenditures:

> Before the creation of CCEPOC, there was a pool of money, and these were the designated projects. There was a lack of accountability

and efficiency. Now there is a line itemized capital construction budget enacted by the legislature. And if a project has not been itemized, it cannot be built. Also, capital construction activities are now out in the open to public scrutiny. The committee looks for a better way to do things; it reviews all capital construction budget requests. Certain projects have been deferred or eliminated. I can remember only one time when the Secretary of Finance overruled the committee's recommendation.

This oversight committee has been able to delay controversial projects. According to one representative and staffer, the committee held up the issuance of $1 million in economic development bonds for the city of Carlisle. The project was delayed until there was a proper accounting of how the money would be spent. Another delay concerned the developers of the Riverfront in Louisville; the committee refused to approve a "blank check." Another recent problem concerns the garage cost overruns on the Festival Marketplace in Lexington; the developers underestimated their costs. In this case the CCEPOC has acted as a middleman between the developers and the secretary of finance who was asked by the developers to allocate more economic bonds to pay for the overruns. Since the secretary did not make a recommendation for it, the developers came directly to the oversight committee—an out-of-order procedure. As of yet, the problem has not been resolved.

The CCEPOC chairman is particularly excited about the committee's current endeavors regarding a comprehensive study of all space requirements for state government: "There has never been a long range plan. The state did not even have an inventory of properties leased. There is no central store for the state; every agency has its own warehouse. This study represents a tremendous, painstaking undertaking by our staffers. We need to consolidate everything in the lab. Another major state office building which brings together some isolated state agencies should be constructed."

There is an excellent working relationship between the staffers and the committee's chairman. The chairman has high praise for the technical skills of his staff who often make a list of five or six puzzling questions they feel should be addressed concerning particular capital construction outlays and equipment purchases.

When asked about the role of minority committee members, one representative noted that a Republican senator was the member who first "jumped on state leases" and has been given the credit of fathering state lease reforms. This minority member was recently elected vice-chairman of the committee—an unusual occurrence. Generally, there are no partisan issues, and minority members are treated very fairly.

ADMINISTRATIVE REGULATIONS REVIEW SUBCOMMITTEE

Executive agencies are often given authority by statute to promulgate administrative regulations in implementing legislation. Administrative regulations are legally binding and are of interest and concern to many citizens. In 1972 the General Assembly passed legislation making the procedure for promulgating administrative regulations more open to the public and subject to legislative review. Proposed regulations must be filed with the Legislative Research Commission for printing and public distribution. Concerned citizens have the opportunity to request a public hearing to voice their objections to a proposed regulation.

The Administrative Regulations Review Subcommittee (ARRS) meets monthly and reviews proposed regulations to determine whether the state agency proposing the regulation has the statutory authority to do so and whether the regulation is consistent with legislative intent. Unacceptable regulations are returned to the state agency for possible revision; however, the governor may issue an executive order promulgating a regulation for up to 120 days while the committee considers it. This joint interim subcommittee consists of seven members: four representatives and three senators. Later in this chapter we will provide a case study of the 1983 proceedings of the Kentucky ARRS.

Each state administrative body exercising its prerogative to adopt regulations implementing its legally assigned functions must submit to the LRC the original and four copies of each proposed regulation. All such regulations, except those of an emergency nature, must be reviewed by the ARRS before they may be deemed "filed" and become effective. Upon filing of regulations, the LRC compiles, prints, and distributes these documents annually as the *Kentucky Administrative Regulations Service*, which constitutes the official state publication of administrative regulations. In addition, the commission publishes a monthly *Administrative Register of Kentucky*, which contains all proposed regulations filed with the commission.

One ARRS staffer describes how the ARRS process operates:

> When we get the regs initially, we send them to the staff of the appropriate substantive interim committee (e.g., Education, Human Resources, etc.). We have two staff attorneys who then review the regulations and the comments from interim committee staffers. They deal with the more legal aspects, and subject matter of regulation. The staff attorneys will alert the ARRS to any problems that they see with the reg; the attorneys are alert to political aspects as well as the legal aspects. And they recognize what might concern the subcommittee members. Sometimes the members will see problems that staff members

don't see. If our staff finds a problem with a regulation, we will send a letter to the agency well before the subcommittee meeting, inviting them to call our staff. They often do, and often work out the problem before the subcommittee meets, and sometimes they will withdraw or defer a regulation. Sometimes the interest group gets involved in this. Though our staff does not alert the interest group to the problem—it is the interest group that initiates the problems.

The ARRS committeemen generally accept the staff's recommendations. One Senate long-term member commented: "Usually the ARRS members accept staff recommendations because it is so hard for committee members to be informed on every regulation. But sometimes the LRC staff gets carried away and does not take into consideration the political problems associated with particular regulations." Another Senate member remarked: "Generally ARRS accepts the staff recommendations unless there is some pressure from some powerful interest or individual outside the ARRS. Politics plays an important role in ARRS decisions." A veteran representative voiced a similar response: "Most of the time ARRS accepts staff recommendations, but committee members may reject one if the political consequences are severe. The staff sometimes do not understand about ARRS's suffering the political consequences of a decision."

When questioned about the kind of interaction between the agency and the staff and/or ARRS, one lawmaker responded: "Usually the agency communicates with the staff and chairman of ARRS, but not directly with committee members. There is a great deal of compromising and working out the problems between the first and second ARRS meetings—because of conflicts between staff, agency, and interest groups."

The ARRS members have become frustrated by the increasing practice of agencies of incorporation by reference in the administration regulations. One staffer asserted: "Sometimes the subcommittee doesn't know the details of what is being referenced—for example, the fire code, building code, state correctional facilities' manuals, or the child care facilities will reference their policy manuals."

At different access points, various interest groups attempt to influence the ARRS process. There is not a lot of formal, regular contact between legislators and interest groups until the ARRS meeting. There are primarily letters to the staff who act as intermediaries with the committee members; the input of the interest group letters is often realized. Staff attorneys and other staffers have frequent contacts with nursing homes, coal mine interests, environmentalists, and education people. There is not much face-to-face contact since lawmakers are not in Frankfort very often. But certain groups such as the Kentucky Chamber of Commerce, Kentucky Retail Organization, and Kentucky Coal Association are in the capitol frequently and do regularly lobby legislators. Also, state employee groups (e.g., concerning personnel rules and retirement matters) and industry groups are fairly visible. There are informal visits and telephone calls. Moreover, some legislators contact interest groups first when a particular administrative regulation is coming before the ARRS. Interest groups have also become more involved in the public hearing process involving agencies formulating regulations.

According to several ARRS members, their contact with interest groups is primarily infrequent and informal. One senior member asserted: "Interest groups might come to me before a meeting and present their case, but usually they do not." In contrast, another seasoned lawmaker acknowledged having considerable contact from interest groups about regulations. Groups will call or write or stop by the capitol to inform him of their positions. This member is considered a very powerful seasoned legislator who is very antiregulations; he seems to have a sympathetic ear. Another veteran member with a pro-business stance also complained about too many stringent regulations: "We almost lost the Jockey Underwear Plant because the regulations were too stringent."

Another experienced Senate member said that he may hear from interest groups before a meeting if an issue is particularly hot. His contact is usually in the form of phone calls, and occasionally a few letters. According to this legislator: "Environmental issues are always hot issues. The Chamber of Commerce and business and industry groups are very visible on environmental issues. The business and industry groups' input is helpful in understanding regulations. The most controversial agencies are Human Resources and Natural Resources." A Republican newcomer commented that the members of ARRS will contact interest groups to make sure they are aware that a regulation that is of concern to them is coming before the ARRS.

Efforts to Strengthen Oversight of Administrative Regulations. Prior to 1982 the LRC and its Administrative Regulations Review Subcommittee lacked the authority to veto or indefinitely postpone administrative regulations with which they disagreed. They could criticize an administrative regulation and ask an agency to reconsider or amend it, but in the last analysis, neither the subcommittee nor the LRC could prevent it from taking effect, nor could they delay it until the legislature had an opportunity to overturn it by legislation.

In 1982 the General Assembly enacted a law providing that no administrative regulation could take effect until it had been reviewed and accepted by the LRC or until it had been placed before the legislature and not disapproved. The actual responsibility for reviewing regulations and making recommendations to the LRC was delegated to the ARRS. If the agency refused to change the regulation to meet the objections of the LRC, the regulation would be postponed until the legislature met in regular session and had a chance to reject it. The governor could make regulations effective immediately in case of an emergency.

Governor Brown challenged the law and tested its constitutionality in the state courts. A 1983 U.S. Supreme Court decision in the Chadha case, holding the legislative veto exercised by Congress to be unconstitutional as a violation of separation of powers, cast some doubt on state laws that appeared to be legislative vetoes. Several constitutional challenges to legislative rules review as a violation of separation of powers have had similar results in other states, but not all such challenges have been successful. Legislative review of administrative rules appeared to have the strongest constitutional basis when it was done on an advisory basis backed up by the power of the legislature to amend the law if compliance is not forthcoming (Pound, 1984: 83).

The Kentucky Supreme Court, in *Legislative Research Commission* v. *Brown*, ruled this law unconstitutional, declaring that it had "the effect of creating a legislative veto of the actions of the executive branch." It declared that the adoption of administrative regulations is "executive in nature and ordinarily within the constitutional purview of the executive branch of government." It reaffirmed the importance of the doctrine of separation of powers, emphasizing the the power of the General Assembly is "*legislative power and legislative power only.*" In the same decision, the Court overruled a 1982 law that defined the LRC as an "independent agency of state government," with authority to conduct all business of the General Assembly except passing legislation. The court held that this was an unconstitutional effort to prolong the life of the General Assembly beyond adjournment. As a consequence of this decision, neither the LRC nor the ARRS can veto or indefinitely postpone administrative regulations.

Several members of the 1983 ARRS were interviewed concerning the effects of *Brown* v. *LRC* (Mahoney, 1987). A Democratic senator who has served on the ARRS for several years commented: "The committee is not as effective as before. It can now only point out problems with the regulations, but it cannot keep them from taking effect." A Republican representative who recently joined the ARRS responded: "ARRS now has very little power. It cannot stop a regulation from going through." The Republican Senate minority leader who resigned from the ARRS remarked: "The *Brown* v. *LRC* decision completely devastated the ARRS . . . I became so upset by the decision because it deprived ARRS members of all power; thus I removed myself from the ARRS after the Supreme Court ruling." In contrast, a seasoned Democratic Senate member answered somewhat optimistically:

ARRS's power has been lessened only somewhat by the *Brown* v. *LRC* decision. Before the decision, agencies used Emergency Regulation procedure for implementing an emergency regulation, and this bypassed the oversight committee; for the governor had the authority to enact the emergency regulation. There was no indication of opposition from ARRS about these enacted emergency regulations. Quite a lot of antagonism developed between committee members and Gov. Brown. But now, as a result of *Brown* v. *LRC*, there is documentation of ARRS's opposition—by utilizing *attachments* of the committee's dissent to the regulations. Attachments are useful, especially if the case goes to court. With this documentation of opposition, ARRS's dissent is given some weight with the judges.

One of the last actions of the 1986 General Assembly was to require state agencies to submit all regulations as potential statutes, stipulating that any regulation not put into law by the 1988 General Assembly would expire. With no votes to spare, 20-16, senators overrode Governor Martha Layne Collins's veto of House Bill 310; the House had earlier voted 52-44 to override the veto. The Senate Democratic leadership, which split 4-1 in favor of Collins's position on HB 310, appeared to make little effort during the roll call to peel away the one vote needed to sustain her veto. According to the Majority Leader Joe Wright: "I might have been able to switch two or three votes, but I didn't have the compulsion to try."

In vetoing the bill, Governor Collins said it would rob state agencies of the flexibility they need "to react to changing situations that occur after adjournment of the General Assembly." Once regulations would be adopted into law, the executive branch could not modify them to fit circumstances. Agencies need to be able to change regulations, particularly those required under federally mandated programs dealing with such topics as welfare, surface mining, air and water pollution, and occupational safety and health. But Collins said she sympathized with lawmakers who fear agencies will adopt regulations "thwarting or misinterpreting legislative intent."

The legislation was the latest round in a long-running fight between legislators and executive agencies over regulations that the agencies establish to implement laws enacted during the session. Kentucky's 3,000 administrative regulations take up seven volumes containing about 4,200 pages. The regulations include, by reference, other documents that cover more than twenty feet of shelf space in an LRC office. Under the provisions of the 1986 law, executive-branch agencies were required to identify the regulations that they wished enacted into law, and the agencies designated 2,739 such regulations. Those regulations were grouped into 496 bill drafts, many of which ran hundreds of pages. The attorney general's office released an opinion that there was nothing to prevent agencies from making more regulations after the legislature adjourned, even with the provisions of the new law.

The 1986 law produced a flood of paper work that threatened to swamp lawmakers. One Republican representative said, "It seemed like a good idea

at the time. I'm sorry I voted for it. We've got a stampeding elephant here."
When questioned about the problems with the law, the Senate President
Pro Tem John "Eck" Rose remarked: "You're looking for good regulations,
when in the past all you had to do was look for a few bad ones." Expressing
his opposition to the legislation, Senator Mike Moloney, chairman of A &
R warned: "Senators will rue the day we did this, and we will spend 10 years
trying to repair the damage to our environment and to our citizens' health,
among other things that will ensue from the administrative chaos caused by
the law." Early in the 1988 session, the legislature repealed the law.

There also is substantial support in the legislature for doing something
about regulations. According to House Speaker Pro Tem Pete Worthington,
"A lot of agencies are writing a lot of laws that we didn't authorize." One
senator who strongly favored the legislation remarked: "A regulation promulgated by an unelected person without a hearing . . . is just as much a
law . . . as any statute we pass here. It's time we reassert control by the
elected representatives of the people over what shall be the law of this
commonwealth." Another senator commented, "Small business operators in
Kentucky feel choked to death by regulations and need some relief."

Many of the private interests that must deal with the regulations ap-
plauded the bill. The head of the Western Kentucky Coal Association commented: "I personally think it's a good piece of legislation. It's an opportunity
to get a total review of the regulations that are there and eliminate duplications and conflicts."

Administrative Regulation Review in Practice: A Case Study. The dispute
over methods of reviewing administrative regulations is not merely a conflict
between the legislative and executive branches. If legislative bodies such as
the LRC and the ARRS have more authority over administrative regulations,
interest groups can use this arena in efforts to change, or to support, such
regulations. Ultimately, this aspect of legislative oversight can have important policy implications.

A recent study of the review of administrative rules and regulations
(Ethridge, 1985) is one of the first to analyze the effects of oversight on policy
outcomes. Little or no theory exists that specifies the probable policy consequences; thus, Ethridge posits three possible policy consequences of oversight. Legislative review of administration rules and regulations conceivably
could result in increased regulatory stringency, decreased regulatory stringency, or no patterned effect on levels of stringency. He tests the relationship
between a legislative committee's willingness to approve administrative rules
and regulations. He found that, though legislative committees in several
states would approve restrictive regulations at times, in general, as the involvement of the legislature increased, the stringency of regulations decreased. Ethridge concludes that "new oversight powers may simply create

a new access point for interests already successful in obtaining influence" (1985: 19).

The existing literature on bureaucratic-legislative-interest group relations supports the plausibility of Ethridge's contention that the review process may provide an additional access point for interested parties. According to Zeigler and Baer (1969), lobbyists most effectively communicate their viewpoint to legislators in face-to-face contact and in public hearings. Several case studies indicate that in situations in which agencies and interest groups conflict, legislators support interest groups of major importance (Foss, 1960; Freeman, 1965). As legislative review of administrative rules and regulations provides an additional opportunity for interest group communication with legislators, they are likely to influence legislative decision making.

To evaluate the consequences of administrative regulation review in Kentucky, we will review a study by Mitzi Mahoney (1985) of operations of the ARRS in 1983, based on data from tape recordings of the monthly ARRS meeting and interviews with subcommittee members, staff to the ARRS, and personnel of agencies that submit regulations to the ARRS. She found that the subcommittee focused most of its attention on a small proportion of the regulations. Out of 165 proposals submitted to it, the committee recommended for approval without discussion 115 (70 percent). ARRS members explain the large percentage of regulations recommended without discussion by citing the routine, noncontroversial nature of many of the regulations and by their limited authority. The subcommittee only has the statutory authority to recommend rejection of a regulation when it exceeds statutory authority or violates legislative intent.

Figure 7 illustrates a simple model of the legislative regulation review process. A number of factors complicate the process. For example, legislators' responses likely will vary depending upon the agency proposing the regulation. Agencies' relations with the legislative review committee, and with the legislature as a whole, vary. Relations may vary because of the nature of regulations they promulgate, their willingness to compromise, or the perceived quality of their work. Legislative staff affect policy outputs. Because their recommendations are legislators' most important source of information, staff perceptions of agencies' regulations influence legislative decision making. Parties (individuals or groups) interested in the policy outcomes of the legislative review process also may exert influence on legislators. But their impact depends on the type of interest sector they represent. For example, business and industry interests may be more influential than some public interest groups. Communications with legislators as well as the size and status of membership of interested parties affect policy outcomes. Finally, characteristics of legislators will influence decision making—their perceptions of their role in legislative review, their policy preferences, their expectations of other actors' responses to their output, and their status rela-

Figure 7. Model of the Legislative Regulation Review Process

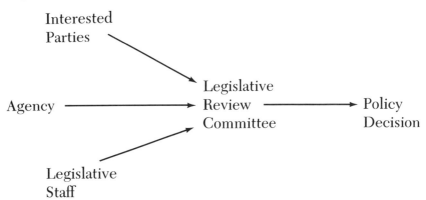

tive to other actors in the process. Complex interactions among agencies, staff, interested parties, and legislators characterize and determine policy outcomes of the legislative review of administrative rules and regulations.

The following findings are analyses of the fifty proposed regulations that the ARRS discussed in 1983, with particular attention to the thirty that attracted the attention of interested parties. The frequency distributions of proposals by policy area are shown in table 21. Almost one-third of all discussed proposals are business related, and one-fifth are welfare related. These two areas plus state administration (appropriations) and environmental policy proposals constitute over 75 percent of all regulations discussed.

Of the ARRS members, staff, and agency personnel, all agreed that two cabinets generate the majority of the controversial regulations: the Cabinet of Human Resources and the Cabinet of Natural Resources and Environmental Protection. In 1983 the Finance Cabinet submitted a number of controversial regulations, though this is not typical. Seldom were the Transportation Cabinet or the Department of Insurance parties to controversy. Again, members of the committee, staff, and agencies agreed that the regulations were controversial because of the costs imposed upon certain parties, usually interest groups (though a few exceptions exist). Occasionally, public/cause interest groups objected to regulations that shifted the burden of the cost of care from the state to the individual.

The Administrative Regulations Review Subcommittee rejected only six of the fifty proposals it discussed; this is 12 percent of those discussed and only 3.6 percent of all regulations reviewed. With one exception, all ARRS recommendations for rejections were proposed regulations that were highly restrictive. Of the fifty proposals, eleven may be considered highly restrictive, eighteen are moderately restrictive, fourteen are not very restrictive,

Table 21. Proposals by Policy Area

	Number	Percentage	Number of Proposals for Which Interested Parties Appeared
Business/ occupations	16	32	7
Welfare	10	20	8
Environmental policy	6	12	5
State admin./ appropriations	6	12	5
Education	5	10	3
Public employees	3	6	0
Crime/corrections	2	4	2
Taxation	1	2	0
State administration/ general	1	2	0

and seven are actually permissive. Half of the negative recommendations were of government sector proposals and half were of business sector proposals. One minor government proposal, strongly opposed by local government officials, was recommended for rejection. Five of the six rejected proposals would have imposed significant costs on business. For example, two rejected proposals altered the process by which banks are selected as depositories for state funds. Kentucky banks likely would have lost significant deposits if the regulations were implemented. The ARRS also rejected oil shale regulations that would have imposed very stringent and costly data collection requirements as a requisite to the issuance of a permit. One minor regulation, the requirement that all county governments submit a waste management plan, was rejected because local officials perceived the plan as costly (though the Department of Natural Resources and Environmental Protection was insistent that the plan need not be costly to prepare).

We can understand the review process better by looking more carefully at the role of interested parties at the ARRS hearings. The last column of table 21 shows the frequency with which interested parties appeared at hearings on particular categories of regulations. The parties mentioned most frequently by interviewees as likely to attend ARRS meetings include business groups such as the Kentucky Chamber of Commerce, the Kentucky Coal Association, Kentucky Association of Health Care Facilities, and the Kentucky Retail Association; public/cause groups such as the Long-Term Care Ombudsman Program, Audubon Society, and the Sierra Club; and

Table 22. Interest Groups' Attendance and Success Rates at Hearings

	Number of Times Groups Appeared	Number of Times Groups Were Successful	Success Rate (%)
Business	22	20	90
Professionals	2	0	0
Farming	2	2	100
Local government	52	52	100
Public employees	2	2	100
Public/cause	38	8	21

government interest groups such as the Kentucky Association of Counties and state employee groups.

Table 22 shows how often groups representing particular interests appeared at hearings to express views on issues and how often they succeeded in getting the changes they sought in regulations. The 100 percent success rates of three sectors (farming, local government, and public employees) does not reflect consistent, repeated success with the ARRS; rather, they appeared before the ARRS for no more than two proposals each. (There were a large number of local government groups at a hearing on one measure.) Conversely, business interests appeared for many more proposals and were consistently successful twenty out of twenty-two times. The one instance in which the ARRS approved a regulation that business interests opposed involved health care cost containment measures opposed by long-term care health care facilities. Public/cause interested parties were significantly less successful, with a 21 percent success rate. Only eight of thirty-eight public/cause parties were successful. Examples of instances in which public/cause interested parties were not successful include the rejection of restrictive oil shale regulations designed to protect the environment and rejection of handicapped facilities regulations requiring that all buildings be handicapped-accessible before leases are renewed.

From analysis of interested parties' success rate, business interests are most successful over repeated appearances. At least two explanations are plausible. One, the appearance of interested business parties and the influence they exert on the members of the ARRS may affect the willingness of the members to accommodate business interests. ARRS members state that interested parties often provide them with useful information about the impact of a regulation on their interests. For example, county judge executives informed the ARRS that the regulation requiring the preparation of a planning document would be too costly. This information was instrumental in the ARRS's negative recommendation of the regulation. At times, the involvement of interested parties directly determines the policy impact of legislative review. Certainly the appearance of interested parties enhances the salience of proposals.

One reason more regulations are not challenged by interest groups or criticized by the ARRS is that, prior to review by the ARRS, the agencies hold public hearings at which some problems are worked out. Agencies are required by Kentucky Revised Statutes to publish all proposed regulations. At the request of any party, they must hold a public hearing to receive comments from any interested parties. Often, as a result of public hearings, agencies will accommodate interested parties by incorporating their suggestions and/or by changing the regulations. Agency personnel cited the public hearing stage as crucial for reaching agreements with interested parties. Without these hearings, the ARRS process would be much more conflictual. Only rarely do agencies and interested parties fail to reach an acceptable compromise.

In 1983 public hearings were held by agencies for 21 of the 165 proposals the ARRS subsequently reviewed. In five instances agencies substantially altered proposals to accommodate interested parties. Agencies accommodated business interests five times, at the expense of environmentalists, long-term ombudsmen organizations, and professional groups. The ARRS approved all proposals that were altered to accommodate business interests. In four instances agencies refused to incorporate the comments of interested parties. Twice the ARRS rejected proposals that reflected no agency accommodation, once to the benefit of local government officials and once to the benefit of business interests. Only once did the ARRS approve a proposal the agency refused to alter and business interests opposed (the health care containment measure). Public/cause parties were less able to extract concessions from agencies during public hearings than were business interests.

It is clear that the ARRS does not utilize its authority to recommend rejection of regulations as extensively as it might. Though many of the 165 proposals reviewed do not constitute important substantive policy, the ARRS could have exercised more control over bureaucratic policymaking if it had wished. Several ARRS members stated that they would not recommend rejection of a proposal that was to be reviewed in a legislative standing committee or that was to be the subject of litigation. They leave some conflictual policy decisions to other policymakers.

But occasionally the committee considered exercising its oversight authority more actively than by approving regulations without discussion. Of the fifty proposals the ARRS discussed, interested parties appeared for twenty-seven. Had interested parties not attended the meeting, some of these twenty-seven proposals would not have been discussed. The appearance of interested parties generated discussion and closer scrutiny of some proposals than might have otherwise occurred.

But if the appearance of interested parties alone guaranteed their success, then public/cause parties would not have such a low success rate. From comments of committee members, a second explanation seems warranted. Business parties' success might be explained by committee members' positive business orientations that make them sympathetic to the concerns of business. Members explicitly stated throughout the meetings that if business opportunities were enhanced and costs kept low, the tax burdens on individuals would decline. They viewed it as their responsibility to maintain a favorable business climate in Kentucky. Once an ARRS member chided a Cabinet of Natural Resources and Environmental Protection staff member for writing a regulation that would hinder easy extraction of oil shale. When the staff person replied that he did not feel it was his responsibility to enhance business opportunities, the ARRS member stated that the *only* purpose of the bureaucracy was to enhance business opportunities to reduce the tax burden.

Local government parties are also likely to be successful before the ARRS. Though they came before the ARRS only once, the members seemed ready to accommodate their interests. Members seemed respectful of the political power that county judge executives are able to muster "back home." Even though the ARRS disagreed with the local government officials that the proposal would be costly, they rejected the proposal to appease the interested parties.

The 21 percent success rate of the public/cause interested parties should not be construed to mean that the ARRS is hostile to public interests. In fact, many times the ARRS approved regulations favored by public interest groups. But when public/cause interested parties conflicted with business interested parties, public/cause parties inevitably lost. The ARRS supported public/cause interests to the extent that they did not extract costs from business interests. Some ARRS members explained that the agencies and some public/cause interest parties did not understand that unreasonable and costly regulations would drive business out of the area. Thus, some members claimed that it was their responsibility to protect the commonwealth's interest of maintaining a positive business climate.

Perhaps as important an access point for interested parties seeking concessions from agencies is the public hearing process. Agency personnel and legislative staff repeatedly emphasized that as a result of public hearings, compromise and accommodation occurred. It appears to be in most parties' interest to compromise. Interested parties extract some concessions; agencies are likely to receive a positive recommendation from the ARRS when they have compromised; the ARRS members do not have to expend valuable political resources by opposing either agencies or interested parties. All parties agreed on the value of accommodation.

The data support Ethridge's suggestion (1984) that legislative review of administrative rules and regulations may provide an additional access point for interested parties to influence bureaucratic decision making. That business interests are more consistently successful suggests that they have learned how to utilize the additional access point to their benefit. Public/cause interests are less successful. In the case of the Kentucky ARRS, legislative review of administrative rules and regulations seems to have made bureaucracies marginally more responsive to and less independent on the legislature. The data suggest that business and governmental interest groups are especially successful in obtaining a less stringent policy after legislative review.

It is difficult to assess the effectiveness of the Kentucky legislative oversight committees for a number of reasons. The responsibilities of the committees vary in scope and complexity; the agenda of the Personal Services Contract Review Committee, for example, is much narrower and more specific than that of the Program Review and Investigations Committee. The priorities set by a committee and the aggressiveness with which it acts often depend very much on its chairman; changes in the chairmanship may lead to significant changes in committee effectiveness. Moreover, it is impossible to measure most of the accomplishments of committees in precise terms or in dollars and cents.

The Program Review and Investigations Committee has the greatest potential for impact on state programs and priorities. Although it has carried out some valuable studies and saved the Commonwealth considerable money, the committee appears to have fallen short of its potential. The Personal Services Contract Review Committee has been more successful in accomplishing its much narrower objectives. It has established some clear standards for personal service contracts and forced administrative agencies to justify deviations from those standards. The fact that contracts will be subject to public scrutiny has doubtless discouraged agencies from negotiating a number of contracts that could not stand a public examination. In a state with a long tradition of patronage, the success in placing restraints on public service contracts is a notable achievement. Similarly, the questions raised by the Capital Construction Committee have forced the executive branch to proceed with greater care.

By describing the Administrative Regulations Review Committee in some detail, we have demonstrated the complexity of the review process, and at the same time have shown the difficulty of making an accurate assessment of oversight. The work of that committee has forced the executive agencies to justify administrative regulations and has undoubtedly restrained the zeal of some bureaucrats. At the same time, this process has provided interest groups with a new arena in which to seek modifications in administrative regulations, and this has generally benefited business interests. Members of the committee differ in their priorities and their attitudes toward various interests.

Despite the successes of this committee, many legislators (both members and nonmembers of the committee) believe that the bureaucracy is not sufficiently responsive to the legislature and too often ignores legislative intent. This frustration led legislators to adopt legislation giving the Legislative Research Commission the power to cancel administrative regulations. After this initiative was invalidated by the Supreme Court, the General Assembly adopted a plan to require that all administrative regulations be enacted into law, a plan that was repealed before it could be implemented. Based on the assessment of legislators, it appears that the review of administrative regulations has been, and will remain, one of the most difficult and frustrating techniques for achieving effective oversight of the executive.

Part Four
Changes in Politics
and Policy Making

The trend toward more professional legislators and legislatures is common to most states, but there are some important differences among the states in how power is organized and how decisions are made.

In many state legislatures there has been a trend toward longer tenure for legislative leaders, particularly in those chambers where there used to be a tradition of rotation after one or two terms. At the other extreme, it is now very rare to find a presiding officer or floor leader serving in that post for more than four or five terms. There has clearly been a trend toward providing leaders with more staff assistance. There are major differences among leaders, however, and a major reason is variation in the skills and styles of individual leaders.

Party leaders today have bigger staffs, more resources, and perhaps more political skills than in the past. In many states party loyalty remains strong, but party discipline has weakened as individual members have grown independent. An Ohio legislative leader, complaining about the decline of party discipline, once told us that there were now too many chiefs and not enough Indians or, in other words, too many who wanted to lead and not enough followers.

One of the most significant differences among state legislatures that remains is the balance of power between the parties and the importance of parties in the decision-making process. There has been an increase in the number of states having competitive legislative parties, but there are some, primarily in the South, that are still dominated by a single party—a situation that minimizes the importance of party in decision making (Jewell and Patterson, 1986).

There are some common trends in the roles played by governors in the legislative process. With rare exceptions it is accurate to say that there are no more weak governors (Sabato, 1978). Governors today have more political and constitutional resources, as well as much larger staffs, than in the past. Most modern governors play an active and powerful role in the legislative process. On the other hand, few if any governors have the power that some governors—particularly in the South—once had to dominate the legislature. Despite these common trends, important variations remain among governors in the way they carry out their legislative responsibilities. Some have more formal power than others, some make greater efforts to exercise partisan leadership, some propose ambitious legislative programs, and others are more cautious (Morehouse, 1981: chap. 5).

Finally, there are differences among the states in interest groups. Political scientists are just beginning to make cross-state comparisons of groups and lobbying (Hrebenar and Thomas, 1987). Today there are fewer examples of state legislatures being dominated by a few powerful interests; a common pattern is the proliferation of interests represented in state capitols. The lobbying is more open, with a wider range of interests represented at formal hearings and in informal negotiations. In some states political action committees organized by interest groups are beginning to play a major part in financing legislative races. Variations remain, of course, partly because of differences in the major economic and social interests in each state, and partly because of differences in legislative norms regarding lobbying, the resources of specific groups, and the skills and tactics of particular lobbyists.

Kentucky is one of the states having fundamental changes in the selection and tenure of leaders. Democratic governors in the state used to select the presiding officers and Democratic leaders, who normally served only for a four-year term. Now the legislature independently selects its leaders, and longer terms are common. There has been no important change in the lopsided Democratic majorities in the Kentucky legislature. The Kentucky governor used to be one of the most powerful in the nation, vis-a-vis the legislature. The balance of power has changed because several recent governors have either not tried or not succeeded in using these powers and because the legislature has gradually developed its own resources and enhanced its power. Kentucky is also a state in which there has been a proliferation of interest groups, as well as greater attention by lobbyists to legislators and not merely to the governor.

8. Leadership and Political Parties

The influence of legislative leaders in the American states rests on both their formal powers and their skill in developing and using informal tools of leadership. In nearly all states, the Speaker of the House has a broad range of formal powers. He appoints and removes chairmen and members of committees, occasionally with the assistance of a leadership committee. He has some discretion in sending bills to committee and often chairs a rules committee that controls the movement of bills from committee to the floor. As presiding officer he has considerable discretion in recognizing members and controlling the tempo of the session.

In the Senate the most powerful figure may be the presiding officer, the president pro tem, or the majority leader. In slightly more than half of the senates, including Kentucky, the lieutenant governor is the presiding officer. Power over committee assignments is often shared, or given entirely, to the president pro tem, the majority leader, or a leadership committee. Where the presiding officer of the senate is elected by the membership, he usually has more power but may have to share control of committee assignments with a committee.

There is much greater variation in the informal tools and techniques of leadership used by presiding officers and floor leaders; it varies not only from state to state but from one leader to the next. The informal power of leaders has been enhanced in many states by the trend over the last decade or two to longer leadership tenure. Leaders have not only gained more experience, but they are less often operating as lame ducks. The size of the leadership staff has grown in most states. An increasing number of leaders have begun raising campaign funds for legislators in their party, a practice that has the potential for increasing their leverage over members, but a practice that has not yet spread to Kentucky. In some of the legislatures where partisanship used to be weak, there has been a trend toward stronger party leadership and structure—but this development has also bypassed Kentucky.

The leadership of the Kentucky General Assembly is organized like that in most other states. The Speaker of the House is not only the presiding officer but is in effect the leader of his party in the House. The House majority floor leader is responsible for conducting legislative business on the floor and serves as the second ranking leader of his party. There are three other members of the majority leadership team: the Speaker pro tem, majority whip, and caucus chairman, all of whom serve on leadership committees in addition to their other responsibilities. The minority leadership also includes the floor leader, whip, and caucus chairman. For the last seventy years, the majority leadership in the House, as well as the Senate, has been Democratic.

Senate leadership is organized differently, and the distribution of power is more difficult to define. The presiding officer is the lieutenant governor, and in Kentucky—unlike some states—the norm is for the lieutenant governor to actually preside over the Senate most of the time. Until recently the lieutenant governor sat on major leadership committees (and until 1974 presided over the Legislative Research Committee). Because the lieutenant governor is not chosen by the senators, he or she does not have legislative influence comparable to that enjoyed by the House Speaker. The influence of the lieutenant governor also depends on his or her initiative and efforts and political relationships with both the governor and the legislative majority.

The president pro tem presides over the Senate in the absence of the lieutenant governor and sits on major leadership committees. The political influence of the president pro tem depends largely on his own goals and skills. Only two persons held that position from 1968 through 1986, William Sullivan and Joe Prather, and neither of them exercised as much influence within the legislative party as does the Speaker of the House. There is also an assistant president pro tem, who serves on leadership committees. In recent years the most powerful Senate leader has been the majority floor leader, with that influence being based both on formal responsibilities and political skills. The remainder of the leadership structure parallels that in the House: there is a minority floor leader, and both parties have party whips and caucus chairmen.

THE SELECTION OF LEADERSHIP

Democratic Leadership. In January 1985, during the brief organizational session of the General Assembly, the House Democratic caucus elected a new team of leaders. Don Blandford defeated Speaker Bobby Richardson, and Greg Stumbo replaced Majority Leader Jim LeMaster. It was an important milestone in the legislative independence movement: the first time in modern history that Democratic legislators in the House had replaced their leadership without the governor playing any role in the transition.

Traditionally, one of the strongest sources of the governor's power in legislative affairs has been his influence over the choice of legislative leaders. Of course, the constitution and the rules of the General Assembly say nothing about such authority. The governor's ability to select his own leaders rested on the legislature's willingness to accept his recommendations. At one point during the Breathitt administration, the governor was having difficulty deciding whether to recommend a change in the speakership. One impatient legislator was heard to say, "I wish he would make up his mind and tell us who he wants." It never occurred to this member, or to his colleagues, that the governor's indecision gave them an opportunity to make their own decisions.

Table 23 illustrates the effects of gubernatorial control through the 1978 session. The normal pattern was for new legislative leaders to be selected at the start of a governor's term and to serve for only four years.

During the 1968 and 1970 sessions there was a Republican governor, Louie Nunn, who followed tradition at the start of his term by selecting Republican legislative leaders. In the 1968 session the Democratic legislators had to make their own leadership choices, and they chose a new team of leaders in both the House and the Senate. In the 1970 session House Speaker Julian Carroll and most of his leadership team were reelected, but in the Senate Lieutenant Governor Wendell Ford played a key role in putting together a new slate of leaders, although there was no change in the president pro tem. When Ford was elected governor in 1971, no serious thought was given to challenging his right to select leaders. It was during the Nunn administration that some of the early steps toward legislative independence were taken, but these did not include greater independence for the leadership.

In 1972 Governor Wendell Ford selected a new team of House leaders, headed by Norbert Blume as Speaker, and he endorsed for another term the existing Senate leaders whom he had helped to select two years earlier. Of course this latter group had not been associated with a previous Democratic governor but had won positions on their own during the Nunn administration.

When Julian Carroll took office, he had an unusually strong legislative background, having been elected Speaker (on his own) in 1968 and 1970 and having presided over the Senate as lieutenant governor in 1972 and 1974. Although he made statements in public about the importance of legislative

Table 23. Changes in Democratic Legislative Leadership

Governor and Year	House Leaders				
	Speaker	Speaker Pro Tem	Floor Leader	Caucus Chairman	Whip
Nunn					
1968	Carroll	McBrayer	Morgan	Reynolds	—
1970	Carroll	Blume	McBrayer	Reynolds	Prather
Ford					
1972	Blume	Paxton	Swinford	Reynolds	Harris
1974	Blume	Paxton	Swinford	Reynolds	Harris
Carroll					
1976	Kenton	Clapp	Richardson	Donnermeyer	Wells
1978	Kenton	Clapp	Richardson	Donnermeyer	Wells
Brown					
1980	Kenton	Hancock	Richardson	Donnermeyer	May
1982	Richardson	Thomason	LeMaster	Donnermeyer	Dunn
Collins					
1984	Richardson	Blandford	LeMaster	Donnermeyer	Dunn
1986	Blandford	Worthington	Stumbo	Donnermeyer	Rapier
Wilkinson					
1988	Blandford	Worthington	Stumbo	Richards	Rapier

	Senate Leaders			
	President Pro Tem	Floor Leader	Caucus Chairman	Whip
Nunn				
1968	Sullivan	Frymire	Huddleston	Lewis
1970	Sullivan	Huddleston	T. Garrett	Stacy
Ford				
1972	Sullivan	Huddleston	T. Garrett	Stacy
1974	Sullivan	T. Garrett	Stacy	Gentry
Carroll				
1976	Prather	T. Garrett	Yocum	Friend
1978	Prather	T. Garrett	Yocum	Friend
Brown				
1980	Prather	Berry	Karem	Hughes
1982	Prather	Wright	Karem	H. Garrett
Collins				
1984	Prather	Wright	Karem	H. Garrett
1986	Prather	Wright	Karem	H. Garrett
Wilkinson				
1988	Rose	Wright	Karem	H. Garrett

independence, Carroll wanted his own set of legislative leaders in the 1976 session, and he worked effectively to get them. It must be remembered that he had not been closely aligned with Wendell Ford during Ford's term as governor. In the House Carroll selected William Kenton as Speaker and Bobby Richardson as majority leader. Norbert Blume, the incumbent Speaker, campaigned to keep the job but eventually withdrew because he did not have the votes to challenge the governor. In the Senate Carroll picked Joe Prather as president pro tem, but retained Tom Garrett as majority leader. Except for Garrett there was a complete turnover of House and Senate leadership.

The tradition of gubernatorial selection of the leadership ended not because the legislators revolted and chose their own leaders, but because Governor John Y. Brown, Jr., gave up the prerogative. After his election in 1979, he made it clear that he would make no effort to influence the choice of leadership. Although legislators enthusiastically welcomed Brown's decision, most of them could not understand how he would be able to exercise influence over the legislature if he did not control the leadership.

When the Democrats met in December 1979 during the prelegislative conference, the leadership selection patterns were quite different in the House and the Senate. William Kenton had been selected as Speaker by Governor Carroll, and for four years had worked faithfully to carry out Carroll's programs in the legislature. But Kenton had also built a strong base of support among legislators and had worked hard to upgrade the House and open up its activities to the public. He was well prepared to win reelection on his own. Kenton became the first Speaker in the state's history to win a third term when he defeated Don Blandford, by a comfortable margin of 52-22, after a third candidate dropped out of the race. Majority leader Bobby Richardson was reelected without opposition, but there were contests for the other leadership positions.

In the Senate Joe Prather had served four years as president pro tem, having been chosen for that post by Governor Carroll. But Prather had split with Carroll late in his term (because Carroll refused to support him for lieutenant governor), and Prather won reelection to his leadership post independently, defeating his predecessor in that office, William Sullivan.

Most of the new Senate leaders who took office in 1980 were members of the "Black Sheep Squadron." This was the term applied during the 1978 session to a group of senators who were identified as mavericks. They were supporters of greater legislative independence and critics of the Carroll administration. Some of them had been strong supporters of Governor Ford and had lost major committee assignments when Governor Carroll took office. John Berry, the acknowledged leader of the Black Sheep, was elected majority leader by a vote of 18-11. (The majority leader's position was vacant because of the death of Tom Garrett.) The other top leadership posts were filled, sometimes after contested races, by senators who were prominent in the Black Sheep Squadron.

At the half-way point in Governor Brown's administration, Bill Kenton was firmly entrenched in the House leadership and was unopposed for re-election as Speaker. But in November 1981, at the age of 40, Kenton died suddenly. Bobby Richardson moved up from majority leader to Speaker without opposition. Jim LeMaster was elected majority leader in a close race, 40-33, after several other candidates withdrew and supported him. There were also very close, wide open races for the other major leadership posts, and one incumbent, Speaker Pro Tem Hank Hancock, was replaced by David Thomason. In the Senate Joe Wright was elected without opposition to replace John Berry, who had retired from the Senate, and there were few serious contests.

As Democratic legislators have acquired more experience in choosing leaders, they have begun to change the selection procedures. In 1980, for the first time, the House caucus elected its leaders by a secret ballot. This system obviously prevents legislators from being intimidated either by the governor or by incumbent leaders, and it presumably makes incumbents more vulnerable to challenge. In 1982 the House Democratic caucus adopted a runoff system for leadership elections. They were trying to prevent a recurrence of choices like that in 1980, when Hank Hancock was elected speaker pro tem by a plurality vote of 18-17-16-16-6. In the 1982 caucus, Hancock led by one vote on the first ballot, but lost the runoff.

By the end of the Brown administration, Democratic legislators had become accustomed to choosing their leaders without interference, and it seemed unlikely that they would surrender that authority once again to a governor. But it also seemed plausible that a future governor who wanted to establish a strong position of legislative leadership might try to have some influence over the choice of some leaders.

There was, however, a new obstacle to gubernatorial influence: the new timetable for legislative elections and sessions established by the constitutional amendment adopted in 1979. The leadership used to be chosen in a prelegislative conference, at the beginning of a governor's term, in December 1979, for example. Under the new schedule, legislative leaders are elected at an organizational session in January of odd-numbered years, whereas the regular sessions are held in even-numbered years. When a new governor takes office, the new legislative leadership will have been in office for a full year, though the governor might have a chance to influence the next selection, which occurs after one year of his or her term.

When Governor Collins took office, the leaders for the 1984 session were already in place. With one exception these were the same leaders who had served during the 1982 session. However, Speaker Pro Tem Thomason had been beaten by Don Blandford, a change that foreshadowed more important changes to come. If Governor Collins had been able to select the leadership, she probably would have made no changes in the Senate, whose top leaders had been active in her campaign. She might have wanted to make a change in the House, because Speaker Bobby Richardson had been the campaign manager for one of her opponents in the primary, and during the general election campaign had suggested that the office of lieutenant governor (which she held) ought to be abolished because it served no purpose except as a launching pad for gubernatorial campaigns.

A constant undercurrent during the 1984 legislative session was the forthcoming battle for the speakership between incumbent Bobby Richardson and Don Blandford. Richardson, a lawyer from Glasgow who entered the legislature in 1972, was serving his second term as Speaker and his fifth term in the leadership. Blandford, a former meat cutter from Philpot who entered the legislature in 1968, had first sought the speakership in 1979 and had won the job of Speaker Pro Tem in 1983. During the 1984 session, Richardson supported the governor's education program, though not very effectively, whereas Blandford opposed it. Some observers felt that the polarization that was occurring over the speakership contributed to the defeat of Governor Collins's program.

When the Democratic caucus met in January 1985, Blandford defeated Richardson by a substantial 42-31 margin. Majority Leader Jim LeMaster, who was allied with Richardson, lost by a similar margin. Governor Collins apparently made no effort to influence the speakership race, although several of her cabinet secretaries supported Richardson. One sign of the changing times was that several former governors made phone calls on Richardson's behalf, without success.

There was no single explanation for the turnover in leadership, but during his two terms as Speaker Richardson had alienated a number of members. They criticized him for making decisions "behind closed doors" and for using heavy-handed tactics to win votes for his position on bills. Blandford took advantage of these resentments. He promised to treat members fairly and without pressure and to make decisions openly, minimizing use of the Rules Committee to kill bills. Blandford campaigned aggressively for the speakership and visited the newly elected members in their home districts to seek support.

Because the caucus vote was secret, it is impossible to describe the voting alignments exactly. The alignment was neither ideological nor regional (both candidates being from western Kentucky); it was based more on class and status. Richardson apparently drew support from most committee chairmen and from members who were lawyers, other professionals, and business persons. Blandford had strong support from legislators who had close personal or constituency ties with organized labor (particularly in Louisville) and with agriculture. In addition to the unions, several other interest groups tried to influence the outcome, including some associated with the horse business, but it is not clear how much influence such groups had.

The most intriguing aspect of the race for the speakership was the decisive role played by a group who came to be known as the Young Turks. This was a group of six or seven legislators who had been developing a reputation in the last couple of sessions as bright, hard-working, and independent. As a group they had a particularly strong interest in improving education, and several of them serving on the Education Committee in 1983-84 had made major contributions to reform proposals drafted by that committee. They had supported the governor's education and tax package in 1984 and were sympathetic to most of the viewpoints of the Kentucky Education Association.

Anyone who understood the alignments in the Speaker's race would have assumed that the Young Turks would support Richardson. But this group was frustrated by Richardson's leadership and believed that they could play more important roles in the legislature and advance the cause of education more effectively if they voted as a bloc for Blandford. Six of the Young Turks announced their public support for Blandford. The support from this group gave greater credibility to Blandford's campaign, and they ultimately provided his margin of victory. Blandford appointed one of them, Roger Noe, to be chairman of the Education Committee; two others won other chairmanships; and several were appointed to the powerful Appropriations and Revenue Committee. The Young Turks' gamble paid off in another sense. As Speaker, during the special session in 1985, Don Blandford supported the new education and tax package proposed by Governor Collins, and it was passed.

During the 1987 organizational session, late in the Collins administration, two veteran leaders were replaced. After serving six terms as president pro tem, Joe Prather retired from the Senate (and briefly entered the gubernatorial race). His replacement, Joe "Eck" Rose, campaigned successfully for the job in a race that lacked either gubernatorial intervention or factional overtones. At the same time, the defeat of House Democratic caucus chairman William Donnermeyer (after six terms in that job) by Jody Richards appeared to weaken Speaker Blandford's control in the House. Blandford had supported Donnermeyer, and Richards had been loyal to former Speaker Richardson; but the turnover seemed to result from personal alliances rather than any basic realignment in the power structure.

What difference does it make whether the governor selects the leadership or whether leaders campaign on their own to win and hold their positions? It is the most important determinant of the governor's influence in the legislature, and it determines the sources of leaders' power. In the next chapter we will describe in some detail the techniques that Kentucky governors have traditionally used to get their programs passed. In order to use these techniques effectively, the governors have depended heavily on leaders who were absolutely loyal to them. The leaders cooperated with the governor in selecting committee chairmen and, for the most important committees, members who were loyal to the governor and would support his programs. The leaders steered the governor's budget and his major legislation carefully through the legislative labyrinth. They manipulated bills sponsored by individual members in order get commitments from these members for the governor's program. The governor had a powerful influence over the legislature because the leadership exercised strong control over the House and Senate—and these leaders were loyal to the governor.

The legislative leaders' power rested on several bases: their control over the selection and removal of committee members and chairmen, their domination of the Rules Committee and the legislative timetable, and their skill in negotiating with members. Their power also rested on their close ties with the governor, and thus their ability to help members get support from the governor for district projects and legislation they had sponsored. The leaders' power was also based on the simple fact that they did not have to depend on the votes of legislators for reelection. As long as they served the governor loyally and effectively they could count on four years in leadership positions. Obviously, it would be possible for a leader to be dropped in midterm if he was inept or had alienated a large proportion of members, but in the last analysis the leader had to serve only one master: the governor.

When the governor's domination of the leadership selection process ended, the nature of legislative leadership changed abruptly. Generally speaking, the leaders try to help the governor in carrying out his or her program, but on occasion leaders balk at some items in the program, seek amendments to bills, or simply present legislation to the Democratic caucus and the House and Senate without working effectively for it. Some of the leaders have had their own legislative agendas and have pushed them with as much or more enthusiasm as they have devoted to the governor's program.

Most importantly, the leaders' ability to win and hold office now depends on their skill in building and maintaining majority support among Democratic legislators. No longer do they have to step aside at the end of a governor's term, but no longer can they be assured of four years in office. In appointing legislators to chairmanships and membership on committee, loyalty to the governor is no longer the most important criterion. Loyalty to the leadership has taken its place. When Don Blandford was elected Speaker, he appointed to some of the major committee posts persons who had been loyal to him in the battle with Bobby Richardson. The legislative leaders may be less likely to put pressure on members to support the governor's program, particularly parts of it, like taxes, that are unpopular. Leaders are particularly cautious about putting pressure on members for commitments if a bill is unlikely to be passed, because those members do not like to take unpopular stands in support of lost causes. Leaders who fail to take into account the needs, problems, and insecurities of members may find that their majority support is slipping away.

Republican Leadership. When Republican Louie Nunn was elected governor in 1967, the legislators in his party approved his list of leaders without any apparent controversy or doubts. Given the state's tradition of strong governors and Governor Nunn's need for maximum support from the minority Republican party, this was not a surprising development. In the middle of Governor Nunn's term, however, the Republicans in the House made some changes in their leadership without the governor apparently playing any role.

During the legislative sessions with Democratic governors, beginning in 1972, there has been relatively little turnover in the top Republican House leadership positions, and it has been rare for an incumbent leader to be deposed by his colleagues. Harold DeMarcus served five terms as House Republican floor leader (1970-78). When he retired from that post, he was replaced by Art Schmidt, who had frequently held other leadership positions and who served as floor leader for two terms before being elected to the Senate. During the 1984 and 1986 sessions, Richard Turner was floor leader. In the 1987 organizational session, however, Turner was defeated by Woody Allen, a veteran representative who had been serving as Republican whip. It took the Republicans four ballots to arrive at that decision, even though there were only two candidates in the race.

Until recently, there has also been stability in the Senate Republican leadership. Eugene Stuart served for five sessions (1974-82) as Republican floor leader. Conflict began in the 1983 organizational session when he was replaced by Jim Bunning. However, Bunning resigned from the Senate later in the year to run for governor, and at the start of the 1984 session Gene Huff was elected floor leader. In the 1985 organizational session the ten members of the Senate Republican caucus found themselves deadlocked 5-5 over the choice of leadership. Eight of the ten Republicans had either held leadership positions in 1982 or 1984 or were seeking them in 1986—a fact that apparently made compromise difficult. The deadlock was finally broken when Huff dropped out of the race and Joe Lane Travis became floor leader. The faction supporting Travis failed, however, in their efforts to replace Clyde Middleton with Jack Trevey as caucus chairman. At a time when the Republicans control only ten of the thirty-eight Senate seats, it is difficult to know what difference it makes who holds which leadership position. The conflicts within Senate Republican ranks appeared to be personal rather than ideological or even regional. The most important consequence of the continuing disagreements within the caucus was that agreement on tactics became more difficult and the potential impact of the small minority of Republican senators on decision making in the Senate was reduced.

When the 1987 organizational session met, there were some changes in the ranks of Republican senators. Senator Middleton had been defeated by a Democrat, and one of his allies, Jon Ackerson, had left the Senate (to run for the House) and had been replaced by another Republican. Senator Travis and his four allies remained. Travis stepped down, and it took only a few minutes for three of his allies to be elected: John Rogers as minority leader, John Trevey as caucus chairman, and Gene Stuart as whip. If the Republicans were not united, at least they were no longer deadlocked.

FORMAL POWERS OF LEGISLATIVE LEADERSHIP

The formal powers available to legislative leadership can be described briefly. Although there have been occasional changes in the rules, most leaders have the same powers and the same institutional machinery available to them. But leaders differ in their tactics, in the choices they make about using the tools available to them, and in the skill with which they lead.

The most important powers of the leadership are:

1. to assign members to committees at the start of a session, and to assign bills to committees;

2. to schedule bills for floor consideration, through the Rules Committee;

3. to preside over the legislative chambers.

Assignment of members to committees is made by the Committee on Committees, made up by the leadership, and dominated in the House by the Speaker and majority leader, and in the Senate by the president pro tem and majority leader. Assignment of bills to committees is also made by the Committee on Committees, which operates within the jurisdictional guidelines spelled out in the House and Senate Rules.

Once a committee has reported on a bill, decisions on the scheduling of legislation on the floor are made in the House and Senate by the Rules Committee. It may delay action on the bill for a maximum of five days and may reassign a bill one time to the committee that reported it or another committee.

The Speaker presides over the House; the lieutenant governor, or in his absence the president pro tem, presides over the Senate. The presiding officer, particularly in the House, has discretion in several important areas. When several members are seeking recognition, he can decide which one has priority. This may be particularly important if members are seeking to make parliamentary motions. The majority floor, however, has priority to be recognized, to carry on the business of the body. The presiding officer has the power to rule on points of order, although his decision may be (and rarely is) appealed to the full membership. For example, legislative rules require that amendments be germane to the bill, and the presiding officer has the responsibility of ruling whether an amendment is germane. The Speaker also has some flexibility in determining how long the voting machine may be open during roll calls, and may delay a roll call while legislative leaders search for additional votes in support of a bill.

THE LIEUTENANT GOVERNOR

There is one person holding a leadership position who is not elected by the members: the lieutenant governor. Kentucky is one of twenty-eight states in which there is a popularly elected lieutenant governor who presides over the Senate. In the Kentucky Senate the lieutenant governor and the president pro tem share legal power. The president pro tem presides over the Senate whenever the lieutenant governor is absent or chooses not to preside. Until recently, the lieutenant governor also served on major leadership committees. Prior to 1974 the lieutenant governor chaired the Legislative Research Commission.

How much formal power and informal influence the lieutenant governor has in practice depends on his or her skills and relationships to the governor and to the dominant party, and perhaps faction, in the Senate. It also may depend on the lieutenant governor's career ambitions. Every lieutenant governor elected from 1967 through 1983 has run for governor: Wendell Ford, Julian Carroll, Thelma Stovall, Martha Layne Collins, and Steven Beshear. A lieutenant governor with higher ambitions may try to further these by playing a more active role in the Senate or by trying to avoid conflict there. Members of the Senate may on occasions try to help or hinder such ambitions by working with or against the lieutenant governor on legislative matters.

During Governor Breathitt's term, the lieutenant governor, Harry Lee Waterfield, was allied with the Chandler faction in opposition to Breathitt. The Senate made some changes in its rules to limit the formal power of the lieutenant governor in the Senate. In the middle of the governor's term, Breathitt and Waterfield backed different candidates in several Democratic senatorial primaries, but Waterfield failed in his effort to change the balance of power within the Democratic senatorial majority.

During the Nunn administration, Lieutenant Governor Wendell Ford, as the ranking Democrat in the state and a skillful politician, exercised considerable influence in the legislature. As we have noted, he put together the leadership slate that ran the Senate in the 1970 session. During Ford's term as governor, Julian Carroll, the former House Speaker, was lieutenant governor. Although he had factional differences with Ford, he cooperated with the governor and the Senate leadership in working for Ford's legislative programs. During Carroll's governorship, the lieutenant governor was Thelma Stovall, who had been elected to lower statewide positions (secretary of state and treasurer) a number of times. Her influence in the Senate was probably less than some of her predecessors most of the time. But in 1979, when the governor was out of the state, she called a special session and persuaded it to make cuts in state property taxes.

During the Brown administration, the lieutenant governor was Martha Layne Collins. She was not regarded as an influential figure in most legislative matters, but she was careful not to obstruct the governor's program. After four years in that office, she was elected governor. During the Collins administration, the lieutenant governor was Steven Beshear, a former legislator and attorney general. He played a more active role than some of his predecessors. He rarely turned over his gavel to the president pro tem, and he chaired meetings of the Committee on Committees, a job his predecessors often delegated to the president pro tem. He was an active member of the Rules Committee. He also lobbied more publicly than is usually done on several pieces of legislation, particularly those concerning regulation of public utilities.

In 1987 the Senate Democratic caucus decided to strip the lieutenant governor of his membership—and chairmanship—of the Committee on Committees (which selects committee members and assigned bills to committees) and his membership on the Rules Committee (which has an influence on the legislative timetable). The move was described by one Senate leader as "removing the last semblance of executive involvement in the legislative branch." The change was not deliberately aimed at Beshear and did not take effect until 1988, but it appeared to be in part a reaction to Beshear's more active role in the legislative process. Whatever the motivation, the consequence will probably be to reduce significantly the lieutenant governor's opportunities for affecting legislative decision making.

LEADERSHIP ROLES

How legislative leaders use their powers depends in part on the role they perceive for themselves as leaders. We can define four distinct roles for the presiding officer and the leaders of the majority party, and we can find examples of each among recent Democratic leaders in Kentucky. It is important to emphasize that these roles are not mutually exclusive, and most leaders play each of these roles at different times, but leaders differ in the emphasis they give to each of the roles.

First, the leader may see his job as trying to accomplish the governor's objectives, gaining passage for the gubernatorial program and helping to block legislation that the administration opposes. Second, a leader's role may be to carry out the goals of the majority party in the legislature and to help his Democratic colleagues formulate their legislative program and unite behind it. Third, a leader may have his own legislative agenda and give priority to passing such bills and defeating others that he opposes. Fourth, instead of trying to get particular bills passed or defeated, a leader may see his role as making the legislative process work in as orderly and equitable a way as possible.

During the period when Democratic governors hand picked legislative leaders, it is clear that the primary role of these leaders was to facilitate passage of the governor's program. They used their formal powers and their negotiating skills to get the governor's bills passed and to block hostile amendments as well as bills to which the governor was opposed. At the same time, of course, they would alert the governor when legislators were strongly opposed to his bills and, if necessary, work out compromises between the governor and a majority in the legislature.

Most of the current Democratic legislative leaders believe that a part of their responsibility is to help pass the governor's program. As one of the leaders put it: "I feel I have a strong obligation to help a Democratic governor pass his or her program, unless it conflicts with my philosophy of governor. With rare exceptions, I try to help the governor." On the other hand, in the words of another leader, "It is not my job to browbeat the members into supporting the governor's position on a bill. I have a responsibility to the membership to carry their concerns to the governor—to act as a conduit. I cannot be one hundred percent devoted to every whim of the governor."

The leader's role of helping to formulate and implement the policies of the majority legislative party is best exemplified by recent Democratic leaders in the Senate. A major technique for accomplishing this goal is to hold weekly caucuses of Democratic members in order to determine the views of Democrats on pending bills and to determine what tactics the leaders should follow. If legislation has strong support within the Democratic caucus, the leadership will bring it to the floor; if not, they will try to avoid floor consideration, even if the bill could probably be passed with Republican votes. We will discuss the use of the caucus more thoroughly later in the chapter.

It seems clear that every leader uses his position from time to time to advance his own legislative agenda. Sometimes this may put him in conflict with the governor or the majority of his partisan colleagues in the legislature.

On other occasions the leader will give priority to bills designed to help his constituents or a particular interest group he supports, bills that are of little concern to the administration or to his colleagues. Leaders differ in the scope of their own agenda and the amount of pressure they are willing to bring on their colleagues to achieve these goals.

Although the Senate leaders have relied heavily on the Democratic caucus to measure viewpoints and formulate a party policy on issues, they have also been willing to use the tools of leadership to advance or defeat bills that were of particular concern to them. During his term as Speaker, Bobbie Richardson did not appear to have a lengthy legislative agenda, but he was criticized by a number of colleagues because of his willingness to use the powers of his office very aggressively to accomplish his own goals.

The final role of a legislative leader might be described as that of a manager. One leader said that his role is "to make sure the process works; you do the things that have to be done, on time." Because the legislative session in Kentucky is relatively short, it is particularly important to move bills expeditiously through the committee system and onto the floor, to avoid logjams at the end of the session. A manager might be described as one who tries to give all legislators a chance to win support from their colleagues for their bills. When the leader is playing the role of manager, he is not promoting his own legislative agenda, nor is he singling out colleagues for particularly favorable—or unfavorable—treatment.

During the 1985 and 1986 sessions of the legislature, it was Speaker Don Blandford who epitomized the role of the leader as manager. This was not the only role he played. He helped the governor pass her school package. He paid attention to the views of House Democrats on certain issues like the lottery, and he worked hard to gain support for the increase in the gasoline tax, which was his top legislative priority. But most of the time, he was a manager. He had campaigned for the office of Speaker promising a change in the tactics of leadership and committing himself to run the House in more open fashion. He promised not to use the Rules Committee as a major device for killing bills that had been reported by standing committees, and he stuck to that promise, making limited use of the committee. For the most part he did not put pressure on committee chairmen either to pass bills or to keep them bottled up in committee. He was particularly concerned with making the system operate in an efficient and orderly fashion, and succeeded in getting more accomplished in the first few months of the session than is usually possible. On several particularly complex, controversial issues, he arranged for committees or task forces to work out compromises during the session or to study the issues in greater detail during the interim— in both cases avoiding bitter fights on the floor. He also tried to protect his colleagues from pressures by not bringing controversial issues to the floor if it was clear that the bills did not have enough votes to be passed.

A leader who emphasizes the role of manager is in a good position to win popular support from his colleagues because he avoids putting pressure on them and seldom uses his power to block legislation they are sponsoring. At the end of his first term as Speaker, Blandford was very popular with legislators, who had grown weary of the pressures and constraints imposed by the previous House leadership.

THE LEADERSHIP AND COMMITTEES

Prior to the committee reforms that started in 1968, it was accurate to say that the majority party leadership controlled the committees. Working with the governor, the leaders selected the chairmen, along with members of key committees, who were completely loyal to them; then they referred bills to the most dependable committees without much regard to jurisdictional formalities. We have described, in chapter 5, how the committees have grown more powerful and more independent since that time. The question is, what influence does the majority party leadership have over committees at present, and how is it exercised?

In chapter 5 we described in considerable detail how the chairmen and members of committees are selected. When new leaders assume office, they have the power to make wholesale changes in chairmanships and in memberships on the most desirable committees, but in practice the leaders have chosen to make much less drastic changes. In 1980, when new leaders took control of the Senate, they replaced only two chairmen, including that for the Appropriations and Revenue Committee and made a few other shifts of members. In 1985, when Don Blandford and Greg Stumbo became Speaker and majority leader of the House, they replaced four committee chairmen who had failed to support their election (in addition to filling two vacant chairmanships). But they also retained three or four committee chairmen who had remained loyal to Richardson in the speakership battle. They placed several loyal members on major committees, particularly Appropriations and Revenue, and Education; but they accomplished this change almost entirely by expanding those committees rather than by dropping members from them (except for two members becoming chairmen of other committees).

There is some feeling among the recent leadership that vindictiveness is a not a wise principle to use in making committee assignments. In choosing chairmen and members, the leadership is particularly concerned with putting highly competent, conscientious members into the major committee posts. Several of the leaders also emphasize the importance of trying to achieve a balance of interests on interest-oriented committees such as Labor and Industry, Banking and Insurance, and Business Organizations and Professions.

This means not only balancing specific interests (such as banking and insurance) but trying to find some members who do not have any vested interest in the issues dealt with by the committee.

There are several steps in the legislative process where leaders have an opportunity to either expedite or obstruct the passage of legislation. They may try to influence committee decisions, take action in the Rules Committee, mobilize support or opposition on the floor, and if the bill passes one house, try to influence the decisions of leadership in the other house and of the governor.

If legislative leaders want to try to influence decisions in committee, they have several sources of power. The fact that leaders choose committee chairmen and members may give them some leverage over them during a session, though this is an advantage that must be exercised with skill and discretion. When leaders want committees to kill a bill, they can always threaten to delay the bill in the Rules Committee or fight it in the caucus or on the floor. The more actively and effectively leaders intervene in the law-making process, the better their bargaining position in dealing with committees; they can promise to expedite or threaten to block bills sponsored by committee members to get their cooperation on bills in committee.

During the years when the Kentucky legislative leaders were acting as agents of the governor, they used these techniques frequently to get cooperation from the committees. In more recent years, the leadership seems to have been less aggressive or more cautious in dealing with committee matters. The Senate majority leader meets regularly with committee chairmen to discuss bills that are in committee. Interviews with chairmen suggest that the floor leader does not apply pressure on them concerning bills in their committee. He may sometimes discuss a newly introduced bill with a couple of chairmen before deciding to which committee the bill should be sent. The Senate leaders occasionally will urge committee chairmen to be more selective in reporting bills and to bury those that will cause obvious problems on the floor or that have no chance of passage.

During the years that Bobbie Richardson was Speaker, he sometimes intervened in committee business, urging chairmen to expedite or kill legislation. Speaker Blandford and Majority Leader Stumbo have followed a very different tactic. During the 1986 session, they held three or four meetings of all the chairmen. These were described as virtually roundtables at which everyone had a chance to discuss important bills in their committees. The leaders used these meetings to urge the chairmen to be restrained in reporting out bills, warning them than any bill they reported would probably come to a vote on the floor, rather than being waylaid in the Rules Committee. Only rarely did the leaders ask specific chairmen to support or kill a bill.

USE OF THE RULES COMMITTEE

At one time the Rules Committee in the Senate and House played a central role in the legislative process. During the last fifteen days of a session it superseded the other committees, exercising virtually life or death power over bills already reported by standing committees as well as those that had been bottled up in committee. The new legislative rules that took effect in 1968 ended the Rules Committee's monopoly power but retained it as an important tool for leadership. Although subsequent changes in the rules have limited its discretion, the Rules Committee continues to provide leadership with a powerful mechanism for controlling the flow of legislation to the floor.

Under the present rules of both houses, all bills and resolutions that have been reported out of a substantive committee are referred to the Rules Committee. Within five legislative days it must either report the bill or resolution to the floor or refer it to the same or a different standing committee, which it can do only once. The Senate Rules Committee can only refer it to the original committee or to Appropriations and Revenue; in the House it can be referred to any committee, but is usually sent to Appropriations and Revenue or the original one.

The House Rules Committee has twenty-one members, including all eight Democratic and Republican members of leadership. The Senate Rules Committee has ten members, including all eight members of leadership. Usually the Speaker and majority leader are in a position to dominate the House Rules Committee, whereas the majority leader usually gets his way in the Senate Rules Committee. Despite the fact that they are proportionately represented on the Rules Committee in each house, the Republicans have little or no chance to mobilize enough Democratic votes to win if they challenge the Democratic leadership on the committee.

The leadership on the Rules Committee may refer bills to committee for a number of reasons, not all of which indicate a desire to kill the bill. If a bill provides for the spending of funds, the standard practice is to refer it to the Appropriations and Revenue Committee. Sometimes the Rules Committee will discover that there are errors in a bill and send it back to committee for revision. The leaders may believe that a floor consideration of a bill must be delayed while efforts are made to mobilize more votes for the bill on the floor.

Often the decision of the Rules Committee to refer to committee is a deliberate attempt to keep the bill from coming to the floor. This may simply reflect the attitude of the legislative leadership toward the bill, but there are several other explanations. Sometimes members of a committee will report out a bill reluctantly because of pressure from lobbyists or from one of their colleagues, and subsequently will ask the leadership to block the bill in the Rules Committee. Interviews with the leadership suggest that such requests are more common than we might expect. Committee chairmen and members who are unwilling to say "No" expect the leadership to have more intestinal fortitude.

Sometimes the pressure to delay the bill in the Rules Committee comes from rank-and-file members who are not on the original committee and who do not want to be forced to vote on the issue. A good example might be legislation that produces strong cross-pressure from interest groups or a bill that legislators believe is poor but popular legislation. In the Democratic caucus, discussion of a bill may demonstrate that most members do not want it to come to a vote on the floor; or a straw vote may show that the bill does not have enough votes for passage. In either case the leadership may refer the bill to another committee to keep it from coming to the floor.

Although the Rules Committee no longer has the power to delay a bill indefinitely, a decision to refer the bill to committee is often a critical setback. The leadership may be able to persuade the chairman of the second committee (or even the original committee) to kill it or to delay action on it for a couple of weeks. The Rules Committee can sit on a bill for five days before referral and another five days if the bill should be reported by the second committee. Time is so short in a session of sixty legislative days, and the agenda is so crowded in the closing weeks, that a delay of two or three weeks resulting from maneuvers in the Rules Committee can often be fatal.

In recent years the Rules Committee has been a major tool of Senate and House leadership, used frequently to block legislation for the various reasons that we have described. Joe Wright, the Senate floor leader, believes that it is a necessary device to overturn unwise committee decisions or conform to the wishes of the Democratic caucus. He also is prepared on occasion to use the Rules Committee to delay a bill when he has serious doubts about it. If Wright decides it is necessary to stop legislation that has been reported by committee, he will try to do so in the Rules Committee rather than opposing it on the floor. He has been very successful in getting his way within the Rules Committee.

During his years as House Speaker, Bobbie Richardson frequently used the Rules Committee to sidetrack legislation; this practice was one of the main reasons Richardson came under criticism from Democratic representatives. They argued that he often blocked bills because of his own preferences rather than in response to requests from substantial numbers of legislators. They also claimed that he acted secretly (though the meetings are open to all members) and failed to explain to legislative sponsors why their bills were being killed.

When Don Blandford ran for Speaker he promised restraint in the use of the Rules Committee, and he has stuck to that promise. The House leaders have warned committee chairmen not to count on the leadership to stop "bad" bills that the committees have hastily or unwisely reported. The Rules Committee continues to refer bills to Appropriations and Revenue if they require spending. The leadership has sometimes delayed bills in order to resolve problems or correct errors, but they have only infrequently used the Rules Committee in an effort to kill a bill. They have made it a point to explain to sponsors why the Rules Committee was delaying a bill or sending it to a committee. The leaders have used discretion in assigning bills to committee, sometimes assigning bills that they opposed to committees that were unlikely to report them hastily, a technique that—when successful— makes it unnecessary to resort to the Rules Committee.

USE OF THE CAUCUS

The party caucus is most likely to serve an important purpose in those state legislatures that have strong legislative parties, ones where there is relatively close two-party competition and each of the parties represents distinctly different interests and policy commitments. Under these conditions the caucus is often a vehicle for developing partisan positions on issues and uniting the party's legislators behind those positions. The Kentucky General Assembly does not have such strong legislative parties and we would not expect its caucuses to assume such an important role.

In a number of other states, the caucus plays a more modest role, facilitating communication between leaders and the rank-and-file members and helping the leadership to assess the opinion of members on pending bills. The Kentucky Senate and House Democratic caucuses generally fit this model. There is one characteristic of caucuses in most states—and certainly in Kentucky: how frequently they meet and how they are utilized depends almost entirely on the preferences of the party leadership. In Kentucky the importance of the caucus has waxed and waned over the years with changes in leadership. The caucus has consistently met at the beginning of a session to select the party's leaders, but the frequency and importance during the session have varied.

During the 1974-78 period in the Senate, when Tom Garrett was the Democratic floor leader, caucuses were held only a few times during the session, despite the desires of some members for more frequent meetings. When the new leadership took control of the Senate in 1980, a decision was made to hold weekly meetings, on Mondays, and this practice has continued to the present. Additional meetings may be held when the workload gets heavy late in the session. Since 1980 the chairman of the caucus has been David Karem, a veteran legislator from Jefferson County.

Most legislation of any significance is discussed in the Senate Democratic caucus before it goes to the floor. The caucus meets behind closed doors, a practice that encourages frank and open discussion and permits members to express views that they would not want to express in public, particularly views that might alienate interest groups. (No written records are kept, assuring even greater privacy of the discussions.) Sponsors of legislation explain bills and answer questions. When problems arise, an effort is made to work out compromises, or the bill may be delayed in an effort to solve the problems. The Senate caucus frequently takes straw votes on bills to determine the sentiment of the members. These votes are not intended to bind the members but to give the leadership an accurate appraisal of sentiment on the bill. If it is clear that there are not enough Democratic votes to pass the bill (without relying on Republican support), the leadership will usually not bring it to the floor for a vote. The bill will be delayed while the sponsors try to work out amendments or generate more support from members; or the leadership will decide to let the bill die, often through use of the Rules Committee.

Both Democratic leaders and members agree that the caucus is not used directly to put pressure on members. If the leaders are strongly committed to a bill and find out in caucus that it lacks the necessary votes, they must either revise the bill to make it more acceptable or persuade additional members to vote for it using pressure, persuasion, or bargaining techniques. If a large majority of Democrats vote to support a bill, those who are in the minority may decide to go along with the bill, but their votes would not be necessary to guarantee a majority on the floor.

Although the caucus is not designed to force party cohesion, the effect of its operation may often be to avoid deep intraparty splits on a bill. The discussions that go on in the caucus may remove some of the causes of disagreement. If the party remains seriously divided on a straw vote, the leadership will not bring the bill to the floor. Sometimes the members will agree that a show of party unity is important. For example, during the 1984 session a Republican senator introduced a right-to-work bill, an issue that had the potential for splitting the Democratic members. In the caucus the Democrats agreed that the bill had been introduced to embarrass Democratic members and that the best countertactic would be to unite against the bill. Nearly all members of the caucus voted to oppose the bill, and the Democrats succeeded in avoiding a potentially divisive issue. Democratic senators are enthusiastic about the caucus, not only because it gives all of them input into the legislative party's decision making but also because it helps the party avoid or at least minimize bitter, divisive floor fights on many controversial issues.

Democratic caucuses have been held spasmodically in the House in recent years, probably on an average of five or six times a session. (Because no records are kept, the exact frequency cannot be calculated.) The tendency has been to hold a caucus when particularly important issues are coming to a vote, including some of the most important proposals by the governor. Occasionally, governors have attended caucuses to make a personal plea for support of their legislative program. Surprisingly, John Y. Brown, Jr., seems to have attended such caucuses more often that his recent predecessors.

Some Democratic representatives believe that caucuses should be scheduled on a regular basis like those in the Senate, and some of them emphasized this point during the leadership struggle in 1984. Some members felt it would give representatives greater input and more influence on the leadership. During the 1985 organizational session, the Democratic caucus established a small committee to recommend changes in both rules for both the House and the caucus. One of the committee's recommendations was that the House caucus meet every Monday during the session.

Speaker Don Blandford opposed the regular scheduling of caucuses, and his opposition was enough to doom the proposal in the 1986 session. Blandford believes that the caucus is an ineffective institution: "In the twenty years that I have been in the legislature, I have never seen anything accomplished in a caucus." Although acknowledging that the caucus may be effective in the Senate, he believes that it is impractical for House Democrats, who usually number about seventy-five. Such meetings are often poorly organized and unproductive, with a handful of members dominating the discussions. Under Blandford's leadership, the caucus met only a few times during a session. One of its purposes was to conduct straw votes and measure membership attitudes. At one of the caucus meetings in 1986, for example, it was determined that sponsors of the constitutional amendment for a lottery did not have enough votes to pass it.

In the last analysis, Blandford opposed the caucus because it did not fit his leadership style, which he described (like a good basketball fan) as "one-on-one." Like many other leaders he concluded, "You do what you are best at."

DEMOCRATIC LEADERSHIP STYLE AND TACTICS

There is no single pattern or norm of legislative leadership followed by everyone who holds the post of Speaker, president pro tem, or majority leader. Leaders are constrained by several aspects of the political environment: the demands made and tactics followed by the governor, the size of the legislative majority, the circumstances of the leader's original selection, and, to some degree, the practices of previous leaders. But each leader also brings to the job a unique personality, a different occupational and political background, and a specific blend of skills and weaknesses.

During the years of gubernatorial domination, and particularly during the Ford and Carroll administrations, the style and tactics of leadership were largely determined by the governors. The leaders' job was to make the administration's policy clear to the members, to persuade and negotiate on the governor's behalf, and to alert the governor's office to problems in enacting his program. The job required considerable skill in dealing with fellow legislators, but the leaders had only a limited amount of flexibility in choosing particular tactics to follow.

Since the start of the Brown administration, the leaders have been able to choose their own style of leadership, and their choices have been somewhat different. Joe Wright, who became Senate majority leader in the second session of the Brown administration, might be described as a strong, quiet leader. His colleagues agreed that he was in control of the Senate. He dominated the Rules Committee and used it aggressively when he believed that bills must be delayed or blocked. Wright seemed to work most effectively behind the scenes, attracting little attention from the media. On the floor, he made his points with a minimum of oratory. He believes strongly in legislative independence from the governor, and his effectiveness as majority leader was based in part on the fact that he had not been closely associated with either Brown or Collins.

Wright, and the other Democratic Senate leaders, have been committed to a partisan strategy of leadership. The caucus has been used to develop as much consensus as possible within the Democratic party before bills are brought to the floor. The leadership particularly has tried to avoid bringing legislation to the floor if its passage is dependent on winning Republican votes. The Senate Democratic leadership has been reluctant to see significant bills passed that have been sponsored by Republicans, and on occasion it has sidetracked such bills so that similar legislation with a Democratic sponsor can be passed. (One Democratic representative commented, "It is tougher to be a Republican in the Senate than in the House," and some Republican legislators agreed to that assessment.)

Bobby Richardson, who served as majority leader under William Kenton, became Speaker in 1982 after Kenton's death and served for two sessions until he was deposed by Blandford in 1985. Richardson believed in being a strong Speaker, and he expanded the professional staff of the Speaker's office to help him maintain contact with members and keep track of legislative developments during the session. He was a strongly partisan leader, but he did not use the caucus very much to assess Democratic sentiment. Richardson worked hard behind the scenes, negotiating to win support for his point of view on legislation. He also used the Rules Committee aggressively to block bills that he opposed. Richardson's speeches on the floor tended to be flamboyant and often caustic; whether they were effective in winning supporters may be open to question.

By the time he was defeated for the speakership, Richardson had many critics. They claimed that too often Richardson carried out his maneuvers in secret, that he was not forthright and direct with members when he opposed or killed their bills. They claimed that he sometimes used his position to violate legislative norms and procedures in an effort to get his way on legislation. Richardson alienated members in part because he was willing to use his power aggressively to block the bills that they sponsored, but he seems to have alienated them even more by the style with which he used this power.

But Richardson also alienated some members during the 1984 session by what he failed to do. During that session he endorsed Governor Collins's education and tax packages, but he seemed to be either unable or unwilling to use the powers of his office and his considerable negotiating skill in an effort to mobilize a majority in support of that program. The forthcoming challenge from Don Blandford for the speakership seemed to have not only divided the Democratic party but to have immobilized its leader on this major issue.

Don Blandford brought an entirely different style to the job of Speaker. He was a veteran member of the legislature (first elected in 1967), who had specialized in the work of the Agriculture Committee. He has never been known as an orator, and did not try to make his case by speeches on the floor or in caucus. Though not a skilled parliamentarian, during the 1986 session he gradually developed greater confidence and poise in presiding over the House. He has been frequently described by his colleagues as "a people person"—most effective in one-on-one conversations and in small meetings. Blandford was highly accessible to members. He thrived on informal contacts, social events, dinners, and party functions, where he had an opportunity to develop friendships and maintain contacts. One reason for Blandford's success in his first term as Speaker was that members found he could be trusted to keep his word—an important asset for any legislative leader. We have described Blandford earlier as a manager, one who was concerned with running the House efficiently and getting the members to work together.

Blandford also tried to protect his colleagues from painful or difficult choices, from having to vote in public on controversial bills that were doomed to defeat. He took a straw vote in caucus on the controversial and emotional lottery bill, and when it failed to get enough support, he let it die without getting to the floor. When strong interest groups made conflicting demands on the legislature, he asked them if possible to work out compromises, in an effort to spare his colleagues from cross pressures. This technique worked in the case of the omnibus bill on the horse industry and the task force that was established to deal with the thorny problem of workmen's compensation. In similar fashion, when political leaders in Louisville and Jefferson County were in disagreement on the terms of an agreement between the city and county, Blandford refused to play the role of referee, and insisted that the leaders develop a compromise bill that would have broad support from the city and county delegation and thus could pass the General Assembly.

It seems fair to say that Blandford's leadership in the House was less partisan than Wright's in the Senate. Blandford did not use the caucus often to formulate a unified Democratic position on issues. He and Majority Leader Stumbo made a conscious effort to treat Republican colleagues better, and they worked more closely with Republican leaders than had been done in the past. For example, they avoided the technique of killing a Republican-sponsored bill that they considered meritorious so that a parallel bill with Democratic sponsorship could be passed. When they expanded the size of two committees, they were scrupulous about giving the Republicans one of the new seats on each. One consequence of this strategy may have been increased willingness of Republicans to support bills endorsed by the governor or the House leadership.

On the major issue with which he was most prominently identified, the increase in the highway tax, Blandford worked very skillfully. He made the decision to seek the tax increase in 1986 after it failed in 1985. He persuaded the transportation secretary to meet individually with members—both Democrats and Republicans—and make specific commitments about road projects in their district, and the Speaker sought firm commitments from members following those meetings. He counted his votes carefully and brought the bill to the floor when he was sure it would pass. Throughout the process, Blandford kept the governor's office informed, but it was his bill, and not the governor's.

Greg Stumbo, who was elected majority floor leader in alliance with Blandford, has similar views about leadership strategy. One of his campaign promises was to broaden participation in the budgetary process, a goal that was partially fulfilled. Another promise, more difficult to fulfill, was to provide each member with a full-time staff assistant during the session. Stumbo is bright and articulate, a good public speaker. Like Blandford he proved to be good at negotiating with members and in avoiding personality conflicts, and skillful in counting votes.

REPUBLICAN PARTY LEADERSHIP

In recent years the Republican party has averaged 22 to 29 of the 100 seats in the House and 7 to 10 of the 38 seats in the Senate. This is the political reality within which Republican leaders must operate in planning their strategy. One possible strategy for the party is to formulate a distinctive position on major legislative issues, such as the budget and the most important components of the governor's program, and to try to unite behind that position. If the Democratic legislative delegation were deeply divided on one of these issues, it is possible that the Republican party could hold the balance of power and get its policies adopted. In practice, this has rarely happened in recent years, because the Republican party holds too few legislative seats, and the Democratic party is not usually deeply divided, at least on legislation sponsored by the governor.

There have been times in the past when the Republican party has been able to hold the balance of power in the legislature. During the 1958 session, Governor Chandler lost control of the Democratic party in the Senate and maintained only a tenuous control in the House. In order to gain adoption of some of his legislative program, he turned to the Republican party for help. Most Republicans supported him and gained some concessions from the Chandler administration. During the Combs administration, most Republicans joined with Chandler Democrats in opposition to some parts of the Combs program, but were largely unsuccessful in their efforts. The Republican party was most successful in the legislature during the administration of Republican Governor Louie Nunn. One reason for this was the larger size of the Republican legislative delegation; during the first session, it held forty-three seats in the House and fourteen seats in the Senate. The Republican party united behind the governor on his major legislative proposals, notably his budget and tax program, and the governor was able to pick up enough Democratic votes to win most of what he wanted. Throughout the Nunn administration, he received strong support from Republican legislators; this was a major reason for his relative success in the legislature.

The Republican legislative party can be expected to play an important role during any future Republican administration, but the decline of Democratic factionalism seems to have ended the Republican party's chances of holding the balance of power during Democratic administrations—particularly because the party has been unable to increase the number of its seats beyond approximately one-fourth.

Under these conditions, if the Republican party develops its own legislative program and attempts to unite behind it during a Democratic administration, the major purpose of this strategy is political: to attract public attention to Republican policies in order to lay the groundwork for the next gubernatorial election. In fact, the Republican legislative party has not very often followed such a strategy. In 1984 a group of Republican representatives, including all of those on the Appropriations and Revenue Committee, developed and publicized an alternative to Governor Collins's budget and tax program. The Republican proposal avoided any new taxes, proposed a gradual expansion of educational spending, and cut spending in other areas. The proposal was defeated in the House on a party-line vote. In the 1985 special session, nearly all Republicans opposed the major increases in business taxes and the increase in the gasoline tax, but most also favored the expensive package of educational reforms. Republicans made no effort in the 1986 session to offer an alternative budget.

There are several reasons, besides the shortage of seats, why the Republican party has seldom tried to unite behind alternative legislative programs. The legislative party draws most of its strength from two geographic areas: traditional Republican counties in Appalachia and the major metropolitan centers. The traditional Republican counties in southeast and south-central Kentucky are among the poorest rural counties in the state. Republican legislators in Jefferson and Fayette counties and in northern Kentucky are elected from the higher income parts of the metropolitan areas. The two groups of Republican legislators represent constituents with different interests and needs and different policy priorities. The political culture in the two areas is quite different.

There is another reason it is difficult for the Republican party to remain united in opposition to policies supported by a Democratic governor or the legislative leadership. Individual Republican legislators need the assistance of the governor and the Democratic leaders to gain benefits for their districts and/or passage of bills that they are sponsoring. During the years when Democratic governors were most powerful, one of their major assets was the ability to provide benefits of various kinds—such as new or improved roads, bridges, parks, and other facilities—to the districts of legislators who supported their programs. Although Democrats benefited most from these projects, Democratic governors sometimes found it necessary or prudent to bargain with some Republicans as well. Because the needs of the rural Republican districts were so great and constituents in those districts put such a high priority on state projects, the Republicans from these counties were more susceptible than their urban colleagues to this kind of temptation from the governor.

In recent years the governor has had fewer opportunities to negotiate because of shortage of funds and more legal restraints on allocation of projects. Moreover, governors Brown and Collins have been much less inclined to bargain with legislators than were their predecessors. Nevertheless, there are still some examples of the administration buying support from Republican legislators. In 1986, when Speaker Blandford was seeking support from legislators for a five-cent increase in the price of gasoline, the secretary of transportation met with legislators and made commitments about roads to be built or improved in their districts, and he negotiated with both Democrats and Republicans. The Republicans provided eleven of the sixty-two votes cast for the gasoline tax in the House, not because the Republican leadership negotiated with Blandford, but because individual Republicans were persuaded to vote for the proposal after negotiating individually about the benefits their constituents would gain from an increase in the road fund.

Although individual Republican legislators may be tempted less often by offers of projects and benefits for their districts, they still want to gain passage for the bills that they sponsor, and this requires the cooperation of Democratic leaders and committee chairmen. An important reason the Republican parties do not consistently challenge major Democratic bills is that Republican members want to get their own legislation passed.

The Republicans in the House and Senate hold daily, public caucuses, the primary purpose of which is to keep the members informed about bills that are scheduled for consideration on the floor. Because the House Republican delegation is considerably larger than the Senate party, the communications and information functions of its caucus are more important. Pending legislation is explained by members of the committee that considered it or, in the case of local legislation, by members from the affected counties. Members who have sponsored bills get a chance to argue in behalf of them. Occasionally, lobbyists attend the caucus and are given a brief opportunity to state their case. Republicans believe that the information function of the caucus is important because of the variety and complexity of bills that members must deal with every day. The caucus also helps members learn about tactics being used by the governor's office, Democratic leadership, and lobbyists.

The caucus also provides an arena for developing Republican positions on issues and endorsing amendments to Democratic bills, as in the case of the Republican budget alternative developed in 1984 under the sponsorship of the caucus. From time to time the discussions that occur in the caucus lead the members to agree on tactics, such as supporting an amendment to a Democratic bill, or lead to consensus about a particular issue. But it appears that the caucus is less important as a vehicle for developing Republican policy alternatives than as an arena for keeping members informed about legislation.

VOTING IN THE LEGISLATURE

One of the most important variations among American state legislatures is in the role that partisanship plays in decision making. There are a few states in which most important controversial issues are fought out along partisan lines and others where partisanship is virtually irrelevant to decision making. Of course, there are many state legislatures that fall somewhere between these two extremes (Jewell and Patterson, 1977: 381-88).

The level of partisanship can be measured most directly in the roll call votes taken on the floor of the House and Senate. In Kentucky (as in most states) roll calls are required by the constitution on the final passage of all bills and are also taken frequently on controversial amendments and motions;

the constitution specifies that a roll call vote be taken whenever requested by at least two members.

Because roll calls are required, even on noncontroversial bills, there are many lopsided and even unanimous roll call votes recorded. Even controversial issues may lead to lopsided roll calls if the controversial aspects of the bill have been worked out in committee. On the other hand, some bills never get to a vote on the floor because crucial decisions (perhaps on party lines) are made in committee. We will be examining a small sample of legislative roll calls, selecting those on issues of some importance that produced nonunanimous roll calls.

Partisanship plays some part in roll call voting in Kentucky, but not a dominant part—as we shall demonstrate. The reasons for the weakness of partisan voting alignments in Kentucky are quite clear. First, in recent years the Democratic party has held a large majority in both houses, usually approximating three-to-one. Consequently, the Democratic legislative leaders do not usually need to strive for a high level of party cohesion in order to gain the legislative outcomes they favor and get the governor's program passed. On the other hand, the Republican party has little incentive to strive for unity because it cannot usually expect to win by maintaining such unity.

There is a second, less obvious reason for the low level of party cohesion: each of the legislative parties represents heterogeneous interests in the state. The Democratic legislators represent many districts in the larger cities and also most of the rural counties—in parts of Appalachia, most of the Bluegrass region, and nearly all of western Kentucky. The much smaller number of Republican legislators represent the higher-income urban and suburban districts in Jefferson and Fayette Counties (Louisville and Lexington) and in northern Kentucky; they also represent some rural counties in southeastern and southcentral Kentucky, some of the poorest areas of Appalachia.

Despite the numerical imbalance and the heterogeneity of both legislative parties, there are reasons for expecting some efforts at partisan cohesion. The governor might be expected to seek as much support as possible from his or her party on major parts of the administration program, particularly the state budget. The Republicans might be expected to take a stand against the governor's program, or propose alternatives to it, either to challenge and possibly embarrass the governor, or to stake out a position or image for the party that might prove to be helpful in the next election. Most obviously, when the governor recommends an increase in taxes, he or she may need to mobilize as many Democratic votes as possible, and the Republicans may perceive political advantages in opposing the tax increase.

We have selected for analysis a total of 46 Senate and 48 House roll calls for the 1982, 1984, and 1986 regular, and 1985 special, sessions. The roll calls were chosen because they dealt with some of the most important and controversial bills in these sessions. In most cases we have chosen ones on

Table 24. Indexes of Difference Produced by Partisan Divisions (percentage voting yes)

Index of Difference	Democratic	Republican
0	75	75
0	25	25
10	55	45
25	75	50
50	100	50
50	50	0
100	100	0

which there there was some significant opposition in the vote in one house
or both.

We are primarily concerned with evidence of partisan alignments in
voting. How often, and on what kinds of issues, can some evidence of partisan
alignment be found? A second question is whether any other noteworthy
patterns of voting can be found on these roll calls where partisanship is weak.

What do we mean by a partisan alignment in roll call voting? There are
several levels of partisanship that we can use. The most dramatic evidence
of partisanship occurs when every Democrat who is recorded votes on one
side of an issue and every Republican votes on the other side, what is often
called a party-line vote. In most state legislatures it occurs on only a few
roll calls. Among the roll call votes we examined in the four sessions there
were only four cases, three of them in the House, on which all the Democrats
voted against all the Republicans. A second level of partisanship occurs when
all the members of one party vote on one side, and a majority of the other
party votes on the other. There were four roll calls in the Senate and one
in the House on which all the Republicans voted against bills supported by
a majority of Democrats. There was one roll call in the Senate and one in
the House on which all Democrats voted favorably and a majority of Republicans voted negatively.

A much looser standard of partisan alignment is one on which a majority
of Democrats vote against a majority of Republicans. This occurred on 30
percent of Senate votes (14 out of 46) and 58 percent of House votes (28 out
of 48). Although this is an easy measurement to calculate and understand,
it is also very imprecise. It counts as a party alignment a roll call on which
the Democrats vote 74-1 and the Republicans vote 1-24, but also one on
which the Democrats vote 38-37 and the Republicans vote 12-13. In fact,
there was one Senate roll call on which Republicans supported a bill by a
5-4 margin and Democrats opposed it by 14-15.

What we need is a measurement that is more precise and that also
provides an average or median measure of partisanship that can be used for

Table 25. Partisan Index of Difference on Sample of Controversial Bills in
Legislative Sessions, 1982, 1984, 1985, 1986

Index of Difference	Distribution of Votes on Bills			
	Senate		House	
	(N)	(%)	(N)	(%)
0 - 10	10	21.7	12	25.0
11 - 20	8	17.4	10	20.8
21 - 30	7	15.2	9	18.8
31 - 40	8	17.4	3	6.3
41 - 50	7	15.2	4	8.3
51 - 75	2	4.3	4	8.3
76 -100	4	8.7	6	12.5
Total	46	100.0	48	100.0
Median		26.5		23.5

comparative purposes. To accomplish this, we can calculate an index of
difference. We simply calculate the percentage of Democrats and of Republicans voting yes on measures or motions, and then subtract the smaller
percentage from the larger. This gives us an index that ranges from 0 to 100.
Table 24 illustrates what types of partisan divisions can produce particular
indexes of difference. Although there are many combinations that can produce a small index of difference, there is of course only one set of percentages
that can produce an index of 100.

When we calculate an index of difference for each roll call, we find that
the index usually ranges from low to moderate (table 25). There were four
roll calls in the Senate and six in the House on which the index of difference
was 76 or more, and two more in the Senate and four more in the House
with an index over 50. At the other extreme, there were ten roll calls in the
Senate and twelve in the House with an index of difference of 10 or less.
On some of these roll calls the differences were very small because most
members of both parties favored the bill, but that was not always the case—
as we can illustrate by three House roll calls on which the index of difference
was 0. The proportion of representatives voting yes on the three bills was
71, 64, and 48 percent. The index of difference on the median roll call in
the Senate was 26.5, and in the House, 23.5.

We cannot compare partisan alignments in Kentucky with those in other
states by using the index of difference, for two reasons. In recent years there
has been an acute shortage of roll-call studies in state legislatures. Also, we
have selected only a small sample of important, controversial issues in Kentucky. Someone studying another state would be unlikely to use exactly the
same criteria in sampling roll calls. If we were to count every nonunanimous

roll call, the median index of difference would be lower because on a large proportion of roll calls a very small proportion of legislators oppose the bill.

We are less interested in calculating either a range or a median index of difference than in determining what kinds of issues produce the most partisanship and on what issues there are few if any partisan differences. Even if strong partisan alignments are infrequent, we want to know on which issues partisanship is relatively strong. We will begin by looking at the issues involved in seventeen Senate and sixteen House roll calls that were the most heavily partisan. (In the Senate the index of difference ranged from 34 to 100 and on most a majority of the two parties were opposed. In the House it ranged from 36 to 100, and the two parties were opposed on all.)

Two of the perfect party-line votes (index of difference of 100) concerned amendments to the executive budget proposed by the House Republican party. On several roll calls involving final passage of the budget, the Republicans were sharply divided and the Democrats were all or nearly all supportive. In 1986, however, nearly every legislator in both parties voted for final passage of the budget.

Most of the other bills with the strongest party alignments concerned taxes. All Republican senators and most Republican representatives voted against increased business taxes, during the 1985 special session, to finance Governor Collins's education program. All Republican senators and a large majority of the representatives opposed an increase in the alcohol beverage tax, and nearly all Republicans opposed a truck weight-distance tax. In the House, but not the Senate, most Republicans opposed postponing implementation of a more liberal business depreciation policy based on changes in the federal law. On one other tax bill the partisan differences were smaller but still noteworthy. In 1985 in the House a small majority of Democrats and a large majority of Republicans opposed an increase in the gasoline tax. In 1986 most Democratic senators favored the gas tax and seven of ten Republican senators opposed it; but partisan differences were not so sharp in the House.

The remaining roll calls with evidence of partisanship include a wide variety of issues. In 1986 there were perfect partisan votes in both houses on the bill to reintroduce a presidential primary, which the Democrats favored and the Republicans opposed. Senate Republicans unanimously supported a resolution favoring a balanced budget amendment for the U.S. Constitution (one that did not come to a vote on the House floor). Most Republicans in both houses supported a bill changing the requirement that the prevailing wage must be paid on local government construction projects, an issue that sharply divided Democrats. A majority of Republicans in each house either opposed a more generous legislative retirement bill in 1982 or voted to uphold the governor's veto of the bill. In 1986 nearly all Democrats favored, and a substantial majority of Republicans opposed, a bill to float a bond issue to help the new Toyota plant in central Kentucky. Almost all Republicans in both houses favored, and Democratic majorities opposed, a motion to override the governor's veto of a bill requiring that all administrative regulations be written into law to become effective.

There were several issues, however, on which the Senate and House Republicans took distinctly different positions, weakening their leverage and their ability to use the issue for campaign purposes. Narrow majorities of Republicans supported the Senate reapportionment plan; the House reapportionment plan had the support of nearly all Republican representatives, whereas their Senate colleagues were split 4-4. House Republicans unanimously passed a constitutional amendment to ease the restrictions on mayoral succession, but the House Republicans were split 5-5.

The major package of educational reforms was passed in the 1985 special session with the support of a large majority of Republican representatives but the opposition of six of the ten senators. Two other educational reform bills produced unusual partisan splits. A bill requiring more local tax effort to support education had the support of most Republicans but only a minority of Democrats in the Senate; in the House it won support from more than two-thirds of the Democrats but only nine of twenty-two Republicans. A bill permitting the state to intervene in cases where local school boards were "bankrupt" won strong support from both parties in the Senate and from House Democrats but was opposed by thirteen of twenty-three House Republicans.

One incentive for the minority Republican party to vote cohesively on an issue is the possibility of winning if the majority Democrats are badly enough divided. In reality, this happens only infrequently. Among the 96 roll calls that we examined over four sessions, there were no bills that were defeated on which the Republicans provided the margin for defeat. There were, however, five roll calls (three in the Senate and two in the House) on which the Republican party provided the margin of victory. In each case the Republicans were nearly united in support of the bill and the Democrats were opposed, usually by narrow margin (or in one case were tied). In three of these cases the legislative body voted to override a veto of bills that tightened legislative control over administrative regulations. The House passed a bill changing the law on prevailing wages in government contracts despite Democratic opposition; in the Senate a majority of both parties favored the bill. The strangest example occurred on a bill requiring local school districts to impose at least a fifteen-cent property tax to support education. It passed in the Senate with Republican support and narrow Democratic opposition; in the House it passed with Democratic support and Republican opposition.

We turn now to look at issues that can properly be called nonpartisan because there was little difference between Republican and Democratic voting patterns. The most interesting example of an issue that was highly controversial but nonpartisan is the multicounty banking bill. This complex measure was designed to permit large, well-financed banks to acquire smaller ones in other counties. It appears that most legislators voted in support of the banking interests that were strongest in their counties. The bill came to a vote in 1982, was narrowly defeated, and was passed in 1984. In the House, in the two sessions, the Democratic margins were 39-35 (1982) and 46-30 (1984), whereas the Republican votes were 11-12 and 10-12. In the Senate the Democratic votes were 14-15 and 16-12, whereas the Republicans voted 5-4 and 5-5. It is worth noting that, although Republicans in both houses remained almost evenly divided in both sessions, it was a shift of the Democratic votes that brought about passage of the bill.

Other examples of bills that caused deep divisions on roll calls within one or both houses, but virtually no differences between the parties, include a Senate vote to permit Sunday liquor sales in urban restaurants, a vote in the Senate to keep an experimental career ladder plan for teachers, and a bill to permit reorganization of Jefferson County. A proposed constitutional amendment to appoint rather than elect the superintendent of public instruction had strong bipartisan support in the Senate and nearly as strong bipartisan opposition in the House.

In those states where party alignments are more frequent they usually arise on three types of issues: bills that are part of the governor's program (or are strongly opposed by him or her), bills that particularly affect the two party organizations, and bills that embody economic and social issues of particular concern to those interests closely allied with each of the parties (Jewell and Patterson, 1977: 394-402).

Partisanship in the Kentucky legislature most often arises from the differing roles and responsibilities of the majority and minority—or administration and opposition—parties. As the majority party, the Democrats often feel obliged to support tax increases, particularly those proposed by the governor. The Republican party has the luxury of opposing those tax increases and often exercises that choice. Similarly, the Republicans occasionally support (and the Democrats oppose) amendments to change budgetary priorities. Despite some doubts about the program, Democrats felt obliged to support the governor's plan for a state bond issue to facilitate the building of a new Toyota plant in Kentucky. The Democrats have an incentive to uphold gubernatorial vetoes, and Republicans have no reason to do so.

Another category of bills on which partisan differences occasionally arise in Kentucky are those affecting the interests of party organizations. The bill to reestablish the presidential primary and bills to change the date of the state primary are good examples. Most votes on reapportionment, however, did not follow party lines.

It is the third category of issues, those involving economic and social interests, that cause partisan alignments less often in Kentucky than in many other states. We have attributed this to the fact that each of the legislative parties represents a heterogeneous collection of interests. We cannot describe the voting record of one party as liberal and the other as conservative. One of the few economic issues causing a partisan alignment was the question of changing the prevailing wage law for governmental contracts. There were partisan differences on a few educational issues, but no consistent pattern of party alignment, even on issues of particular concern to the Kentucky Educational Association. There were no major differences between the two parties on some of the most important and controversial issues faced by the legislature, including multicounty banking, restrictions on abortion, and very often the final passage of the budget bill.

When divisions in the legislature do not follow partisan lines, there is no other consistent pattern of voting. Instead, there is a shifting pattern of coalitions from one issue to another. On some issues there are differences in voting between urban and rural legislators; this would include some of the social and "moral" issues. Groups of legislators can be identified who support the position of organized labor or the Kentucky Education Association on issues of concern to them. Other legislators are responsive to other organized interests. Depending on one's definition of "reform," it is possible to identify some legislators as relatively consistent "reformers." Some Democrats, as well as many Republicans, have voted with some consistency against major tax increases. But because these coalitions shift from one issue to the next and there are relatively few sharply divided roll calls on important issues, it is difficult to discover continuing patterns of voting, other than party voting, on a significant number of issues.

Since 1979 the roles of the presiding officers and majority floor leaders in the Kentucky General Assembly have changed fundamentally. As long as the leaders were, in fact, selected by the governor, their major responsibility was to get the governor's program enacted. Now that leaders are selected by the membership, and specifically the Democratic members, they have more independent power, but ultimately they are responsible to the membership. They feel an obligation to help the governor get his or her program through, but they are sensitive to the needs and concerns of their colleagues.

The leaders now can define their own roles and styles of leadership, and, not surprisingly, they have done so in different ways. The Democratic leadership in the Senate has emphasized the importance of maximizing unity within the legislative party and has used the caucus as well as the Rules Committee to achieve this. Bobby Richardson, the first "independent" House Speaker, was an activist who was willing to put pressure on members and to use the Rules Committee aggressively to achieve his objectives. His successor, Don Blandford, sought to maximize consensus and minimize pressure on the members. He preferred informal, personal techniques of persuasion rather than using the caucus or making vigorous use of the Rules Committee.

The large Democratic majority in both houses enables the leadership to follow a strategy of building legislative majorities largely from Democratic members. But an analysis of roll call voting shows that there are relatively few bills that produce strong party-line voting. This is because the Democratic majority is so large that neither party needs to maintain a high level of discipline and because each of the parties represents a wide diversity of constituent interests.

9. The Governor as Legislative Leader

PATTERNS OF GUBERNATORIAL LEADERSHIP IN AMERICAN STATES

A decade ago Larry Sabato (1978) wrote a book entitled *Goodbye to Goodtime Charlie: The American Governorship Transformed.* The theme of this book is that American governors, most of whom used to be "ill prepared to govern and less prepared to lead," have become "vigorous, incisive, and thoroughly trained leaders," "skilled negotiators and, importantly often crucial coordinators" at both the national and local levels. "Once parochial officers . . . whose responsibilities frequently were slight," today's governors "have gained major new powers that have increased their influence in national as well as state councils" (p. 2).

Sabato describes a number of reasons for this growth of influence and respect. The terms of governors in most states have been extended, either by permitting a second consecutive term or by raising the term from two to four years. Governors have become more successful in winning reelection. Constitutional changes and administrative reorganizations in most states have given them more effective control over the executive branch. The office of the governor has become better staffed. Governors have become more skillful in using the media to lead public opinion. Perhaps the most important trend, however, has been the growing importance of state government, as the federal government has begun to transfer responsibilities back to the states. As the demands on state government have increased, it is the governors who have undertaken the responsibility of meeting these challenges.

Differences remain among the states in the formal powers of the governor. A few serve two-year terms or cannot succeed themselves. A few cannot control the executive budget. States differ in the extent of gubernatorial authority over the executive branch and the power to hire and fire officials with policymaking functions. Some governors are given greater flexibility in the use of the veto (Mueller, 1985). Equally important are political differences among the states that affect the governor, including the level of two-party competition in elections and the normal balance of parties in the legislature, as well as the availability of patronage. There are also variations in custom, the traditional influence of the governor.

There are significant variations and trends in the relationship between the governor and the legislature—the topic of immediate interest to us. Thirty years ago some states had strong governors and weak legislators; others had weak governors and strong legislatures. Today there is more nearly a balance of power between governors and legislatures and fewer differences among the states. The weakest governors have become stronger. At the same time, the legislatures that used to be the weakest have become stronger and more professional, with fewer constitutional limits on sessions, longer tenure and better salaries for members, and larger, more qualified staffs.

There are also significant political changes affecting gubernatorial-legislative relations. Reapportionment of legislatures has meant that essentially the same electoral majorities choose both the governor and the legislature, reducing one of the causes of deadlock between the two. There has been a growth of two-party competition in most parts of the country. At one time some southern governors were very powerful in legislative affairs because the legislature met relatively briefly and had no effective opposition party. Today southern governors, whether Democrats or Republicans, often have to forge bipartisan coalitions to govern effectively. At one time some northern governors could depend on the support of highly disciplined legislative parties, as long as their party held a majority. Today, party discipline has been eroded, and northern governors must often rely on other tools of leadership.

The pattern of gubernatorial-legislative relations in American states today is a complex one. Both governors and legislators are more professional and less partisan; they serve longer terms; they have better staffs; and their effectiveness depends more on their political, administrative, and legislative skills than on traditional bases of power.

We shall find that some of these national trends are at work in Kentucky. There is a more even balance of legislative-gubernatorial power because the legislature has grown more professional and more powerful, whereas there has been less change in the governorship. Some of the traditional bases of gubernatorial power in Kentucky have been eroded and newer techniques have been developed only gradually. In Kentucky, as in all states, the effectiveness of the governor varies with the goals and skills of the individual who holds that office. The single-term limit has led to frequent turnover and major differences in the style of gubernatorial leadership.

THE GOVERNORSHIP IN KENTUCKY

Traditionally, Kentucky has had a strong governor, but the sources of this strength are less constitutional than political. In one recent study of the formal powers of state governors, Kentucky ranked below the average; on a twenty-five-point scale, the average was nineteen and the governorship in Kentucky was seventeen (Beyle 1982). The most obvious constitutional weakness is the fact that Kentucky is one of only three states in which the governor cannot serve a second consecutive term. (In three other states the governor is handicapped by two-year terms.) As a consequence, the governor's political influence over the legislature often appears to be diminished during the second legislative session of his or her term.

The Kentucky governor has relatively strong control over the executive branch, except for those officials who are elected by the voters. The governor can hire most of the important officials, without legislative confirmation being required, and can fire them at will. The Kentucky governor does not face the problem of major functions being run by boards whose members serve fixed, staggered terms. The governor is handicapped by the fact that there are more elected officials than in some states and the fact that the governor and lieutenant governor are not elected as a team. On balance, the Kentucky governor has about as much formal control over the executive branch as the average governor.

When a governor has firm control over the executive branch, he or she is better able to present a coordinated legislative package to the General Assembly, and members of the executive will speak with one voice on legislative issues. Where the governor's control is weak, the heads of executive agencies may engage in lobbying efforts at cross purposes to those of the governor. We should recognize, however, that effective coordination of the executive branch depends much on the governor's political skills as on formal powers.

No aspect of formal power is more important than the governor's control over the budget-making process. In the vast majority of states, including Kentucky, the governor has complete authority over the executive budget and has the power to hire and replace the officials who direct preparation of the budget. The Kentucky governor's control over the executive budget remains unchanged; what has changed, as we have described in chapter 6, is the legislature's ability to review and revise that budget.

The governor in every state except North Carolina has the veto power, and governors of most states (including Kentucky) have the item veto over appropriations bills. In Kentucky a veto can be overridden by a majority of the membership in each house; those states where more than an absolute majority is required are ranked ahead of Kentucky in the strength of the veto. The governor has ten days to veto a bill, however, and until the schedule of legislative sessions was changed a few years ago, most bills did not gain final passage until the last ten days of the session and the governor did not have to veto bills until after adjournment. Consequently, it did not matter how many votes were required to override. Since the legislature gained greater flexibility in scheduling its session, it has regularly adjourned for ten days and returned for two legislative days to deal with vetoes. The governor's veto has become less absolute because of the change in legislative sessions, but this has not been reflected in the indexes of formal gubernatorial powers that are constructed for American states. On the other hand, the veto may have become a more important weapon because the governor's political control over the legislature has become less absolute.

This leads us to consider the most important characteristic of the Kentucky Constitution that affects gubernatorial-legislative relations, one that is never mentioned in indexes of formal power: the limitation on legislative sessions. The legislature can meet on sixty days every two years, and only the governor can call special sessions and determine their agenda. The governor's political influence over the General Assembly rests in large part on the fact that legislative time is so limited and the members must rely on the governor to provide leadership. As we have repeatedly emphasized, the legislature has developed a thriving interim committee system in an effort to overcome this limitation; the success of that institution has strengthened the legislature and reduced the governor's constitutional advantage.

In reality, the Kentucky governor's strength in dealing with the legislature has largely been political: his leadership of the party and his utilization of patronage, his control over the budget and the budgetary process, his influence over the choice of legislative leaders. Because this strength has been political, it has been subject to variations depending on the skills and resources of individual governors.

In order to understand the changing relationships between the governor and the legislature, we must examine the interactions between individual governors and the legislature. The growing independence of the legislature, which we have been tracing throughout this book, has constrained the governor in the exercise of political power. Moreover, the reluctance of some governors to exercise strong leadership in legislative affairs has provided the legislature with greater opportunities to exercise its own political power.

Over a twenty-year period, from 1959 to 1979, Kentucky had a succession of of strong governors: Bert Combs, Edward Breathitt, Louie Nunn, Wendell Ford, and Julian Carroll. They differed in their tactics, and each had particular strengths and weaknesses, but each worked vigorously to gain legislative support for his programs, and each had considerable success. The successes of Nunn, Ford, and Carroll were achieved in the face of a gradual but persistent drive toward greater legislative independence. The next two governors, John Y. Brown, Jr., and Martha Layne Collins, were less effective in dealing with the legislature. They did not fully utilize the political resources available to a governor nor did they employ many of the tactics perfected by their predecessors. This benign neglect gave the legislature further opportunities to assert its authority, and it made good use of these opportunities.

During the 1960s and 1970s, the power of the governor vis-a-vis the legislature was stronger in Kentucky than in most other states—both because of the political skills of a series of governors and because of the constitutional and political weaknesses of the legislature. Although there were variations among the states in the political skills and resources of individual governors, in nearly all of the states the legislature was stronger than that in Kentucky, particularly during the 1960s. The legislative reform and revitalization movement came more gradually to Kentucky than to most other states.

During the 1980s the Kentucky legislature, despite the brevity of its regular sessions, has been comparable to many other states in its professionalism, resources, and political independence. At the same time, recent Kentucky governors have not made effective use of many of the political resources commonly employed in other states. Consequently, the Kentucky governor now appears to be weaker in legislative relations than would be true in the average state.

This appearance may be deceiving. We have not yet seen an example in Kentucky of a strong and politically skillful governor, determined to carry out an ambitious legislative program and willing to use all available resources to serve that purpose, confronting the more professional and more independent General Assembly. To put it more simply, we do not know how independent the legislature has become.

THE STRONG-GOVERNOR MODEL IN KENTUCKY

Building the Model. To understand the previous pattern of strong gubernatorial leadership and assess its potential for the future, we need to examine how the tools of political leadership have been employed by Kentucky governors in the recent past.

The model of a strong governor was not invented by Bert Combs in 1959. Because the legislature was so weak and dependent on outside leadership, it was not difficult for a governor to gain a dominant position in legislative matters. The best example of effective gubernatorial leadership prior to Combs's term was provided by Earle Clements, who served from 1947 until his election to the Senate in 1950. Combs's immediate predecessor, A.B. Chandler, used many of the tools of political leadership, but ran into serious resistance during his second session because of sharp factional divisions that pervaded the legislature.

Combs had an ambitious legislative program, and he demonstrated great skill in using the resources and tools available to a governor to win passage of most of his program. Combs's hand-picked successor, Edward Breathitt, got off to a slow, uncertain start and faced factional opposition led by Lieutenant Governor Harry Lee Waterfield. But Breathitt followed the example of Combs and used his political power with increasing skill to win a number of legislative victories.

Louie Nunn, the first Republican governor to be elected in twenty-four years, faced the obvious problem of a Democratic majority (though a smaller one than usual). Concentrating on a limited agenda, primarily his budget and tax program, Nunn commanded the nearly unanimous support of Republican legislators and succeeded in winning enough Democratic votes to gain most of his limited objectives.

The strong-governor model reached its peak during the administrations of Wendell Ford and Julian Carroll. The factions that had divided Democratic legislators had disappeared, and normal Democratic majorities of at least three-to-one in the legislature had been restored. Both Ford and Carroll were skillful politicians who had been elected by comfortable margins in the primary and general elections. Both had served in the legislature, Carroll had been Speaker of the House, and both had presided over the Senate as lieutenant governor. Carroll probably understood the legislative process better than any Kentucky governor in modern times. Both as Speaker and as lieutenant governor he had contributed to the growing effectiveness and independence of the General Assembly. It was ironic but not surprising that, with this background, Carroll was more persistent than his recent predecessors in exercising influence over the legislature.

The modern strong-governor model was developed initially, by Combs and Breathitt, at a time when the legislature was weak, lacking time, resources, staff, and experienced members. The model was developed to perfection by Ford and Carroll at a time when the legislature was growing stronger, gaining more time through the interim committee system, increasing its budget and its staff, and getting more experienced members. We have described in earlier chapters some of the conflicts that resulted from these two trends.

Kentucky governors, from Combs to Carroll, had a number of tools at their disposal in exercising influence over legislative decision making. Some of these tools are still being used today. Others may be obsolete because of changes in the legislative process or in state politics. Still others have grown rusty from disuse. We will describe how these tools have been used in the past and explain how some of them have grown obsolete or rusty.

Party Leadership. The Kentucky governor is the leader of his party; when the governor is a Democrat, he or she leads a party that normally holds a majority of at least three-to-one in each house of the General Assembly. From research in other states, we know the conditions under which party leadership can be an asset to a governor, as well as its limitations. Generally speaking, members of a governor's party are more likely than opposition members to support gubernatorial programs. Thus a governor is better off when his or her party holds a majority in the legislature, but the governor does not necessarily benefit from a large majority. When the majority is large, party discipline—being less essential—tends to be become slack. Moreover, the larger the partisan majority of legislators, the greater diversity of interests they are likely to represent.

The large majority usually enjoyed by Democrats in the Kentucky legislature gives a Democratic governor a comfortable cushion, but does not guarantee him or her disciplined partisan support for a legislative program. In seeking support the governor can appeal to party loyalty, but the bonds of such loyalty are likely to be weaker than in states with closer party competition.

In theory at least, there are more tangible aspects to party leadership. A governor might have some influence over the nomination and election of legislators in his party, and might be expected to control patronage that could be distributed to legislators as well as to other loyal members of the party. In practice, it is quite rare for a governor to have any significant influence over the nomination and election of legislators, whereas the extent of patronage available to a governor differs considerably from state to state.

During the 1950s and 1960s, Kentucky was one of the very few states in which the governor played a direct, and sometimes powerful, role in the nomination of legislative candidates and the renomination of incumbents. This occurred because the state Democratic party at that time was deeply divided along factional lines, and this factionalism extended to both local and legislative politics. The leaders of the two factions were Earle Clements and A.B. "Happy" Chandler. The highlights of their factional battles can be briefly summarized by looking at a series of gubernatorial primary elections.

Clements was elected governor in 1947; when he was elected to the Senate in 1950, he was succeeded by his ally, Lawrence Wetherby, who was elected to a full term in 1951.

In 1955 Chandler (returning to Kentucky politics after a term as baseball commissioner) won the gubernatorial nomination over Bert Combs, who had been selected by the Clements organization. After Clements sought to prevent Chandler from gaining control of the party machinery, Chandler helped defeat Clements's bid for reelection to the Senate.

In the 1959 primary, Bert Combs, with Clements's support, defeated Chandler's ally and lieutenant governor, Harry Lee Waterfield.

In the 1963 primary, Edward Breathitt, selected and endorsed by Combs, defeated Chandler, who was seeking a third term; but Harry Lee Waterfield was again elected lieutenant governor.

In 1967 Breathitt's anointed successor defeated Chandler, Waterfield, and a few others, but factional divisions were so deep that a Republican was elected in November.

During this period the factionalism that permeated gubernatorial campaigns carried over into the legislature. The governor could normally depend on loyal support from legislators who were members of his faction, but often faced opposition from those who had been allied with the other faction during the primary. During the 1958 legislative session, Chandler was confronted by a Democratic legislative party controlled by Clements-Combs supporters and was forced to make an alliance with Republicans to pass his budget.

Under these conditions the governor had an incentive to intervene in Democratic legislative primaries in an effort to increase the proportion of legislators who would be loyal to him. It was usually impractical for gubernatorial candidates to try to influence legislative primaries; they were too busy trying to win their own nominations. But in the mid-term primary elections, incumbent governors provided support to factional allies who were incumbent legislators, who were running against incumbents, or who were running for open seats. The purpose was to strengthen their political position in the second legislative session when they had the disadvantage of being lame ducks. Chandler's efforts to elect more factional allies failed in 1957. Combs made extensive efforts in 1961 to replace Chandler supporters with members of the legislature who would be loyal to him. In 1965 Governor Breathitt concentrated his electoral efforts in the Senate because Lieutenant Governor Waterfield was trying to gain control over that chamber.

Surveys of legislative candidates in the 1961 and 1965 Democratic primaries show the extent of gubernatorial endorsements. In each year data were collected from candidates in four-fifths of the contested legislative primaries (Jewell and Cunningham, 1968: 155-78). Respondents reported that the administration endorsed a candidate in each contested Senate race both years, and it endorsed a candidate in three-fourths of the House races in 1961 and in nearly all of those in 1965. Our data suggest that four-fifths of those endorsed by Combs and two-thirds of those endorsed by Breathitt were nominated. In addition, in some of the uncontested primaries, the governor's support of particular candidates appears to have been important in discouraging any opposition.

The endorsements usually were a product of alliances between the governor and his factional supporters in the counties. Word of the endorsement was passed to local party activists and to state workers. The endorsed candidates found it easier to raise campaign funds. The administration also raised and distributed campaign funds to the endorsed legislative candidates, but only on a small scale. One insider estimated that in 1961 no more than $15,000 was distributed by the administration, with no more than $500 going to any single candidate. In short, the major effect of endorsements was organizational: to mobilize the administration loyalists on behalf of the legislative candidates. In most of these races it was unlikely that most voters would know or care that one of the candidates was endorsed by the governor.

In 1965, however, Governor Breathitt campaigned openly for a number of the candidates he had endorsed—particularly in senatorial primaries. He campaigned in a number of counties, and in a television broadcast he asked voters to support senatorial candidates who would support the administration. Ten senatorial primaries became the focus of a factional battle between Governor Breathitt and Lieutenant Governor Waterfield; Breathitt's candidates won seven of these races.

The 1971 gubernatorial primary between Wendell Ford and Bert Combs (who had been factional allies) marked the end of the traditional Democratic factions in Kentucky, and it also presaged the end of gubernatorial endorsements of legislative candidates on an extensive or systematic basis. The endorsement of legislative candidates was an important tool of partisan leadership employed by the governor. During the Combs and Breathitt administrations, at least, a large majority of the endorsed candidates in contested races were nominated. Those endorsed legislators who were elected to the second session of the Combs and Breathitt administrations could be depended on to provide loyal support to the governor's programs.

We must recognize, however, that legislative primary endorsements were an outgrowth of the factional system, and legislative factionalism presented obstacles to the governor. He could not assume that most Democrats were predisposed to support his program; rather, he faced an organized opposition bloc within the majority party in addition to the opposition of the minority party. On rare occasions, as in the 1958 session, the factional opposition was strong enough to control the leadership and committee chairmanships. One consequence of legislative factionalism was that governors often negotiated with Republican legislators for support on important issues. Another consequence was that governors were forced to rely on other tools of leadership, beyond partisan loyalty. These tools were abundant and powerful, as we will describe.

Patronage and Projects. Kentucky governors were in a position to offer legislators a wide variety of personal favors, usually described as patronage. The administration might employ one of the legislator's relatives in a state job. A number of legislators were lawyers or ran insurance companies of other businesses. The state might negotiate a person-service contract with the legislator's law firm or buy insurance or other services or products from his firm. In 1960, however, the legislature adopted a merit system and also passed a conflict of interest law applying to legislators. These reforms significantly limited the governor's ability to win legislators' votes with personal favors—but they did not abolish personal patronage. The administration could arrange with a company doing substantial business with the state to hire a legislator's relative, to engage the services of a legislator-lawyer, or to place contracts with legislators in various businesses. Although the merit system covers most full-time state jobs, there are large numbers of boards and commissions that are prestigious or powerful or both. The administration could appoint friends and relatives of legislators to some of these positions.

It is possible, of course, that legislators can become indebted to the administration without intending to. Many years ago one legislator complained: "When I first came up here I used to boast of how independent I was: I didn't have any relatives on the payroll and I had only a small law practice. They snuck behind me and put my sister-in-law on the payroll without my knowing it and she thought I was responsible. And then I have had my business clients come to me and express the hope that nothing that I do in Frankfort will put them in an embarrassing position with the state."

Despite such examples it is generally true that the value of patronage depends on the extent of legislators' interest in benefiting from it. During the 1950s and 1960s, when most legislators served short terms and had no long-term political ambitions, it was easier to influence a member by offering him some form of assistance with his business or profession. Today, when more members are interested in long-term political careers in, or beyond, the legislature, they are less likely to be bought with promises of help to their nonlegislative careers.

Although legislators might differ in their vulnerability to pressure through the use of patronage, all legislators share an interest in gaining benefits for their district—benefits that are determined through the budgetary process. As we have seen, one characteristic of the strong-governor model was the governor's control over both the formation of the budget and its prompt passage by the legislature. If legislators wanted to gain something for their district—a new bridge, a rebuilt highway, a new lodge for a state park, or new facilities at a community college—they had to come to the governor to make their request. There was no realistic opportunity to add these projects by amending the budget bill in committee or on the floor.

The districts of Republican legislators had as many needs as Democratic districts, and usually more, because they had been generally ignored by Democratic administrations. Republican legislators could not afford to wait until the next administration might be elected to gain assistance for their districts. Consequently, Republican as well as Democratic legislators were willing to bargain with the governor to gain projects for their districts.

During the 1966 session, a Republican legislator from Casey county explained on the House floor why he was supporting the administration's budget. When he had presented a petition from eight hundred constituents asking to have an aging bridge rebuilt, the governor's assistant had asked him to support the budget. Said the legislator, "If you fight the administration, you won't get too much for your people. I'm a Republican—what do I have to work with? And if I come into the House and vote against the Democrats I'll get mud in my face for my people—that's all I'll get. What can I do? If I go against them I'll have no chance of serving my people." One Republican legislator said he supported the governor's budget in return for a written promise of a road. "That's what you call reciprocity. My people need that road. . . . If I get it for them, they don't care how I vote on matters such as the budget."

During the 1958 legislature, when Governor Chandler had lost the support of Democrats, he won a number of legislative struggles because most Republican legislators supported him. When a highway construction bill was pending, Chandler met behind closed doors with the House Republican caucus and promised support for projects in the members' districts in return for their support. He got twenty-one of the twenty-four votes for the bill, which passed by a one-vote margin. One Republican legislator, explaining why a new National Guard armory was built in his district, said "Why was I able to get it? Chandler's budget passed by one vote and I voted for it."

Republican Governor Louie Nunn was equally effective in using budgetary control to win votes for his programs from both Republicans and Democrats. In 1968 Nunn won legislative passage of a two-cent increase in the sales tax. At one point during the proceedings, the House adopted by a one-vote margin an amendment to exempt food, clothing, and medicine from the sales tax (without providing alternative revenue). The next day the vote on the amendment was reconsidered and reversed by a margin of twenty-five votes. In the interim the administration had explained to a number of legislators what projects would have to be eliminated from their districts to make up for the revenue lost.

One Democratic legislator had brought a number of civic leaders from his county to meet with the governor and celebrate legislative approval of a new community college for his city. At the meeting Governor Nunn bluntly informed the legislator that this provision would be vetoed if he failed to change his vote on the sales tax exemption. The next day the legislator spoke on the floor to explain his reversal. He described a number of projects planned for his district that would be lost if the amendment passed and the budget had to be cut: the community college, a new airport, and increased funding for a vocational school and a mental hospital. He said that he had voted for the exemptions to the sales tax as a matter of party loyalty, but he now understood that what was at stake were the interests of his district, not his party.

The governor, of course, has never had complete freedom to hand out projects to state legislators, and over the years the freedom has been restricted in a number of ways. Since many projects are built with the aid of federal funds, the federal government has a voice in their location. Very often, new projects must be preceded by advisory panels, feasibility studies, and hearings. Economic circumstances have cut back the number of new projects that some governors can initiate.

Despite the limitations the governor's office remains at the center of the decision-making process in planning the budget. The best chance any legislator has for gaining a project in the district is to win the support of the governor. In the words of one political leader who has served as both a legislator and a governor's aide: "The governor giveth and the governor taketh away; blessed be the name of the governor."

Controlling the Legislative Process. In chapter 8 we described the influence that the governor traditionally had over the selection of legislative leadership. Legislators had become accustomed to accepting the preferences of Democratic governors for the choice of the House Speaker and Senate president pro tem and the majority leaders. These leaders consulted with the governor on the choice of committee chairmen and the membership of the most important committees. This practice was based on tradition, not on the constitution or the legislative rules. During the Nunn administration, although the governor chose Republican leaders, Democratic legislators chose the presiding officers and their own party leaders; but none of them objected when Governor Wendell Ford resumed the traditional practice of selecting the leadership. It was not until 1979, when John Y. Brown, Jr., opted out of the selection process, that the governor's power faded away.

Because the governor selected the leadership, he could count on their full cooperation in maneuvering his program through the legislature. The rules and procedures were designed to facilitate passage of the governor's programs. Administration bills were steered to committees packed with loyalists, and bills the governor opposed were sent to committees that could be counted on to bury them. The Rules Committee was used to speed action on the administration bills and delay or refer to committee bills that the administration opposed. The legislative rules made it easy to cut off debate and amendments and act quickly on the governor's program. Because the governor and his leaders controlled the legislative timetable, they could determine the fate of bills filed by individual members, and this of course increased their bargaining power in negotiating with such members. It was common to keep many individual bills bottled up in committee until the governor's budget had been passed, simply to guarantee votes for the budget.

The brevity of legislative sessions played into the governor's hands because it gave legislators little time to conduct research, collect evidence, or even hold hearings; consequently, they had to turn to the governor and experts in the executive agencies for advice.

In earlier chapters we traced the reorganization of the committee system, the gradual growth of interim committee activities, and the expansion of staff. These trends, which started during the Nunn administration, were all designed to give legislators more opportunity to make their own decisions, and thus more independence of the governor. We have seen how Governor Carroll, through his influence over the legislative leadership, interfered with the growth of a strong staff, particularly for the Appropriations and Revenue Committees.

In fact, during the Ford and especially the Carroll administrations, the committee system was considerably stronger than it had been in the past; members were better informed and had more time to conduct their business, and the legislature was taking seriously its responsibilities for budgetary review and legislative oversight. Despite these new realities, governors Ford and Carroll maintained strong control over the leadership and worked tirelessly to enact their programs.

The Carroll Administration. Governor Carroll provides the best example of strong gubernatorial leadership in dealing with a resurgent legislature. Publicly he talked about the need for an independent legislature. Behind the scenes he worked tirelessly to control the legislative process. One of his assets was the huge majority he had won in the primary and the general election. If most of the tools and tactics that he employed were familiar, he brought to the job an intensity and an attention to details of the legislative process that were unusual. His style of leadership was characterized by a high level of personal involvement with both leaders and members.

Kentucky governors have not been timid in their personal efforts to lobby legislators. Earle Clements used to sit beside the Speaker and watch the House conduct important roll-call votes, occasionally gesturing at a member whose vote displeased him. On the final day of the 1966 session, Governor Breathitt spent the morning talking to senators in and around the Senate chamber, and the afternoon just outside the House chambers calling members off the floor one by one. His purpose was to salvage a public utilities tax measure that appeared doomed, and he was successful. Julian Carroll occasionally testified in person before legislative committees on behalf of his bills. But the center of gubernatorial activity has usually been the governor's office on the first floor of the capitol.

During the Carroll administration, the governor's office was the focal point of the legislative process. Lobbyists centered their efforts on the governor because his endorsement of a bill, or his commitment to oppose it, was the most important determinant of its fate. Members who were having trouble getting their bills passed came to the governor's office for the same reason.

Carroll relied heavily on a strong staff whose members monitored the legislative process carefully. Jackson White, the governor's general counsel, prepared legislation in the governor's program and reviewed the substantive content of all bills that were introduced. Finance Commissioner William Scent examined all proposed legislation for its financial implications. Serving as Carroll's chief legislative lobbyist in the first session was William Cox, his campaign manager in the primary and a former legislator—a man reputed to be skillful as a negotiator and willing to crack the whip when necessary.

Every morning during the session, these three would meet with Governor Carroll to decide what stand would be taken on bills that had been introduced. The legislative leaders would then be provided with lists of bills that the governor favored, those he opposed, and those on which he was taking no stand. Carroll took a position on more bills than most activist governors had done. Using the governor's lists, the legislative leaders prepared notebooks that included the governor's wishes on each bill, information about the position taken by executive agencies, and suggestions about tactics that should be followed on legislation, such as timing and committee assignment. They prepared similar lists for each committee chairman concerning bills pending in that committee.

During the session Carroll met at least once a week with his legislative leaders. This gave him the opportunity to find out how much opposition there might be to his wishes on legislation, and he discussed with the leaders tactics that should be followed and steps that might be taken to change the minds of recalcitrant legislators.

Carroll kept careful track of what was going on in the legislature. A sound system was installed so that the proceedings in the two chambers could be piped into his office. The story was told that while one representative was making a speech in opposition to an administration bill, he received a note from one of the governor's aides telling him, "If you want your bill passed, sit down and be quiet"; the legislator sat down. On one occasion the Carroll administration was trying to gain reconsideration and passage of a bill that had been narrowly defeated in the House the previous day and found itself one vote short. One of the opponents was called off the floor and asked to come down to the governor's office; while he chatted with the governor, the bill was reconsidered, passed, and sent to the Senate.

Cox was a careful vote counter, both in committee and on the floor, who knew exactly how many votes needed to be changed and therefore how much persuasion and bargaining was necessary. Sometimes an opponent who would not change his or her vote could be persuaded to leave the chamber until the roll call was over. According to Cox, "There has never been a day in the history of the General Assembly when you cannot get one legislator to leave the floor long enough to keep something from happening."

When he felt it was necessary, Carroll called legislators into his office to persuade, bargain, or threaten, depending on the situation. Carroll prided himself on his ability to persuade and his willingness to compromise on bills, so that he seldom had to use threats. He complained that his major liability was a shortage of time, saying that sometimes he had to simply insist that he wanted a bill passed because he lacked the time to explain the measure in detail.

Because Carroll maintained tight control over the flow of legislation, in his negotiations with legislators he was able to promise help in passing their bills or threaten to block them. Nearly every legislator comes to Frankfort with a few bills that he or she wants to get enacted. They recognized that Governor Carroll could facilitate passage of all but the most controversial or expensive bills and could usually block even the most innocuous ones.

THE RECENT GOVERNORSHIP

When John Y. Brown, Jr., became governor in 1979 he abandoned the practice of choosing legislative leaders, and Martha Layne Collins made no effort to reinstate it. During the eight-year period of their terms, the legislature continued to exercise greater independence. Neither Brown nor Collins tried to emulate Julian Carroll's model of gubernatorial leadership. Neither took a stand on a large number of issues, and neither engaged in day-to-day negotiations with legislators to get their programs passed.

Brown did not have an extensive legislative program. He was primarily concerned with getting his budget enacted and with getting a change in the basis for computing the gasoline tax in an effort to increase revenue as gasoline prices rose. He suggested various possibilities for tax reform, but never pushed for them in the face of legislative resistance. As we have noted earlier, the Appropriations and Revenue committees thoroughly reviewed Brown's budgets and made some modest changes in them. After a close battle, the legislature adopted Brown's change in the gasoline tax.

Governor Collins had both more defeats and more victories in dealing with the legislature. After a late start in the 1984 session, she proposed major tax increases to finance educational reforms and was turned down flatly by the legislature. In a special session in 1985, however, she won support for a different tax package, one that centered on businesses and major increases in spending for education. In the 1986 session she won backing for her commitment of support for the Toyota plant in central Kentucky and got an increase in the gasoline tax without being publicly committed to it.

After eight years of low-profile gubernatorial leadership in the legislature, it is time to take stock of the governorship. Because the tools of gubernatorial leadership are largely political, their utilization and effectiveness differ from one governor to another. The fact that a particular tool or technique has not been used much recently does not necessarily mean that it has lost its potential utility. What tools of leadership that characterized the strong-governor model have been lost or weakened, and which ones remain available for other governors to use?

We know that the legislature is a very different institution from what it was during the Combs and Breathitt administrations. This is most obvious in the performance of the committee system, with better use of the interim and higher quality staffing, and and of the budgetary and oversight processes. Sharply reduced turnover has led to more experienced members. These developments are not going to be reversed. The legislature will never again be forced to rely so heavily on the governor and the executive branch for advice, information, and leadership.

It is most unlikely that future governors will be able to select the legislative leaders. A skillful governor might be able to influence a few votes in a close struggle for a leadership post, but there is no reason to expect the legislature to abandon its prerogative to choose its own leaders. Consequently, governors are no longer able to control the selection of committee chairmen or LRC staff. When the governor negotiates with legislators, he or she no longer can—with any certainty—offer to get a member's bill passed or threaten to block it. It is now unrealistic for any governor to expect the executive budget to be passed without detailed hearings and some modification. It would be surprising if we found another governor becoming directly involved in legislative primaries.

If the Kentucky governor today no longer has the potential to dominate the General Assembly, he or she still has most of the political resources that are available to governors in other states. Governors across the country face legislatures that are better informed, more experienced, and more independent than they used to be. Governors in many other states are more likely to face legislatures that are controlled by the opposition party. In short, the governorship in Kentucky resembles that found in other states—except for a prohibition on consecutive terms. American state governors who are skilled in the use of political techniques can have a powerful impact on legislative decision making.

We turn to an examination of the political resources that remain available to Kentucky governors and an assessment of their use in recent years. The governor remains the head of the Democratic party, with the de facto authority to select the party chairman and set priorities for the party organization. Although John Y. Brown, Jr., selected the several chairmen who served during his term, he took very little interest in the activities of the state Democratic party organization. Martha Layne Collins, on the other hand, maintained much closer contact with the party chairman and took more interest in party activities.

If a governor chooses to be an active head of the party, what leverage does he or she gain in dealing with members of the General Assembly? It is rare today for the governor of any state to intervene in legislative primaries. It is generally assumed that probable risks outweigh the possible benefits, the most obvious risk being that legislators whom the governor has opposed will be reelected and become staunch opponents. Unless the Democratic legislative party were once again divided into factions, it would seem unlikely that a Kentucky governor would make any serious effort to influence legislative primaries.

It would be possible, however, for the governor to use the party organization to help elect legislators in the general election, and the governor could be selective in deciding which legislators to assist. It must be realized that most Democratic legislators do not need much help because most come from safe districts. In chapter 2 we described the effort made by the state Democratic party in 1986 to aid Democratic incumbents and new candidates with fund raising, polling, precinct targeting, and other forms of assistance. The technique was not, however, used to reward or punish incumbents; all legislators who had any significant opposition in the fall election were offered assistance.

As head of the party, the governor controls patronage. We have noted that most state jobs are under the merit system, but—in addition to top policymaking jobs—that there are many appointments to boards and commissions that the governor can make with a free hand. There are also many deserving Democrats, and particularly financial contributors to the campaign, who are eager to serve in such positions. In recent years there has been little evidence that the relatives of legislators are getting appointed to many of these desirable positions. On the other hand, it is inevitable that some persons seeking appointments will seek help from their legislators. A governor who chooses to give priority to such requests gains bargaining chips that may be useful in the next legislative session. Governor Brown campaigned against the patronage system and tended to ignore political considerations in making appointments. Governor Collins took a more traditional attitude toward the patronage system, but there is no reason to believe that she gave particularly high priority to requests from legislators.

A Democratic governor in Kentucky leads a party that normally controls at least three-fourths of the legislative seats; this is one asset of gubernatorial leadership that has not diminished in importance. It is true that the size of the margin and the diversity of constituency interests weaken Democratic party discipline. But the Republican legislative party is too small to pose a serious challenge to the governor. When the governor takes a strong stand on an issue, the responsibility of challenging the position rests with the opposition, but it is difficult for minority leadership to mount a plausible challenge when the Republicans are so badly outnumbered.

For the same reason, the governor can often win some Republicans when they are needed on controversial issues. Republican legislators still need projects for their districts, and the norms of partisanship in Kentucky do not prohibit Republicans from making such trades, even if they are less frequent than in the days of Governor Chandler.

The governor retains complete control over the executive budget and may choose to include projects that are sought by legislators. In recent years, with funds in short supply, governors have had to be more conservative about allocating resources for such projects, but the power is still important. Legislators, particularly those on the Appropriations and Revenue committees, now have the alternative of seeking to get projects added while the budget is in committee, but any project has a better chance of surviving if it is in the executive budget.

In the closing days of the 1980 session, the House of Representatives was considering Governor Brown's proposal to raise revenue as gasoline price rose by changing the gasoline tax from nine cents a gallon to 9 percent of the wholesale price. After two hours of debate, the roll call machine was opened for voting—and stayed open for an hour while members "explained" their vote. One by one, the leaders called legislators off the floor and into the Speaker's office to speak in person with Secretary of Transportation Frank Metts and on the phone to the governor. The legislators bargained with the administration for specific projects in their districts, and the bill was passed 52-48. The administration was cautious in making its commitments and refused, for example, to make commitments on completion of the Jefferson Freeway to a bloc of legislators from southwest Jefferson County—thereby losing their votes.

In the 1985 special session, the House defeated a proposed increase in the gasoline tax advocated by both Governor Collins and Speaker Blandford. In the 1986 session Blandford was determined to pass the tax increase. When he turned to the administration for support, the governor took no public stand but authorized Secretary of Transportation Leslie Dawson to negotiate with legislators. Dawson spent several days in the Speaker's office negotiating with both Democratic and Republican legislators and made commitments to legislators of both parties about the highway project that they could expect. The five-cent tax increase passed 60-36 in the House and 25-13 in the Senate.

Bills affecting the gasoline tax are particularly appropriate vehicles for negotiations and specific promises. Tax increases are unpopular, and legislators can legitimately argue that they must be able to explain to constituents what specific improvements they are getting for their money. The administration, in turn, can make promises because the money must be spent somewhere and there are always more legitimate highway projects being studied than can be immediately funded—and someone must set priorities.

During the 1960s and 1970s Kentucky built a statewide system of community colleges, numbering fourteen. Several were built in the hometowns or immediate areas of new governors. By the 1980s both the need for new community colleges and the available resources had diminished, but in Owensboro (the third largest city in the state) there was a strong demand for a community college. In 1985 the new Speaker of the House, Don Blandford, was from Owensboro. Governor Collins needed his support for her ambitious program of tax increases for education. The governor decided that Owensboro needed a community college and made a commitment to include it in the 1986 budget. The Speaker provided full support for the education and tax packages in the 1986 budget. There were those who saw this as symbolic of the changing power relationships between the governor and the legislature; the hometown of the Speaker was now as important as the hometown of the governor in determining high-cost spending priorities.

Through control over appointments and the budget, the governor is in a position to coordinate the legislative efforts of executive agencies. The governor may choose to let agencies initiate and support legislation on their own, providing a personal endorsement only if it becomes necessary. But the governor cannot afford to have agencies lobbying for legislation that is contradictory to his or her program or that will distract attention from that program; nor can the governor tolerate agency support for bills with price tags that exceed the financial commitments in the executive budget. When an executive official testifies on legislation before a legislative committee, there must be no misunderstanding about whether the individual is speaking for the governor or simply for the agency.

The difficulties that arise when a governor fails to maintain control over executive agencies were illustrated during Martha Layne Collins's first legislative session. She did not come into office with a legislative program, but was preoccupied with developing a tax and education package. Individual agencies promoted their own bills in the legislature, and she neither endorsed these nor made any effort to discourage these efforts until late in the session. Although she studiously avoided taking any stand on the multicounty banking bill (which became law without her signature), some of her top officials were working behind the scenes for its passage. The transportation cabinet prepared a bill to gut the state's auto title law, enacted in 1982, and the deputy transportation secretary successfully urged a House committee to report the bill, before the governor stepped into the situation and made clear her opposition. This kind of confusion and contradiction weakened the credibility and effectiveness of the Collins administration in dealing with the legislature during its first session. By the second session, the administration appeared to be better organized and more experienced, and the governor more often reviewed bills proposed by agencies. But the governor continued to take the position that in most cases agencies were on their own in trying to get legislation enacted.

Recent governors have not followed Julian Carroll's example of presenting legislative leaders with lengthy bills they approve and oppose. Such lists would be pointless when the governor no longer controls the legislative machinery. But all governors have a budget to enact and have legislative programs, whether narrow or broad in scope, and they are likely to be opposed to some legislative proposals. To accomplish their objectives, governors are heavily dependent on the cooperation and advice of legislative leaders. Most Kentucky governors have held regular meetings with the top leadership during the session, but this has not been the practice of recent governors.

John Y. Brown, Jr., met intermittently with his leaders. During her first session, Martha Layne Collins held weekly meetings with the leadership. She also had several meetings with members of the House Education Committee leading up to the 1985 special session. But during the entire second session, she held only three or four meetings with leadership, and in some cases weeks went by in which the leadership had no direct contact with the governor. At the end of the 1986 session, when Governor Collins vetoed a bill to require that all administrative regulations be written into law, she did not ask the leadership in either house to make an effort to sustain the veto; consequently, it was overridden by the narrowest of margins in each house. One leader told us, "The governor is intimidated by confrontation and will go to any length to avoid having to debate and discuss issues, even in private."

Democratic governors in the past have attended Democratic caucuses to make personal pleas for support of their most important bills. During the 1984 session, Governor Collins met with the Democratic caucus to urge support for her education and taxation package, but the caucus eventually turned her down. In the 1986 session she made no appearances before the caucus, the first recent session in which a governor had failed to do so.

Kentucky legislators have been accustomed to "hands-on" governors who would be accessible, would ask their support for legislation, and would help them get bills passed. Obviously, when the governor no longer controls the legislative machinery, he or she has less to bargain with in such meetings. But neither Governor Brown nor Governor Collins showed much interest in frequent interaction with rank-and-file legislators. Governor Brown was preoccupied with other matters and was out of the state at times during legislative session. He tended to work through the leadership rather than showing any interest in bargaining with individual legislators. Martha Layne Collins brought to the governorship more familiarity with state government and politics than did Brown, but she had little inclination to bargain with individual members. It was rare indeed for members to receive a summons to the first floor.

Perhaps the most important power available to a governor in Kentucky, or any state, is the power to focus public attention on an issue. If a governor emphasizes an issue during the election, he or she can claim a mandate from voters to act on that issue, whether or not there is any evidence that the voters were endorsing the governor's position. In a state of the Commonwealth address to the legislature, and subsequently in the budget message, the governor has an opportunity, and an obligation, to set an agenda and establish priorities for legislative action. The governor can propose an extensive legislative program or concentrate attention on a few priority issues. The legislature can expand the agenda and it can modify or reject the governor's proposals, but it rarely ignores them.

The governor's message is delivered not only to the legislature but to the public at large. The governor can call press conferences, which are often covered on the front page and at the top of the evening television news. The governor receives more invitations from across the state to speak to groups than can possibly be accepted. The governor can use these occasions to sell a program of educational reform, better roads, or a new program of health care. The governor can generate editorial support for these programs. He or she can mobilize citizens' committees and study groups to give greater public attention to the issues. The goal of these activities, of course, is to persuade legislators that the governor's proposals have enough public support so that they should vote for them. This strategy of building public support is time consuming and often difficult, but it is very nearly indispensable when the governor is trying to passage legislation that is controversial or that will require tax increases.

Every governor sets priorities, makes proposals to the legislature, and seeks public support for his or her program. Governors differ in the skill and persistence with which they focus attention on issues and generate public support for them.

In her 1983 campaign for governor, Martha Layne Collins did not propose any major breakthrough in financial support for education, and she assured voters that her programs could be implemented without tax increases. In her State of the Commonwealth address to the legislature early in January 1984, she proposed a number of relatively inexpensive educational reforms and warned legislators, "No windfall of money will be available to solve our problems in education. For now we must find ways of improving our schools that don't take lots of money." Ten days later, confronted with more pessimistic revenue projections, she changed her mind and decided that a substantial tax was necessary to continue existing programs and to finance a more ambitious, expensive educational program. On January 26 she proposed tax increases that would produce over $300 million in new revenue, with more than two-thirds of the new funds going to educational improvements. Two months later the program was a shambles; the House Democratic caucus had rejected the tax increase program (changed several times by the governor over a period of several weeks), and the Appropriations and Revenue committees were writing a budget that included few of the educational reforms.

At the time, critics compared Governor Collins's failure with the success of governors in Arkansas, Mississippi, and Tennessee who had won approval for large-scale, expensive educational reforms. But every one of these governors had carried out prolonged speaking and media campaigns, some extending for more than a year, on behalf of their programs. Collins had no time to mobilize public support and no experience in doing so. She was unable to enlist the support of groups such as labor unions, the chamber of commerce, and the Kentucky Education Association for her program. She spoke to a few forums around the state organized by parent-teacher associations, where she was largely preaching to the converted. She resisted proposals from her staff to undertake a more extensive speaking program, and she lacked the time for a statewide tour on behalf of education. In mid-March her office sent out letters to state newspapers and public service announcements to radio stations, and she gave a speech on the state educational television network to defend her program. But it was too little and too late.

In the summer of 1985, she called a special session in which her educational package and a revised tax package passed the legislature by comfortable margins. In earlier chapters we have explained some of the reasons for the turnaround, particularly the work of the House Education Committee, which reshaped her package, partly to make it acceptable to the Kentucky Education Association. But in the sixteen months between the initial defeat and the eventual success of an education-and-tax program, major efforts were undertaken to explain the state's educational needs to the public. The governor played a significant role in that campaign, speaking frequently around the state about the need for educational reform and the vital link between higher educational standards and economic development in Kentucky. But she had a great deal of assistance. The Prichard Committee, a citizens' group founded by the legendary Edward Prichard, carried on an extensive campaign, featuring citizens' forums throughout the state. The Chamber of Commerce, other business groups, the Ashland Oil Company, and labor unions endorsed educational reform and explained it to various segments of the public. The Kentucky Education Association threw its weight behind the revised program. Major newspapers ran a number of stories on educational problems, documenting the shortcomings in Kentucky and describing the progress being made in other southern states. A continuing theme of much of the publicity was the success that other southern states were having in attracting new businesses and industries to the state. The governor helped focus public attention on the issue and called the special session, but in large measure she was responding to the pressure from organized groups, the media, and the public.

The decline in the governor's dominant role in the legislative process is the most dramatic recent change in Kentucky's political system. The immediate cause was the change in leadership style adopted by Governor Brown and followed by Governor Collins. But it is important to understand that the balance of power would not have shifted if the legislature had not been gradually developing its capacity and asserting its independence over more than a decade.

It is also important to recognize that there are many techniques and resources still available to a governor who wants to play an active role in the legislative process and who understands those tools and that process. In the years ahead, each governor will bring to the job a unique combination of experience, skills, and goals that will largely determine his or her success in legislative leadership. Kentucky appears closer than ever before to achieving a balance between a strong governor and a strong legislature—the pattern that is increasingly common in other states.

10. The Legislature as a Broker of Interests

Kentucky, more than most states, is often described in terms of stereotypes: the Bluegrass State, famous for bourbon, fast horses, burley tobacco, and coal mining. In the late nineteenth and early twentieth centuries, the Louisville and Nashville Railroad appeared to be the strongest single interest in the state. During the first quarter of this century, Kentucky politics was dominated by a "Bipartisan Combine," an alliance of political leaders with the major racetrack, liquor, and coal-mining interests in the state; the Jockey Club was reported to be more directly involved in financing political campaigns. During the New Deal period, labor unions, particularly the United Mine Workers in the coal fields, challenged the dominant business interests in the states and were prominently involved in several statewide races.

But Kentucky, like most southern and border states, is becoming more diverse and outgrowing the stereotypes of the past, with a wider range of interests and a much larger number of interest groups represented in Frankfort. The interests that assume the greatest importance in Kentucky are those that are broadest in scope and affect the largest number of bills and the most important portions of the state budget. In recent years when legislators have been asked to name the most powerful or more influential interest groups, they have most often named the major agricultural, labor, educational, and business groups—the same ones that are likely to assume importance in most states.

Kentucky is changing in a number of ways that affect the influence of interest groups in the state. There has been a gradual shift of population to metropolitan areas (despite a back-to-the-country movement in the 1970s). Although coal production doubled between 1960 and 1980, there has been a decline in the number of persons employed in coal mines, and in recent years there has been a slump in coal income. The major industrial center of Louisville has lost some of its employment in heavy industry (such as automobiles and appliances), but Lexington and surrounding communities continue to grow—most notably with the recent acquisition of the Toyota plant in Scott County, just outside Lexington.

The recent changes in gubernatorial-legislative relations—the shift in the balance of power between the governor and the legislature—have had major, far-reaching implications for interest groups. In the past lobbyists devoted much of their time to trying to persuade the administration to support or oppose bills. This meant contacting the governor if possible, as well as his aides and the heads of agencies. Only if the governor was unwilling to take a stand, or asked for help in getting a bill passed, was it necessary to devote time and effort to legislative lobbying.

Legislative reform has led to changes in the tactics of legislative lobbying. Over the last twenty years there has been a steady increase in the frequency and length of committee hearings, making it possible and necessary for all groups to present testimony at such hearings. The growth of legislative independence and power has made the job of the lobbyist more complicated. More decision makers must be contacted over a longer period of time. These changes have also made the decision-making process more open, enabling a wider variety of groups to participate in the process. These changes in the legislative system, together with the growing complexity and variety of issues considered by the legislature, have contributed to the growing numbers of interest groups represented by lobbyists in Frankfort.

THE ROLE OF INTEREST GROUPS IN ELECTIONS

Interest groups may participate electorally in several ways, such as endorsing candidates or mobilizing their members to vote in particular ways. The most obvious, and most easily measured, method of participating in elections is through political action committees, commonly called PACs. We are interested in the level of PAC contributions in both Democratic primaries and general election campaigns; Republican primaries are seldom competitive. Because both governors and legislators play roles in the legislative process, we will examine PAC contributions to candidates for both offices.

Beginning with the 1968 election, the Kentucky Registry of Election Finance has served as a repository of campaign reports for all state and local offices. Contributions of individuals and groups of more than one hundred dollars must be recorded by campaign treasurers and submitted to the registry. Before 1968 there were artificially set limits on contributions and haphazard, minimal reporting; thus, there was a dearth of comprehensive and accurate campaign finance data. During the period covered by this study, the maximum contribution an individual could make to a candidate in one

Table 26. Interest Groups and Their Contributions to House Legislative Candidates

	Primary Election				General Election			
	1975 ($)	1979 ($)	1981 ($)	1984 ($)	1975 ($)	1979 ($)	1981 ($)	1984 ($)
Education	550	23,100	32,156	34,730	2,150	8,405	16,400	73,107
Labor	12,820	5,216	18,000	36,287	3,575	8,323	14,025	33,917
Public employees	—	—	375	905	—	—	150	1,200
Professionals	200	450	900	200	—	150	5,450	2,750
Health and medical	1,350	4,550	26,650	23,950	4,000	13,300	25,470	38,550
Insurance	—	900	1,400	750	—	200	1,550	3,075
Real estate	—	—	11,700	4,200	—	6,300	13,900	18,600
Construction	500	—	1,700	7,750	2,300	1,400	3,600	4,100
Banking and finance	400	12,900	15,720	23,455	200	5,000	18,400	23,670
Business and industry	2,300	9,400	14,650	14,400	1,000	9,200	23,598	14,800
Horse industry	—	2,400	25,800	17,500	—	8,000	17,000	29,700
Transport	1,200	—	1,850	2,500	200	500	1,325	5,150
Utilities	—	1,950	1,080	1,450	—	150	550	9,500
Oil and gas	—	—	900	800	—	—	600	200
Coal	—	—	—	4,700	—	—	—	2,150
Liquor	—	—	875	—	—	—	200	150
Special issues	—	350	1,400	800	—	600	1,900	6,350
Total Group Contributions ($)	19,320	61,216	155,156	174,378	13,425	61,528	144,118	266,969
Total Contributions to House Candidates ($)	300,406	449,426	674,351	944,670	149,356	261,184	431,967	749,037
House Contributions from Groups (%)	6.4	13.6	23.0	17.5	9.0	23.6	33.4	35.6

state or local election was three thousand dollars, and there was no cap on PAC contributions.

Legislative Races. In this section we analyze trends in PAC contributions to legislative races over several elections (1975, 1979, and 1981 Senate and House; 1983 Senate; and 1984 House). Several broad questions concerning PAC contributions need to be addressed: What kinds of PACs contribute the most funding to legislative races? Most importantly, have some groups substantially increased their funding to legislative races since the balance of power has been shifting from the governor to the legislature? What choices do PACs make in putting resources into the primary and/or general election? Do PACS follow the strategy of concentrating their funds on one candidate or hedge their bets by spreading contributions among several candidates? Do PACs follow the general strategy of supporting the favored winner (usually the incumbent), or do they try to change the outcome of a race?

We show in tables 26 and 27, by type of interest group, how much the PACs spent in legislative races over the period 1975-84. Seventeen interests were identified, and money given by PACs within each group was aggregated. Most of the categories in the tables are self-explanatory; the special issues include such things as right-to-life and gun regulation. The business and industry category is a residual one, excluding such specific groups as coal and insurance. Although these categories do not include all potentially significant groups, they were chosen because of their recognized political and economic power in Kentucky, the frequency and total sums of their giving, and—in most cases—their unity on issues affecting them.

Tables 26 and 27 show that the cost of legislative campaigns for all the House seats and one-half of the Senate seats quadrupled between 1975 and 1983-84, with total campaign receipts increasing from $722,195 to $2,613,000. During the same period the amount of funds received from PACs grew more dramatically, from about $40,000 to nearly $700,000, with the proportion of money contributed by PACs increasing from 5.6 percent to 26.4 percent. In 1983-84 PACs contributed 20.3 percent of the total receipts of legislative primaries and 37.2 percent of those for general elections. The rapid increase in the rate of PAC contributions to legislative campaigns reflects the growing power of the legislature vis-a-vis the governor, a trend that a number of the interest groups have clearly recognized.

Overall, the leading PAC contributors to House and Senate electoral campaigns have been education, health and medical, labor, horse industry, banking and finance, business and industry, and real estate interests. The education lobby, through its statewide and county Kentucky Education Political Action Committees (KEPACs), has been in the forefront for targeting funds to legislative candidates. For example, in the 1983 Senate primary, KEPACs donated more than $31,000 to legislative campaigns. Two-thirds

Table 27. Interest Groups and Their Contributions to Senate Legislative Candidates

	Primary Election				General Election			
	1975 ($)	1979 ($)	1981 ($)	1983 ($)	1975 ($)	1979 ($)	1981 ($)	1983 ($)
Education	—	6,850	28,368	31,320	200	5,900	14,350	17,657
Labor	1,550	2,450	1,600	9,234	—	2,975	2,000	16,915
Public employees	—	—	—	—	—	—	—	1,000
Professionals	—	—	—	3,650	—	—	1,050	1,750
Health and medical	1,650	5,400	31,000	31,150	1,800	13,350	10,950	26,576
Insurance	—	1,200	—	1,400	—	600	1,000	200
Real estate	—	2,000	5,500	10,000	—	4,475	6,500	4,000
Construction	200	1,050	250	250	450	500	1,050	3,200
Banking and finance	600	4,700	14,700	20,250	1,200	3,050	9,520	4,350
Business and industry	—	6,400	10,800	8,150	200	9,700	12,750	5,650
Horse industry	—	600	6,100	12,500	—	1,900	4,950	12,600
Transportation	—	—	1,400	2,800	—	400	650	—
Utilities	—	950	2,900	5,850	—	950	1,950	3,600
Oil and gas	—	400	400	700	—	—	—	—
Coal	—	—	3,200	3,200	—	—	3,500	1,000
Liquor	—	—	1,000	1,600	—	—	200	1,450
Special issues	—	—	2,100	—	—	—	1,800	6,750
Total Group Contributions	4,000	32,000	109,318	142,054	3,850	43,800	72,220	106,704
Total Contributions to Senate Candidates	220,869	434,576	434,719	613,287	51,564	181,610	193,391	255,782
Senate Contributions from Groups (%)	1.8	7.4	25.1	23.2	7.5	24.1	37.3	41.7

of the figure went to three Democratic candidates—challenger Bob Chambliss in the fifth district, incumbent Benny Ray Bailey in the twenty-ninth, and incumbent John Doug Hays in the thirty-first. Bailey was the only one of these candidates who prevailed in the primary. In the 1983 general election campaign, KEPACs donated more than $17,000, of which Democrats received better than 90 percent. Moreover, in the 1984 House primary and general elections, KEPACs contributed more than $34,000 and $73,000 respectively; education funds went to legislative leaders, key education committee members, and other targeted friends of education (incumbents and challengers).

Health and medical PACs put their funding primarily in legislative races rather than statewide races. The health industry consists of a diversity of practitioners and interests, including physicians, dentists, pharmacists, optometrists, chiropractors, nurses, hospitals, and nursing homes. At times, these different groups are on opposing sides on particular legislative issues. There have been bitter legislative battles concerning licensing and regulating health professionals (e.g., optometrists versus ophthalmologists). Also, with the decreasing government funding for health care (e.g., Medicaid and Medicare), these groups must compete for their share of the pie (e.g., nursing homes versus hospitals). Because of growing conflicts within the health industry, and particularly the increased competition for shrinking governmental funds, health and medical PACs have dramatically increased their funding to Senate and House legislative leaders, members of key committees (e.g., Health and Welfare, Appropriations and Revenue, Banking and Insurance), and other incumbent friends of the health profession.

Labor has also increased substantially its funding of legislative races, with most of its funds going to Democratic candidates in targeted House and Senate races. In 1975 labor PACs contributed fewer than $18,000 to all legislative races; by 1983-84 this figure had increased to almost $97,000. Besides increased funding to legislative leaders, key committee members, and incumbents, labor unions have begun to formally endorse more candidates; also, labor's members play active volunteer roles in legislative candidates' campaigns.

One of the most dramatic changes among interest group contributors is found among horse industry PACs. In the past horsemen and race tracks traditionally relied on governors to take care of their needs, and campaign contributions to gubernatorial races were made primarily by individuals rather than by PACs. The Kentucky Horsemen's Benevolent Protective Association (trainers, small owners, an so on) took the lead in beginning to donate PAC resources to legislative races. Recently, the Kentucky Thoroughbred Association (including breeders and large owners) has begun to target some PAC funds to House and Senate races. Unlike the health and medical industry, where there are eight or ten groups who make significant

Table 28. Comparison of Total Group Contributions in Primary and General Elections

	Senate, 1983 ($)	House, 1984 ($)	Gubernatorial (D), 1983	Gubernatorial (R), 1983
Primary Election				
Total group contributions	142,054	174,378	356,705	
Total receipts in races	613,287	944,670	4,408,910	
Total funds received from groups (%)	23.2	17.5	8.1	
General Election				
Total group contributions	106,704	266,969	147,900	29,961
Total receipts in races	255,782	749,037	1,770,551	1,221,617
Total funds received from groups (%)	41.7	35.6	8.4	2.5

PAC contributions, the horse industry is represented by two or three powerful groups, and these groups contributed a total of $72,300 to legislative candidates in 1983-84; in contrast, these horse interest groups contributed nothing to legislative candidates in 1975.

Banking and finance PACs have also increased substantially their contributions to legislative candidates. Most of the state's large banks have formed PACs that try to affect legislative electoral outcomes. The more independent legislature plays a crucial role in formulating state regulatory and licensing banking policies (e.g., the multibank legislation). Total spending by bank PACs for legislative races increased dramatically from $2,400 in 1975 to almost $72,000 in 1983-84.

Comparing Legislative and Gubernatorial Contributions. For summary purposes it would be interesting to compare group contributions to legislative and gubernatorial candidates in the 1983-84 electoral period (see table 28). In the primaries PACs contributed slightly more money to the gubernatorial races, but their funds constituted 20.3 percent of the total receipts of legislative candidates compared to 8.1 percent of those for Democratic gubernatorial candidates. In the 1983-84 general elections, PACs contributed twice as much money to legislative races as to gubernatorial candidates; this constituted 37.2 percent of the total receipts of legislative campaigns compared to only 5.9 percent of those for the gubernatorial candidates—8.4 percent for the Democrat and 2.5 percent for the Republican.

There were some noteworthy differences among the groups in priorities between legislative and gubernatorial primary campaigns. The leading PAC contributors to the House and Senate electoral campaigns were education, health and medical, labor, horse industry, banking and finance, and business and industry groups; whereas the major PAC contributors in the 1983 Democratic gubernatorial primary were labor, education, and business and industry. Certain PACs earmarked their limited funds largely to legislative candidates—notably health and medical groups, the horse industry, and banking and finance. Labor PACs were the only large contributors giving much more to gubernatorial than to legislative candidates. The groups making substantial and relatively equal contributions to both types of races included education and business and industry.

Targeting Funds to Legislative Candidates. In recent years some attention in the literature has been focused on interest groups' financing of legislative campaigns. These studies suggest that success in an election is correlated with spending, that special interests frequently concentrate their contributions on members of committees that handle legislation of concern to them, and that there may be a correlation between receiving such contributions from a specific interest and voting on legislation related to that interest (Jacobson, 1980; Welch, 1980; Patterson, 1982; Drew, 1983; Jones and Borris, 1985). ·

We have examined contributions for the 1979-84 period to members of four standing committees that seem particularly likely to be targeted by PACs because of the issues under their jurisdiction: Labor and Industry, Education, Business Organizations and Professions, and Banking and Insurance. We find that only a few specialized PACs target funds to chairmen and key members of these committees. For example, although in 1981 the House Chairman of the seventeen-member Labor and Industry Committee received more labor PAC funds than any other committee member, only three other committee members received any labor PAC contributions; in contrast, more than twenty noncommittee candidates received primary and general election labor funding. It is apparent that education PACs do target their limited resources to chairmen and other members of the House and Senate Education committees. In 1981 seven of nine members of the Senate Education Committee ran for reelection. Of the six who had primary and/ or general election opposition, state and/or county KEPACS made sizable primary ($10,650) and general election contributions ($11,250) to five members and to the opponent in the other contested race. In assessing business and professional PAC contributions to the 1983 campaigns of members of the Senate Business Organizations and Professions Committee, we find that every member who ran did receive primary and/or general election funds from such groups as the Optometric PAC, Kentucky Ophthalmological PAC, and the Louisville Area Business PAC. Moreover, of the seventeen members of the House Banking and Insurance Committee, more than 50 percent received 1981 primary and/or general election contributions from various banking and insurance PACs (e.g., Credithrift of America, Kentucky Bankers Committee for State Government).

It is particularly interesting to examine how groups make their decisions about investing in campaigns. Obviously, interest groups want to maximize their influence in the legislature. One method is supporting the candidates most likely to win—usually incumbents—in order to maximize the number of legislators who feel indebted to the interest group. The second method is attempting to increase the proportion of sympathetic legislators by seeking to affect the outcome of elections. This means giving financial assistance to those incumbents, challengers, and candidates for open seats who face close competition in primaries or general elections. Obviously, an interest group may use both tactics, but we would expect to find some variation among the groups in their choice of tactics. Although we do not have direct evidence about the tactical decisions of groups, we assume that those groups contributing almost entirely to incumbents are following the first tactic, whereas those who spread their contributions among challengers and open-seat candidates also are making some use of the second tactic.

PACs are more likely than political parties or individuals to give disproportionately to incumbents; this has been shown at the congressional level (Jacobson, 1980; Jacobson and Kernell, 1981), but there is very little data at the state level. Jones and Borris (1985), using data on Minnesota legislative races, examined the relationship between the sources of campaign contributions and state legislative candidates' incumbency status, party, and need for funds. Five sources of funds are distinguished: PACs, parties, individual large contributors, small contributors, and public funding. Their findings indicate that political parties and PACs differ from each other in their patterns of giving when the competitiveness of the state legislative race is taken into account. Parties, not PACs, appear to be the most strategic givers; political parties are more likely than PACs to pay attention to the competitiveness of races. In both years (1976 and 1980) for both houses, PAC funds went disproportionately to incumbents, Democrats, and winners, indicating a rather primitive strategy of giving. Only when PACs gave to their "less targets"—challengers, minority party candidates (Republicans), and ultimate losers—did electoral competition appear to have been related to the level of their contributions. PACs gave the most money where it would provide the least leverage over candidates—to candidates who were in relatively safe districts and to candidates who had been so successful in obtaining funding from a variety of sources that they probably would not have to feel indebted to any one source of funding (1985: 97).

Table 29 presents a breakdown of contributions by major categories of interest groups to legislative candidates—incumbents, challengers, and those running for open seats—in the 1983-84 primary and general elections. The table shows that the Kentucky PACs, like national PACs and those in Minnesota, have contributed disproportionately to incumbents in both primaries and general election contests. Overall, in primary races PACs have given 83.4 percent to incumbents, 8.5 percent to challengers, and 8.1 percent to open-seat candidates; in general elections PACs have given 79.3 percent to incumbents, 5.0 percent to challengers, and 15.7 percent for open seats. The low proportion of funding for challengers in general elections reflects the fact that most seats are safely controlled by one party—usually the Democratic party except in the pockets of Republican strength around the state. The higher proportion of funding for open seats in general elections (15.7 percent) reflects the fact that many of the seats are relatively safe and PACs can predict the likely winner.

Although four-fifths of the PAC contributions go to incumbents, there is some variation among the interest groups in the distribution of campaign funds. We are primarily interested in those groups that provide a significant level of funding. There are several PACs that contribute almost entirely to incumbents. The most important of these is labor (95 percent); others are: transportation (94 percent), banking and finance (90 percent), business and

Table 29. Contributions by Interest Groups to Legislative Candidates, 1983-1984

	Primary Election			General Election		
	Incumbent ($)	Challenger ($)	Open Seat ($)	Incumbent ($)	Challenger ($)	Open Seat ($)
Education						
Senate	19,945	9,925	1,450	10,207	—	7,450
House	26,080	7,350	1,300	64,357	1,400	7,350
Labor						
Senate	9,234	—	—	16,415	—	500
House	34,437	750	1,100	31,317	—	2,600
Public employees						
Senate	—	—	—	1,000	—	—
House	905	—	—	1,200	—	—
Professionals						
Senate	2,800	350	500	1,000	—	750
House	200	—	—	2,000	—	750
Health and medical						
Senate	21,150	4,500	5,500	10,076	3,500	13,000
House	20,700	2,250	1,000	36,400	850	1,300
Insurance						
Senate	1,100	—	300	—	200	—
House	550	—	200	2,475	—	600
Real estate						
Senate	7,000	—	3,000	1,000	1,000	2,000
House	3,200	—	1,000	16,100	1,000	1,500
Construction						
Senate	250	—	—	400	—	1,300
House	7,750	—	—	4,100	—	—
Banking and finance						
Senate	17,250	500	2,500	1,950	600	1,800
House	22,850	200	400	22,520	950	200

Table 29. (Continued)

	Primary Election			General Election		
	Incumbent ($)	Challenger ($)	Open Seat ($)	Incumbent ($)	Challenger ($)	Open Seat ($)
Business and industry						
Senate	7,050	400	700	3,900	550	1,200
House	12,250	—	2,150	13,000	550	1,250
Horse industry						
Senate	10,500	500	1,500	6,000	200	6,400
House	16,700	—	800	24,750	2,050	2,900
Transportation						
Senate	2,650	—	150	—	—	—
House	2,300	—	200	4,900	250	—
Utilities						
Senate	4,250	300	1,300	2,400	300	900
House	1,300	—	150	8,400	900	200
Oil and gas						
Senate	700	—	—	—	—	—
House	800	—	—	200	—	—
Coal						
Senate	2,800	—	400	200	—	800
House	4,700	—	—	2,150	—	—
Liquor						
Senate	1,600	—	—	750	300	400
House	—	—	—	150	—	—
Special issues						
Senate	—	—	—	2,000	2,100	2,650
House	800	—	—	5,150	300	900
Totals	263,801	27,025	25,600	296,467	18,500	58,700

industry (84 percent). The groups making significant contributions but distributing them more broadly are special issues (57 percent to incumbents), health and medical (74 percent), real estate (74 percent), and education (77 percent).

Most groups that give some priority to nonincumbents are more likely to contribute to candidates for open seats than to challengers. Education PACs are the only significant groups giving more to challengers than to open-seat candidates. We see from table 29 that education PACs are more likely to support challengers in primaries and open-seat candidates in general election—presumably because challengers in general elections have little chance of winning. Health and medical groups are also less likely to support challengers in general elections than in primaries, and are particularly likely to donate to open seats in general elections. Almost all of the funds given by PACs to challengers in primaries come from education and health and medical PACs.

The interest groups representing education and labor have much in common. They represent large numbers of individuals, often take "liberal" stands on issues, have been actively involved in electoral politics longer than most groups, and frequently support the same candidates for legislative office. Given these similarities, it is interesting to find them differing in the tactics followed in distributing campaign funds. Labor unions, whose loyalists are generally outnumbered in legislature, follow a "status quo" tactic of supporting incumbents. Educators, who can usually count on a larger proportion of supporters in the legislature, are more willing to support candidates who are not incumbents.

Generally, we conclude that Kentucky PACs usually support incumbent legislators and seldom support challengers. There are very good reasons for such tactics. Incumbents in Kentucky are seldom defeated, as we demonstrated in chapter 2. The domination of most districts by one party has always made it difficult to defeat incumbents in general elections. As incumbent legislators have gained greater visibility and seniority, they have also become less vulnerable to defeat in primary elections.

LOBBYING IN THE LEGISLATURE

Laws Regulating Lobbying. Kentucky's statutes regulating lobbying date back to 1916, and there have been no major revisions since then—a reflection of Kentucky's conservative traditionalistic political culture. According to the Lobbying Act of 1916, "Lobbyist means any person employed as legislative agent or legislative counsel to promote, oppose or act with reference to any legislation which affects or may affect private pecuniary interests as distinct from those of the whole people" (KRS 6.250). Therefore, certain individuals are exempted from the act; these include elected or appointed officials acting in an official capacity, private individuals who lobby about issues without pecuniary interests, and individuals who lobby for issues affecting the "public as a whole." KRS 6.280 to 6.290 require that all lobbyists must file with the attorney general; unlike some other states, there is no registration fee. KRS 6.300 specifies that each lobbyist must file with the attorney general within thirty days after the close of the session a statement of expenses incurred in promoting or opposing legislation. KRS 6.310 prohibits lobbyists' going on the floor of either house while in session, except upon the invitation of that house. KRS 6.320 prohibits any form of corrupt lobbying (e.g., by coercion, intimidation, or bribery).

Since 1916 some legislative sessions have promulgated certain rules for lobbying in order to ensure legislators a measure of protection from the frequent harassment of lobbyists. For example, lobbyists are no longer allowed in the labyrinth of legislators' carrels. Consequently, during a legislative session, many lobbyists just stand around the capitol or cluster inside and outside of hearing rooms in the Annex.

Tabulation of Interest Groups. According to the attorney general, in 1974 there were 215 registered lobbyists in Kentucky. By 1984 the number had more than doubled to 478. Concomitant with this increase in the number of lobbyists has been an increase in the number of registered interest groups, from 162 to 361. Because there have been no legislative changes in Kentucky's lobby law that would account for these increases, the dramatic growth in registered lobbyists and interest groups can be traced to the growing role of state government and growing complexity of society, as well as the increased level of competition for governmental resources as the revenue base comes under increasing pressure. Each piece of the budgetary pie becomes harder to acquire or to preserve.

A list of groups employing registered lobbyists is one indicator of the scope of interest group activity in Kentucky (see table 30). Our focus is on the increase in the number of interest groups represented rather than the number of lobbyists representing each type of interest group, because in Kentucky some interest groups employ many part-time lobbyists whereas others employ one or two full-time agents. Moreover, some full-time lobbyists represent more than one special interest. Therefore, the number of lobbyists employed by particular types of interests would not be an accurate accounting of the power and political clout of those groups.

As depicted in table 30, many types of interest groups have grown substantially in number during this ten-year period in which a more independent legislative body has emerged. The growth has been much less of public interest groups than it has been of specific economic interests. An abundance of trade associations, national corporations, specific individual companies,

Table 30. Interest Group Involvement in the Legislature

	Organizations Represented		
	1974 Only (N)	1974 and 1984 (N)	1984 Only (N)
Agriculture	—	2	3
Banking & finance	19	6	21
Businesses			
Broad purpose			
(Chamber of Commerce)	1	5	5
Single industries			
(Ky Restaurants Assn.)	8	9	16
Individual companies	6	—	54
National corporations	2	3	5
Labor	7	7	16
Professionals (nonhealth)	2	2	7
Education			
Adult groups (KEA)	4	5	4
Student organizations	3	—	3
Energy (coal, oil, etc.)	4	6	22
Utilities	1	6	13
Horse industry	1	—	12
Transportation	3	2	12
Real estate	3	3	4
Government			
Cities & counties	1	1	4
Local officials	1	2	16
Special issues	8	2	19
Nonprofit organizations	5	—	10
Insurance	3	4	13
Health			
Medical facilities	—	1	7
Professionals (AMA)	7	7	22
Total	89	73	288

and other groups have engaged lobbyists to pursue specialized goals of business. The ability of these diverse business groups to turn economic clout into political power has enlisted the time and skills of professional lobbyists and forged relationships with prominent law firms and banking institutions. Medical/health groups and hospital associations have significantly grown in number and political power; health professionals (e.g., doctors, dentists, nurses, optometrists, chiropractors) all compete in the legislature for scarce health-care government funds. Labor groups have increased in number by more than 100 percent; labor's strength has been enhanced by its convergence of interest and activity with education, public employees, farm, and minority groups. Substantial legislative presence also been achieved by groups representing various facets of the horse industry (e.g., horse racing, breeding) and of the energy-related (e.g., coal, oil) and utilities industries. Special issue groups have also demonstrated considerable growth.

The most important interest groups in Frankfort that are not registered are the various agencies of state government. The departments of commerce, human resources, education, and natural resources are among the most active in lobbying the legislature. These agencies are influential in part because of their ability to mobilize skillfully their constituencies and client groups. Moreover, the agencies are respected because they provide the legislators with detailed information and expert judgment on legislation. The University of Kentucky, University of Louisville, and six regional universities are also powerful, partly because of their ability to mobilize faculty and alumni. Legislators are likely to be particularly responsive to concerns of universities in their area and/or the ones they attended. Local governments and organizations of local officials (like sheriffs and county clerks) often have considerable influence over the narrow issues of particular concern to them (though lobbyists for some of these groups are often registered).

Overall, there has emerged a growing pluralism of special interests. That growth shows no signs of abating; nor should a different pattern be expected. Continued slow growth of tax receipts, along with new demands on government, can be anticipated. Old turfs will require more active protection, and new actors will appear at the legislature's door.

Assessing the Power of Interest Groups. What are the most powerful interest groups in Kentucky, the ones best able to gain their objectives, to pass the bills they favor and defeat those they oppose? There is no simple, precise answer to that question.

Perhaps the best way of estimating the strength of interest groups is to ask the legislators, who must deal with them on a continuing basis. Jack Bizzel (1984) who conducted surveys of Kentucky legislators after the 1980, 1982, and 1984 sessions, in each case asked them to list the most powerful or influential interest groups in each session. He then ranked the ten most frequently listed groups in each session. If we combine these rankings for three sessions, we get the list in table 31 of those ranked in more than one session (with top ranking for each year getting a score of ten). Other groups appearing on the top ten list in just one session were Right to Life, United Mine Workers, and Kentucky Municipal League in 1980; Kentucky Coal Association and Kentucky Association of Counties in 1982; Insurance Agents of Kentucky and the Horsemen's Benevolent and Protective Association in 1984.

In order to evaluate interest groups in Kentucky, we will divide them

Table 31. Most Influential Interest Groups as Ranked by Legislators in
          1980, 1982, and 1984 Sessions

	Total Points	No. of Sessions Listed
Ky. Farm Bureau	30	3
Ky. AFL-CIO	24	3
Ky. Education Association	24	3
Ky. Chamber of Commerce	18	3
Ky. Bankers Association	16	3
Ky. Medical Association	11	3
Ky. Utilities Co.	9	2
Ky. Retail Federation	4	2

Source: Jack E. Bizzel, "Interest Groups as Perceived by Kentucky State Legislators" (unpublished paper, 1984).

into several major categories rather than trying to compare groups that differ
greatly in their size and the scope of their agenda. First are the groups that
represent large numbers of persons or businesses and usually take stands
on a wide range of issues, such as the Farm Bureau, the AFL-CIO, and the
chamber of commerce. These groups are ranked first, second, and fourth
by the legislators. It is noteworthy that although the Farm Bureau has been
consistently ranked first, some legislators believe it is now declining in influence. Each of these groups is strong enough that it can often prevent
passage of legislation that it perceives to serious damage its interests. Moreover, when major bills affect the interests of several of these groups, some
kind of compromise is usually necessary to gain passage of legislation.

A second category of groups that we might expect to be important represents particular economic interests especially important in Kentucky, such
as the tobacco, liquor, coal, and horse industries. For several reasons, none
of these groups is quite as influential in Kentucky as we might expect. Most
legislative issues involving tobacco are settled at the national rather than the
state level. The influence of the liquor industry in Kentucky is balanced by
the strong prohibitionist sentiment found in the rural, Bible Belt counties;
and most of the legislative issues are of marginal importance, such as Sunday
liquor sales in larger cities. The coal industry is vitally important to Kentucky,
and the legislature frequently grapples with issues affecting coal—the severance tax, a possible tax on unmined minerals, weight limits for coal trucks,
regulation of strip mining, and compensation for black lung disease, for
example. The Kentucky Coal Association is the most important interest group
representing coal operators, but divisions and conflicting interests within
the industry have weakened its political effectiveness. The horse industry
is even more sharply divided, with different organizations representing the

breeders and larger owners on the one hand and smaller owners and trainers on the other, and with each of the race tracks having its own special interests.

A third category represents interests with major political and/or economic power, groups that are likely to have an interest in major pieces of legislation in every session of the legislature. The most powerful of these, according to legislators, is the Kentucky Education Association. It is powerful because teachers are a significant force in every county in the state, and because they are more politically organized and active than most groups. Another important group, the Kentucky Bankers Association (KBA), is influential because of the economic and political power of its member banks. Some of the most powerful interest groups in Kentucky are those in the health field, and their influence has grown as health issues have assumed higher priority on the legislative agenda.

A fourth category is composed of narrower, more specialized interests, or groups that become active in lobbying only intermittently, as specific issues arise in a particular session of the legislature. Examples might include the state dental association, optometrists, social workers, and chiropractors, as well as individual businesses.

A fifth category represents particular units of government, such as cities or counties, or universities. Recently, legislators have emphasized the relative effectiveness of lobbying efforts by political leadership from the major cities, though being less impressed by the effectiveness of the Kentucky Municipal League. In the area of higher education, each of the state universities tends to have a group of legislative supporters from its own geographic area.

Categories of Lobbyists. The Frankfort lobbying community consists of four categories of lobbyists: in-house, contract, government, and citizen. The largest category of registered lobbyists are *in-house company or association lobbyists*: persons who are employed by or are members of a company or organization and who engage in lobbying as part—often a major part—of their duties. This broad category of lobbyists represents three basic types of institutions: business firms or individual companies (e.g., First Security National Bank or Baker Petroleum), voluntary associations (e.g., Kentucky Education Association [KEA], Kentucky Farm Bureau, or the Kentucky Coal Association), and organizations of local governments or public officials (e.g., Kentucky Municipal League or the District Judges Association of Kentucky).

A few organizations like KEA are large enough that one or more persons on their payroll spend a great deal of time and specialize in legislative matters, year in and year out. But for many other companies and associations, this work is done by various individuals (e.g., company president, in-house lawyers, or public relations experts), and their lobbying efforts, primarily during the legislative session, represent only a small proportion of their overall designated activities. In the last few legislative sessions, there has been a significant growth in the number of individual companies that have registered in-house lobbyists; these businesses want a voice in policymaking that affects their specific interests. Some of Frankfort's most experienced and effective in-house or association lobbyists include the salaried executive directors of large organizations such as Representative Ron Cyrus of the Kentucky AFL-CIO, James Judy of the Kentucky Association of Health Care Facilities, former representative Edward Holloway of Associated Industries of Kentucky, and Nick Nicholson of the Kentucky Thoroughbred Association, as well as the in-house public relations-legislative specialists of companies, such as former legislator Michael Wooden of Humana, Jay Spurrier of Kentucky Utilities Company, and Sara Nicholson of the Kentucky Hospital Association.

Contract lobbyists are individuals who are hired by a client on a contract basis specifically to lobby. Of the 582 lobbyists registered with the attorney general in April 1984, fewer than ten contract lobbyists represented five or more clients. Three of Kentucky's most capable contract lobbyists (and the organizations they represented in 1984) include former high-ranking gubernatorial campaign and legislative staffer William Wester (Alliance of American Insurers, American Sun-Crude Company, Citizens Fidelity Bank and Trust, Kentucky Thoroughbred Owners and Breeders, and Bell South Mobility, Inc.), Ronald D. Adams (People's Security Finance, First City Bank, First Security Bank, Liberty National Bank, Owensboro National Bank, and Covington Trust Bank), and former long-term legislator and House Speaker Norbert Blume (Kentucky Academy of Eye Physicians and Surgeons, Louisville Water Company, Dedicated Alcohol Issues Committee, Committee for Counseling Legislation, Gardner Lose Company, Ashland Oil Company, and Hospital Corporation of America) (*Legislative Record*, April 16, 1984, 218-19.).

Government lobbyists are not officially lobbyists. State and local government entities are represented in the legislative arena by either the department or city/county executive leaders or by designated specialized legislative liaisons. Much of the formal testimony and informal "hard-hitting" lobbying is probably carried out by the powerful, politically experienced agency or local government leaders—the official spokespersons. Although most state employees are not allowed to lobby in their official capacities, the governor's office and the various departments, commissions, and other agencies usually employ at least one person each as a legislative liaison. Legislative liaisons engage in many types of activities: they monitor bills affecting their agencies, testify as specialists in legislative hearings, represent their agency to the legislature and often to the governor's office, and prepare technical information requested by legislative and other executive bodies.

The larger Kentucky local governments utilize the lobbying skills of not only their politically savvy executive leaders, but also specially-trained legislative liaisons. For example, Lexington designated Jane Vimont to be its first legislative liaison in August 1986; she had been serving as research director for their Urban County Council for five years. "The need for her position became evident during the 1986 General Assembly, when Mayor Scotty Baesler sent her to Frankfort to stay abreast of the more than 1,000 bills that directly affected Lexington." According to Vimont, she and Baesler "were able to minimize the problems that some bills would have caused Lexington and to steer some major revisions in planning and zoning laws in the city's favor." Paul Guagliardo, Louisville's legislative liaison since 1982, said that a city's relationship with state and federal lawmakers is "not something you ever take for granted. It helps them to know your face, to give them a quick and reliable answer. The longer you're there, the more credibility you have" (*Lexington Herald-Leader*, August 12, 1986, B8).

Citizen lobbyists generally represent both registered and nonregistered groups that include nonprofit, social service, public interest, and special interest groups such as the state chapters of NOW, the League of Women Voters, and other women's groups; community and neighborhood associations; the state PTA; Kentucky War on Drugs, Mothers Against Drunk Driving (MADD), and other alcoholism and drug-prevention groups; grandparents' visitation rights and grandparents' and grandchildren's rights groups; groups for gifted and handicapped children and for day care; and sports groups such as the League of Kentucky Sportsmen. These groups, which have experienced significant growth in numbers, are largely staffed and run by unpaid volunteers, and they form the core of Kentucky's "citizen lobby."

Lobbyists' Personal Characteristics. What are the personal characteristics of these individuals who lobby in Frankfort? In one study of the background of Kentucky lobbyists, Bizzel (1981) surveyed 194 registered legislative agents and found that their personal traits such as age, sex, education, birth and residence, religion, and occupation were in general terms quite similar to those personal characteristics of legislators in the 1980 General Assembly. The typical lobbyist is forty-five years old, male, white, Baptist, college educated, and a life-long small-town or city resident of Kentucky. Over 90 percent surveyed reside within the state; in-state residence is of particular importance to a lobbyist in order to communicate effectively with state legislators. Over half the lobbyists reported being professional and business people; another large group included retired persons, housewives, and students. Work and background experiences suggest that most lobbyists have not been former legislators (only 3 percent), yet many of them have worked for state government (33 percent) in departments such as human resources, education, transportation, labor, or the Legislative Research Commission.

Most of these lobbyists responded that they lobbied only part-time (75 percent), were generally employed by the group they represented (50 percent), and represented only one group before the legislature (80 percent). Others became lobbyists on their own initiative or because of requests by friends back home. Most had little or no lobbying experience before they took up their present duties.

Spending by Lobbyists. Kentucky lobbyists flocked to Frankfort in fewer numbers for the 1986 General Assembly, but they spent more than ever before. The 440 people who registered as lobbyists for the 1986 session, and the five months preceding it, spent $3,083,325; those lobbyists represented 531 organizations. Two years earlier 582 lobbyists spent $2,991,626, setting what was then the record. In 1986, although most of the money was spent on salaries, hotel rooms, and transportation, lobbyists also claimed as expenses such items as chili dinners, flowers, and candy. The largest single amount in the 1986 reports to the attorney general's office was $82,500, which Buddy Adams of Bowling Green listed as salary and expenses in representing Traffic Safety Now, a Detroit, Michigan, organization supported by the automobile industry that backed an unsuccessful bill to make seat-belt use mandatory. Adams is a former state representative and former secretary of the state Human Resources Cabinet who operates a governmental affairs and public relations firm. He reported a total of $176,430 in compensation and expenses in representing eight companies and trade associations. According to Don Adams, the president of People's Finance and Investment Company, "It's expensive to stay away from home." The bulk of his expenses were for hotel rooms and meals (*Lexington Herald-Leader*, August 12, 1986, B8).

Blue Cross and Blue Shield of Kentucky had seven registered lobbyists who received a total of $104,375 for salaries and expenses, the largest amount being paid to Louisville attorney D. Paul Alagia, Jr. Blue Cross's legislative goals included passage of a bill to allow it to operate as a mutual insurance company and defeat of a sweeping health-care bill that would have required Blue Cross to cover some Medicaid patients as part of its contract for state-employee health insurance. Both of these goals were achieved.

Horse racing interests also fared well in the 1986 General Assembly. The legislature gave a tax break to Kentucky tracks and also approved a betting incentive bill. For its part, the industry spent $136,309. The Keeneland Association contributed $56,440 to the effort, including $19,412 for entertainment.

At the other end of the scale, 60 of the 440 registered lobbyists reported spending nothing. The attorney general's office delineated spending during the 1986 session and interim by categories of special interests (table 32).

Table 32. Spending by Lobbyists in 1986 Session of General Assembly

	Spending Level ($)
Business and industry	$420,485
Health and medical	356,032
Insurance	256,253
Transportation	228,087
Utilities	204,180
Oil, gas, steel	193,787
Banking, finance, collectors	188,926
Public officials, government	173,595
Education	155,980
Contractors, homebuilders, real estate	143,515
Labor	139,441
Equine-racing	136,310
Miscellaneous	130,833
Agriculture	123,925
Coal	95,646
Law	63,826
Liquor, temperance	36,479
Media-communications	15,444
Retirement	15,406
Senior citizens	4,324
Women's issues	853

Source: *Louisville Courier-Journal*, August 12, 1986, Sec. B, pp. 1, 4.

THE LEGISLATIVE STRATEGIES OF INTEREST GROUPS

As the independent influence of the legislature has grown, interest groups have found it necessary to adapt new strategies to accomplish their objectives. It is no longer sufficient to enlist the support of the governor and the pertinent executive agencies in order to get legislation passed or defeated. As we have noted earlier, some groups have used their PACs to channel more funds into legislative races. A greater variety of organizations are sending lobbyists to the legislature, some are increasing the number of their lobbyists, and a few are moving their headquarters from Louisville to Frankfort.

Surveys of legislators conducted by Bizzel (1984b) in 1982 and 1984 found that most legislators have a generally favorable attitude toward lobbyists and few are actually hostile. In 1980 Bizzel (1981) asked both legislators and lobbyists what are the most helpful services that lobbyists provide to legislators. Both legislators and lobbyists emphasized the presentation of information and data on bills, the explanation of complex bills, and keeping track of bills. Lobbyists were much more likely than legislators to mention campaign contributions, letter-writing campaigns, and preparation of speech material for legislators. Both groups gave the least priority to social activities run by interest groups.

Some organizations have tried to play a role in leadership contests, and they are likely to make greater efforts to influence the selection of committee members. As the committees assume greater importance in decision making, membership on those committees assumes greater importance. In examining the membership of House and Senate committees for the 1980-84 period, we find a number of examples of legislators serving on committees dealing with their specialized interests, thus providing interest groups with obvious allies. The executive directors of the state AFL-CIO and the Associated Industries of Kentucky each sat on the House Labor and Industry Committee. Three of the seven members of the Senate Banking and Insurance Committee during this period had strong professional ties to the banking or insurance business. The chairman and vice-chairman of the Senate Education Committee were, respectively, a school principal and a former university president.

The strategies employed by interest groups depend on their resources and goals, as well as the political realities they face in the legislature. The major labor and business groups have broader agendas than individual companies or specific professional groups. Groups that are trying to pass legislation face different challenges, and may need different tactics, from groups supporting the status quo. Some groups are concerned with highly technical issues, whereas others deal with controversial, emotional issues like abortion. We can best illustrate the variety of strategies employed by lobbyists, and assess the effectiveness of each, by examining a number of case studies from recent sessions pertaining to a variety of interest groups and issues.

Labor and Business. The major labor and business organizations are similar in that both of them represent large numbers of persons and become involved in most of the major economic issues that arise during a session—and they usually take opposite sides on these issues. Labor unions are not numerically strong in Kentucky, but in recent years the state AFL-CIO has become better organized for political action and lobbying under a new leader, Ron Cyrus—an experienced member of the legislature. The AFL-CIO and individual unions have been devoting more attention in recent years to legislative elections and to the coordination of lobbying efforts. During the 1986 General Assembly there were fifteen people in the entire labor coalition, representing the various unions; they would meet weekly on Mondays, and sometimes other days, to plan strategy. To enhance the lobbying capabilities of organized labor, Representative Cyrus established a group of local communicators—local persons, one in each district, who have close linkages to their legislators. In the 1986 legislature, there were sixty-three local labor communicators, who had earlier experienced training sessions.

Besides its strong financial campaign commitment to targeted legislative candidates each election year, organized labor makes skillful use of public endorsements of favored candidates. With few exceptions, incumbents have the upper hand in winning labor endorsements, which mean support in union mailings, contributions, door-to-door manpower, and the use of phone banks and newspapers. In the 1986 elections, labor, with few exceptions, supported Democratic members of the General Assembly; but here and there, the political arms of major labor groups endorsed Republicans or backed challengers against Democratic incumbents. Only in a few cases did labor find itself split on its endorsements. For example, in Bullitt County's Forty-ninth District, home to a number of union members who work in nearby Louisville, the Kentucky State AFL-CIO endorsed Republican Representative John Harper of Shepherdsville (an unsuccessful gubernatorial candidate in 1987), even though he was opposed by Democrat Frank Smith, a union member and the former legislator whom Harper had defeated in 1984. Harper apparently won the endorsement because of the labor federation's tradition of sticking by friendly incumbents. Also, in the Fourteenth Senate District, the AFL-CIO and the United Mine Workers of America endorsed Bardstown lawyer Ben Haydon, Jr., against Senator Ed O'Daniel of Springfield, the eventual winner, in the Democratic primary. The issue was O'Daniel's sponsorship in the 1986 session of Senate bill 230, which would have changed workers' compensation extensively. "It would tear us all to hell," the UMW's Charlie Head said of the bill, which did not get out of committee.

Two of the major business organizations also have new leadership: the Associated Industries of Kentucky (AIK) and the Kentucky Chamber of Commerce. Business organizations are also giving higher priority to legislative lobbying. AIK, headed by recently retired legislator Ed Holloway, represents a wide variety of industrial and business interests; there is no AIK PAC. AIK takes stands on issues, and its members are encouraged to talk with prospective candidates and support those who are friendly to business interests. Holloway, having served previously for twenty years as AIK's vice-president, feels that business in general has been very slow to get into political activity; in the 1986 legislative session AIK worked with the lobbyists of various companies and other business groups to coordinate informally their efforts.

The Kentucky Chamber of Commerce is also a powerful voice in legislative politics. Although its PAC is inactive, individual members make sizable contributions each year to legislative candidates, and some members keep in close contact with their respective legislators. The chamber and AIK are very similar on most issues; the chamber avoids issues like banking, but it deals with concerns of interest to all business, e.g., tax policies, environment, federal regulations, labor issues, liability insurance, health care, and so on. In the 1986 General Assembly, the chamber had four full-time lobbyists, headed by Anthony Sholar, its director of government affairs. Although the diversity of the chamber may increase the difficulty of making decisions on policy, the staff does not dictate to the board, which is actively involved in policymaking. The chamber also plays an active part in coalitions with like-minded organizations. In 1986 the chamber took an active role in coordinating divergent groups to help defeat the proposed omnibus health care bill.

Not surprisingly, legislators do not like to be caught in the middle of conflicts between business and labor; they prefer to vote for bills that represent compromises between these two groups. The legislative leadership, particularly Speaker Blandford, encourages business and labor to work out their differences in order to minimize the pressures on legislators. Because both labor and business lobbyists have served in the legislature, there have been increased efforts to solve controversial issues through committees or task forces on which the two groups are represented. As a House member, Holloway also worked closely with labor's Representative Cyrus in 1986; "When you can get consensus on an issue it helps in getting it passed because legislators don't have to make choices between business and labor."

One joint study led to nearly unanimous passage of a bill in 1986 to reform the unemployment insurance system. Cyrus and Holloway jointly introduced HB247 on unemployment compensation; once it had been agreed to, labor and business interests resisted any floor amendments and it passed unanimously in the House and 34-2 in the Senate. Similarly, Cyrus and Holloway introduced a resolution to study the whole workmen's compensation issue, and a joint task force was established to examine reforming workmen's compensation during the 1986-87 interim. The result of that study was a bill passed by a special session of the legislature late in 1987 to tighten the standards for workmen's compensation. At the same special session, the legislature adopted a new formula for long-term financing of workmen's compensation, one that placed a larger share of the burden on the coal industry (where a large proportion of the claims arise). The formula was developed by legislative leaders after extensive negotiations with a variety of business and coal industry groups.

The Horse Racing Industry. The pressure by legislative leaders on interest groups to work out their differences is illustrated by the conflicts over the racing industry that came to a head in the 1986 session. The racing industry in Kentucky is a deeply divided one, plagued by squabbling. On the one hand are the major horse breeders, owners, and trainers, with close ties to several of the major race tracks. Traditionally, these groups have sought

political influence by supporting candidates for governor, but in 1983 they
established the Kentucky Thoroughbred Association (KTA) in order to increase their influence in the legislature. The KTA, with its roots in the
Kentucky Thoroughbred Owners and Breeders (a trade association), hired
Nick Nicolson, a former aide to U.S. Senator Wendell Ford, as its lobbyist
and executive vice-president.

On the other hand are the smaller horse owners and trainers, who have
been organized for a longer period of time as the Horsemen's Benevolent
and Protective Association (HBPA). This organization began active lobbying
of the legislature in 1978, and also began funding legislative candidates earlier
than the KTA did. Since 1983 the KTA PAC has become a major contributor
to legislative candidates, topping donations by the HBPA in 1984 races. The
two organizations disagree on a number of economic issues and on the role
the state should play in the horse racing industry. In addition, each of the
state's race tracks has its own interests to protect.

The HBPA, with outspoken Ed Flint at its helm, historically has posi-
tioned itself as the protector of small-time horsemen and backside workers—
those who work with horses stabled at the tracks. The HBPA is credited
with helping pass laws aiding transient horsemen, including establishment
of a health and welfare fund and a commission to improve backside work
conditions. But under Flint, who is also its national president, the HBPA
had been criticized for being confrontational, using lawsuits and boycotts to
get its way. Flint resigned as president of the Kentucky HBPA in 1987.

The KTA is viewed as being more cooperative with tracks in contract
talks, particularly with Churchill Downs. HBPA supporters say that is because the KTA mainly represents the "bluebloods," not horsemen trying to
grind out a living with lesser stock.

The two sides, along with the state's race tracks and other horse association officials, were finally able to agree late in the 1986 session on a package
of racing legislation. But legislative and racing officials say the public unity
came about only after back-room battles and threats. Legislators and racing
officials demanded cooperation in 1986 to avoid a repeat performance of the
1984 session, when the two groups fought bitterly. That session ended with
legislators scrapping a massive omnibus racing bill favored by the HBPA for
a much smaller version that essentially extended existing tax credits to the
state's smaller tracks.

The major goal of the horse industry in 1986 was passage of an omnibus
horse racing bill, designed in part to renew and extend tax credits to race
tracks in order to permit larger purses at the tracks to attract better horses.
Because of its more extensive political and lobbying efforts and the assistance
it provided to Don Blandford in his election to the speakership, the HBPA
expected to have a major hand in shaping that legislation. But Speaker
Blandford insisted that the various groups in the horse industry must reach

a compromise on the major issues in the proposed bill, and established an informal committee to accomplish that. The resulting compromise failed to incorporate many of the objectives of the HBPA, but it was endorsed by the Speaker and passed by the legislature.

The 1986 bill again extended the 3 percent pari-mutuel wagering tax credit for the state's two smaller thoroughbred tracks, Ellis Park and Turfway. It also granted a 1 percent credit to Churchill Downs and Keeneland, the first time those tracks received such credits. The HBPA initially opposed credits to the two larger tracks, but it supported that provision in the final bill. Proponents of the bill say that it would have passed without Flint's support and that he jumped on the bandwagon to avoid the appearance of defeat, something the HBPA could ill afford in the wake of a perceived loss of clout with the tracks.

The Health and Medical Complex. There are some policy disputes that the legislature cannot solve simply by insisting that the various interest groups sit down and work out their differences. There may be too many conflicting interests involved, the issues may be too complex, or the financial costs of a solution may be too high. All of these factors help explain the deadlock that developed during the 1986 session over the issue of comprehensive health care costs.

A variety of health organizations have assumed growing importance in the legislature because health issues are becoming more important and the escalating costs of health care are creating staggering problems for state government. These groups—Kentucky Hospital Association (KHA), Blue Cross-Blue Shield, the Humana chain of hospitals (which are powerful in Kentucky), and the Association of Health Care Facilities (representing the well-organized nursing industry)—are represented at legislative sessions by very experienced, effective lobbyists who mobilize their divergent members to assist regularly in contacting their respective legislators concerning crucial health care issues. These varied health organizations have also created PACs that contribute substantial campaign funds each election year to targeted legislative friends of health care priorities.

Although these groups share many common concerns, economic pressures and competition lead them to take opposite sides of some issues. In the 1986 session, several prominent legislators tried to gain passage of a comprehensive health care bill, designed primarily to meet the needs of those persons not adequately covered by insurance. The bill had the support of only one powerful lobby, the Kentucky Hospital Association, which stood to gain relief for its member hospitals' empty beds and mounting debts; a few nonprofit nursing homes; and a few public interest groups. It was successfully opposed by Humana, Blue Cross-Blue Shield, the Association of Health Care Facilities, Associated Industries of Kentucky, the statewide and

Louisville chambers of commerce, and a variety of other health providers and health professional groups. During the 1986 General Assembly, the opposition coalition of lobbyists held frequent informal meetings; although they possessed dissimilar views—different items of the omnibus bill to which their organizations were individually opposed—they worked together to defeat the whole health care reform package.

Controversial aspects of HB 403 included provisions to: impose a 3 percent surcharge on health insurance premiums; penalize hospitals that do not devote at least 3 percent of their total care to indigents; require the insurer of the state's 185,000 workers, teachers, and their dependents to cover some Medicaid patients as well; and allow some empty hospital beds to be used for care like that which nursing homes provide. The Senate companion bill, SB 62, contained neither a tax increase nor the 3 percent surcharge on insurance premiums.

According to one of the bill's legislative sponsors, the major issues included the following:

> The insurance thing was the thing that really got people ticked off. Dual licensure for hospitals was another thing that got the nursing home industry really ticked off. The crazy thing is that we went ahead and passed the dual licensure thing. It is such a complex thing. The 3 percent insurance surcharge was the real problem—we tried to show them intellectually and practically how the 3 percent surcharge would eventually save money for the consumer. We have had in Kentucky over the last 8 years an average rise of 14 percent a year in health insurance premiums. When you combine all the things that the omnibus bill did in terms of health care cost control, then the rise in health insurance premiums should only be 8 percent a year instead of 14 percent. So you put the 3 percent surcharge on, the increase would only be 11 percent. . . . Either they did not understand it, or when are people receptive to change? Hospitals are receptive to change because they are having a very hard time.

When asked to evaluate the influence of the major interest groups involved in the battle over the bill, one of the bill's staunch legislative supporters commented:

> KHA were the only big supporters of the Omnibus Bill. . . . The people who opposed the bill—Blue Cross, Humana, the nursing homes—they're doing quite well and why would they they want to change things? I think the Chamber of Commerce gave lip service to opposition. We even talked to executives of the Chamber and they agreed that something had to be done but their membership would not

let them take a supportive position. We could not even get Blue Cross
to meet with us. . . . Blue Cross and Humana were the primary reasons
it failed. Humana wanted me to come to their head-quarters in Louisville, but I wanted them to come meet with the Health and Welfare
Committee in Frankfort. I was not going to Louisville and get in their
big building and let them beat on me all day."

There are several reasons the bill failed, including its complexity and
its provision for a tax on insurance premiums. But this case illustrates the
difficulty of passing legislation when a coalition of important groups are
organized against it. With 1.2 million subscribers, almost a health-care insurance monopoly in Kentucky, Blue Cross-Blue Shield lobbied relentlessly
for the bill's defeat. The nursing home lobby, which recently had swelled
its ranks, seemed to make its contribution in the form of a delay game. It
reportedly had strung along the sponsors of the reform measures for weeks,
holding forth the prospect of support that never materialized. Humana,
which heretofore had not had much of a presence in the Kentucky legislature,
hired as chief lobbyist a former state legislator and occasionally also sent top
executives to lobby in Frankfort, in addition to hosting a "classy" party for
lawmakers at the Louisville Arts Center. Moreover, the major business lob-
bies contributed their experienced firepower for the defeat.
    This case illustrates the limitation of the legislative strategy of trying to
pass legislation by consensus. It also illustrates one of the consequences of
the shift of power from the governor to the legislature. On any issue such
as this, involving complex issues, strong opposition, and the necessity for
new revenue sources, the best way to overcome strong organized opposition
would probably be for the governor to take a public stand and mobilize
support for the bill, but in 1986 no such gubernatorial action was forthcoming.

The Diverse Banking Industry. The struggles over banking legislation in
the early 1980s illustrate what a well-organized interest group can accomplish
if it is cohesive and how ineffective it can be if it is divided. The banking
industry has long been considered an influential force in Kentucky. Its most
important trade association, the Kentucky Bankers Association (KBA), represents both urban and rural, large and small banks, each with its own
economic and political power base. Several years ago KBA's effectiveness
was seriously limited when its membership became split down the middle
over the multibank holding company issue, which came up in the 1982 and
1984 legislative sessions—defeated in 1982 and passed in 1984.
    The original move to allow multibank holding companies in Kentucky
began in the 1974 General Assembly, where it was perceived to be supported
solely by the large Louisville banks. It was opposed by the KBA, whose

executive committee at that time was dominated by rural banks. By 1981 a strong move was again initiated by the large banks to pass multibank holding company legislation. The Interim Joint Committee on Banking and Insurance and the KBA conducted separate surveys of Kentucky's banks on the issue. Both polls yielded similar results: two-thirds of the banks opposed such legislation. Subsequently, the subcommittee on banks unanimously voted not to change any laws, and the KBA took a public stand against multibank legislation. Noting that the KBA had opposed any change, the Progressive Banker's Association (PBA) was established in November 1981 to lobby for legislative change in the 1982 General Assembly. The PBA comprises mid-sized banks in rural areas as well as the large Louisville banks. Some large Lexington banks—such as First Security—became formidable opponents of any new legislation; they feared the prospect of takeover by the Louisville banks.

In 1982 the press reported intensive lobbying on the bill (the most since the 1976 bail bond issue). The Farm Bureau was reported to be effectively lobbying against it. John Y. Brown, Jr.'s, administration was reportedly supporting the bill behind the scenes; in fact, Brown said that he was. The KBA and PBA became bitter adversaries, continually lobbying their respective legislative friends. Defeated 50-44 in the House, the bill was revived and passed the House. It was defeated in the Senate on a tie vote, with Lieutenant Governor Collins casting a symbolic vote against the measure. At the time, Collins cited the divisive impact of the issue as one reason for voting against the bill. Everyone agreed lobbying was intense, with much pressure brought on members, including pressure from local bankers on their legislators. An excellent example of executive branch lobbying was Governor Brown's last-minute involvement in the HB 194 deliberations. When Representative James Bruce and the PBA struggled to revive the bill in the House, the governor stepped in; several legislators later accused Brown of using coercive tactics in an attempt to elicit promultibank votes from them.

There was a striking shift in sentiment concerning multibank legislation from 1982 to 1984. A number of banks changed their positions because the banking climate changed over this time—due, in part, to federal deregulation—and more banks came to accept the change. Some of the smaller banks decided takeover might be desirable. Lexington's First Security Bank changed its position; one element in 1984 involved credit card legislation that First Security desired. Therefore, First Security made a deal with the Louisville banks: a *yes* for a multibank bill in exchange for a *yes* for a credit card bill. Furthermore, KBA became a supporter of multibank legislation; a change in its rules had ended rural domination and given urban banks more influence. One organization of banks—Independent Bankers—remained opposed to the bill. Also, the Farm Bureau still opposed the legislation because it believed that farm loans would be more difficult to obtain from large banks.

In sharp contrast to the heated battles of the 1982 session, the multibanking bill, HB67, easily passed the House in 1984—55-43. The measure would allow bank holding companies to own more than one bank in Kentucky and to operate across county lines. Before passing the bill for the final time, the House adopted an amendment added the previous week by the Senate before it had approved the measure. The amendment would prohibit any bank holding company from controlling more than 15 percent of the assets in Kentucky banks (instead of a 20 percent limit). The legislation was praised by the bill's supporters as an important step toward the creation of an economic climate that would allow Kentucky to prosper. It was condemned by opponents as a threat to small businesses and farmers. Governor Collins let the controversial bill become law without her signature.

A confusing atmosphere clouded the legislature after the 1984 bill passed the House the first time before being sent to the Senate. Representative Elmer Patrick, R-Williamsburg, signed a criminal complaint asserting that Bank of Louisville lobbyist Russell McClure, one of a number of lobbyists who worked for HB 67's passage, had offered him a $5000 bribe to support the bill. McClure contended that Patrick asked for a cash payment in return for his vote. McClure was charged with bribery of a public servant. McClure's arrest slowed, but did not prevent, the Senate's final action on the multibank bill—a vote of 21-17. McClure was subsequently acquitted by a jury; Patrick was defeated for reelection.

Optometrists and Ophthalmologists. Some of the most heated battles in any legislature involve conflicts between rather narrow, specialized interests. For many years the optometrists and ophthalmologists have been doing battle in Kentucky. The main issue has been the optometrists' effort to gain legal authority to prescribe and administer certain medication for patients. In recent years the optometrists have appeared to be more aggressive both in their political activities and their lobbying efforts. The ophthalmologists have been less effective and have received only limited support from the Kentucky Medical Association. Prior to 1986 the optometrists had been able to win passage for their bill only in the House, but in 1986 the bill passed the House and Senate and became law.

According to a lobbyist for the ophthalmologists, his group had reached an agreement with the House leadership and some legislative supporters of the optometrists that the bill would not be passed in the House (which had passed it before) unless the Senate passed it first. The group thought they had the votes to defeat it in the Senate—a tie plus Lieutenant Governor Beshear opposing—but it passed by two votes when Senator Ackerson shifted at the last moment.

A key figure in Senate passage of the bill was Benny Ray Bailey, chairman of the Health and Welfare Committee, who had opposed the bill in the past but agreed to support it after the optometrists agreed to several amendments he proposed. According to Senator Bailey:

> The Optometrist Bill was not one of the worst pieces of legislation to come before the General Assembly. Since 1982 I have argued about the amendment to the bill—that optometrists could not dispense pills and that 12 hours of educational training was required. Before 1986 the optometrists would never agree to my amendment. Last December they agreed to accept my amendment so I agreed to support the legislation. It passed . . . 19 other Senators plus 67 House members voted for it and the governor signed it. Now somebody thought that was a good bill.

The law, which went into effect July 15, 1986, allowed optometrists who took twelve semester hours of pharmacology training to prescribe drops and ointments for eye ailments.

Shortly after the session, Bailey asked leaders of the optometric association to help raise money for Grady Stumbo, a close ally of Bailey's, who was trying to pay off his debt from the 1983 gubernatorial race in preparation for running again in 1987. In early April Bailey asked Jerald F. Combs of Inez, the president-elect of the Kentucky Optometric Association and London optometrist James E. McCracken, Jr., to tap their colleagues to help Stumbo with his debt. The *Courier-Journal* reported that optometrists and their relatives and employees subsequently contributed at least $133,000 to Stumbo's campaign, more than four-fifths of the total that he needed to retire his debt. Dr. William Offutt IV of Lexington, one of many ophthalmologists who opposed the legislation, said the contributions explained why a bill that had been killed in earlier sessions got passed so easily. But Senator Bailey said he would have voted for the bill "if there had never been a campaign, as long as pills were prohibited. There absolutely was no deal."

This episode calls attention to the fact that funds contributed by individual members of an occupational group may be much larger and more significant than those contributed by any PAC associated with their group. It also is a reminder that, even though the legislature has assumed much greater importance in the decision-making process, it has not entirely escaped from the influence of gubernatorial politics.

Educational Reform and the KEA. The most important issue confronting the Kentucky General Assembly in its 1984 and 1985 sessions was the package of educational reforms and the tax increases necessary to fund it. In order to understand why the education and tax package largely failed in 1984 and succeeded in 1985, we need to understand the role played by the Kentucky Education Association (KEA).

A major source of the KEA's strength is the fact that significant numbers of teachers are found in every county in the state. A second source is its willingness to become actively involved in electoral politics and, most significantly, its recognition of the importance today of legislative elections. As we have noted, the PACs run by KEA and its county affiliates in recent years have made larger donations than any other group to legislative candidates. In addition, they have provided campaign services (such as polls, voter targeting information, and media advisers) as well as volunteer workers to these candidates.

In the 1986 legislative primary and general elections, local KEA activity on behalf of candidates was at an unprecedented level. Contributions by local KEPACs were at the highest level ever. Even more impressive was the people power put into races by KEA members—door-to-door canvassing, stuffing envelopes, preparing mailings, calling other voters, hosting fund raisers, and so on. KEA has been very effective in its targeting of endorsements; for example, in the 1986 primary 92 percent of its endorsed Senate candidates (11 of 12 candidates) and 83 percent of its endorsed House candidates (45 of 54 candidates) were victorious. KEPACs generally like to stay with incumbents, rather than a challenger who may be equally good. Of course, sometimes there are disagreements between the state and local KEPACs about endorsing X or Y; in such cases they endorse no one, rather than each supporting different candidates.

KEA is especially skillful in getting its members mobilized to contact legislators concerning issues; there is a field staff of twenty-one people, each responsible for sixteen hundred to twenty-one hundred teachers, scattered around the state. They set up a contact team made up of five teachers for each legislator. Members of these contact teams all meet before the session to get briefed by the KEA staff, and more than one thousand of these teachers come to Frankfort at a designated time during the legislative session to meet with their legislators. These contact volunteers are individuals who have been active in KEA, held office, been on KEPACs, and have (if possible) worked in campaigns for the particular legislators.

In the 1984 session, Governor Collins endorsed a variety of educational reforms that had been developed by various organizations, study groups, and legislative committees, and she reluctantly proposed a tax increase to pay for the educational package. During that session the legislature passed only a few of the least expensive reforms and rejected the tax increase, but in the 1985 special session it passed an extensive reform package and a tax bill to pay at least part of the costs.

There are a number of reasons failure in 1984 changed to success in 1985, including greater efforts by the governor, growing attention by the media to educational reform, and changes in the tax package to put most of the burden on business. A major reason for success was the efforts by a small group of legislators on the House Education Committee (led by the "Young Turks"), who revised the education package, negotiated with the governor for her support, and worked effectively for its passage. (The role of the committee members was discussed more fully in chapter 5.)

It would be too simple to blame KEA for the defeat of educational reform in 1984 or to give it most of the credit for the successes of 1985. KEA was unenthusiastic about the governor's educational package in 1984 and made no efforts to generate support for it. The legislators who revised the governor's legislative package had close political ties to the KEA. Moreover, as one of them said, "We had to have KEA's support, and therefore the package had to be acceptable to KEA, so that enough legislators would support it." The revisions that they initiated included several that were important to KEA. They gave higher priority to salary increases for teachers, and particularly to a long-term program of longevity pay for those with greater seniority. They gave much lower priority to the plan for a career ladder for teachers, which was opposed by KEA and many legislators—proposing on a small-scale pilot project.

Once KEA's priority items had been included in the educational package, the organization worked enthusiastically for the entire package, along with many other groups that were supporting educational reform. Close observers of the session agreed that KEA's strong support was essential for passage of the educational reforms and the tax package, but they were particularly impressed by its efforts on behalf of its priority items. The most important of these was longevity pay, which came under attack in both houses by the chairmen of Senate and House Appropriations and Revenue committees. KEA showed surprising effectiveness in protecting it from cutbacks. According to one legislator involved in the committee proceedings: "I was surprised by KEA's power on that vote. They got their teachers active in lobbying the legislators. They have a lot of power on the House floor." Another legislator involved in the negotiations remarked: "KEA leaders are not very effective on some things. But on certain issues they can mobilize people—they were able to line up votes for longevity pay versus merit pay."

Higher Education. The powerful higher education coalition is an example of governmental units, somewhat independent of the governor, who are engaged in various forms of legislative lobbying. Each of the state universities—the University of Kentucky, the University of Louisville, Eastern Kentucky University, Western Kentucky University, Morehead State University, Northern Kentucky State University, Murray State University, and Kentucky State University—tends to have a group of Senate and House legislative supporters from its own geographic area. Over the years these universities have been involved in heated battles for budgetary priority and for authority to maintain particular graduate and professional programs—medical schools, dental schools, law schools, and so on. Critics have long argued that the state really does not need three law schools and two dental schools; they cite the tremendous costs and duplication of efforts.

A special legislative committee, named after the resolution that created it—SCR30—was established to investigate duplication of particular state professional schools. The various universities were represented at the hearings by their most experienced lobbyists. One committee member was not convinced there was little duplication of services; he learned that "the universities are at least as powerful a lobby as the teachers." Some legislators had hoped that the committee's study might lead to some meaningful effort by universities to concentrate more on quality rather than quantity. There were some weak promises by the University of Kentucky and the University of Louisville to try to do something in dental and medical areas. The SCR30 committee failed to make strong recommendations; the committee vacillated because of the diversity of its membership and the tremendous political pressures from the universities and their diehard supporters. Because many legislators are parochial in supporting the claims of particular universities in their district or region, it is difficult to change the status quo. No legislator wants to challenge others lest his own university suffer. Many legislators feel more strongly about protecting a dental or law school than do other legislators who want to cut them. Some committee members, at the end of the proceedings, were encouraged by the committee's efforts: "The committee did collect some valuable information, and it also got the Council on Higher Education to push ahead and finally adopt its plan for higher education." The voluminous data revealed that the universities were making concerted efforts to avoid duplications and to find areas where their limited budgets could be substantially trimmed.

Because these various struggles among universities had seriously eroded the political effectiveness of higher education in Kentucky, the divergent competing universities joined together before the 1986 General Assembly and vowed to work more closely with each other. The various university presidents got together and agreed to unite behind the common goal of greater financial support for higher education. The Council on Higher Education held hearings around the state, and the universities mobilized supporters to attend and speak at these hearings. A group of business leaders, with particular support from Ashland Oil, formed an interest group to lobby in behalf of greater funding for higher education. During the 1986 session, there was even a large rally in support of higher education held in Frankfort, attended by several thousand faculty, staff, and students, and featuring speakers, bands, and cheerleaders.

These cooperative efforts help explain a breakthrough in higher education funding in the 1986 legislature. According to the chairman of the House Education Committee, "We kept higher education on the front burner in the 1986 session and got things done on higher education." The governor did not want to put money into higher education across the board; instead she favored the creation of centers of excellence, a program earlier established in some other states. In contrast, the university presidents really wanted more funding for salaries and for formula funding than for the centers of excellence. The 1986 General Assembly adopted the plan for centers of excellence on a reduced scale, while approving more funding for salary increases than the governor had recommended.

Two major trends have been occurring in Kentucky that help explain the current role of interest groups in the political system. One of these trends is political pluralism—the proliferation of organized interests that are represented in Frankfort. Kentucky government and politics are no longer dominated by two or three special interests—coal, horse racing, liquor, or agriculture. Some of the traditionally strong interests, such as the coal and horse industries, have been weakened by division into more specialized and often conflicting interests.

But there are several more important reasons for this new pluralism. The economy of the state is becoming more complex and varied, and Kentucky is gradually becoming more urbanized. The state government now deals with a wider variety of issues (partly because of program cutbacks in Washington), and the interests affected by the issues must make their views known in Frankfort. Some of the major issues facing the state are complex ones on which a large variety of specific interests form shifting and often conflicting coalitions—issues like the costs of medical care, the environmental impact of extractive industries, and restructuring the tax laws.

The proliferation of interests represented in Frankfort is also caused by the second major trend in the state: the shift in power from the governor to the legislature. That trend is not necessarily irreversible, but it is highly unlikely that the legislature will ever be as subservient to the governor as it was as recently as the 1970s. The political system is now much more open. Instead of decisions being made in the governor's office with the participation of a few interests, there are now extensive legislative hearings in which all pertinent groups are represented, and the corridors of the Capitol are crowded with lobbyists seeking out legislators.

This trend toward legislative power has increased the rate of interest group participation and the sheer volume of lobbying, but has it made interest groups more powerful in the political system? It is difficult to say. Political parties in Kentucky are relatively weak, because the Democrats usually hold such a large advantage in state elections and because both of the legislative parties represent heterogeneous interests. In theory, weak parties are supposed to contribute to strong interest groups. It is reasonable to argue that a legislature (particularly with weak parties) is less able than a strong governor to resist interest group pressures.

In practice, the newly independent legislature is still evolving. Critics, including some legislators, believe that the committees are too often dominated by members identified with a special interest and that, even when this is not the case, the committees have not shown enough courage in resisting group pressures. There are differences of opinion about the strategies that legislative leaders should follow to counter some of these pressures. We have noted that the legislators and their leaders often follow the strategy of insisting that conflicting interest groups work out compromises—a strategy that minimizes the cross pressure the legislature must face.

Part Five
Conclusion

The period of greatest change in American state legislatures is over. The years ahead are likely to bring more gradual changes. The least professional legislatures will become more professional; there will be closer party competition in the less competitive legislatures; and the substantive issues faced by state legislatures will grow more important and more complex. This would be a good time to assess the changes of the last few decades and determine what the consequences of change have been.

Reform has come gradually to most state legislatures. Often there has been a lag between the introduction of changes in structure or rules and significant impact on the decision-making process.

There have been significant changes in the composition of legislatures. There has been an increase in minority party members, particularly Republicans in southern legislatures. Changes in apportionment standards mandated by the courts have brought more urban and suburban members. The Voting Rights Act led gradually to more black members, and the equal rights movement has slowly produced more women members. It has taken time for these changes in composition to affect decision making because new members must gain several years of experience before they become most effective.

Some of the changes have resulted directly from deliberate efforts at reform, such as removing constitutional limits on the length of sessions or raising members' salaries. Some changes have resulted from external trends, such as those changing the composition of members. Some changes have resulted from the growing demands of groups in the state, which have recognized the growing credibility and competence of state legislatures as well as the declining role of the national government in domestic programs. Some legislative changes have resulted from a new generation of members, with more interest in public policy, more political skills and ambitions, and with their own agenda for legislative reform.

There have been no national studies and few state studies tracing in any detail these legislative changes. Political scientists have seldom tried to measure the consequences of reform for public policy and have rarely succeeded in providing clear, definitive answers. In the chapter that follows we have summarized for the state of Kentucky what we have learned about the causes and mechanism of change and about the consequences for public policy.

11. Causes and Consequences of Change

Why did reform come to the Kentucky legislature, and why did it start in the late 1960s? Why did it evolve as it did, and why was the process so gradual? What were the interrelationships among the various factors affecting change? What have been the consequences of change? How have policy outputs differed from those that would have occurred with a strong governor and weak legislature? How well does the system work now?

THE CAUSES OF CHANGE

Legislative change in Kentucky has been shaped by at least six major forces. The first three are external forces, over which the legislators have no control: the constitutional framework within which the legislature operates; the court system, which may either mandate or restrict legislative change; and the governor, whose role in legislative affairs varies from one incumbent to the next. The remaining factors are internal: the legislative rules and procedures adopted by the membership; the leadership; and the rank-and-file members themselves.

External Forces Affecting Change. Any explanation of the course of legislative change in Kentucky must begin with the constitutional limitation on legislative sessions to sixty days every two years. No other political institution (except presidential nominating conventions and the electoral college) meets so infrequently. No one would be taken seriously if he proposed that city councils or school boards be prohibited from meeting for periods of twenty or twenty-one months. The Kentucky constitutional provision is so obviously outmoded that anyone interested in improving the legislature must recognize that the first step is to change the constitution. Many other state constitutions used to place unrealistic limits on legislative sessions, and in most of them reformers have succeeded in abolishing or modifying the restriction.

In Kentucky, however, it has proved has impossible to get voter approval for annual sessions or for longer sessions. A revised constitution that included annual sessions was defeated in 1968, and annual session amendments were beaten at the polls in 1969 and 1973. The failure of these efforts has shaped the direction that legislative reform has taken. Members have had to invent mechanisms that would enable them to work productively during the long period of time between sessions, and they have been most ingenious in doing so.

The heart of legislative reform has been the interim committee system; this was the only kind of structure that would enable legislators to study issues, draft and discuss bills, hold hearings, study budgetary questions, and oversee the executive branch on a year-round basis. The importance that members attach to the interim committee system became clear when the schedule of legislative sessions was revised by constitutional amendment in 1979. Because the interim period followed the regular session, the turnover of committee membership following the subsequent election disrupted the work of the interim committees. The new schedule provided for legislative elections in even-numbered years, a brief organizational session, and a year of interim committee meetings preceding the regular session. The schedule was awkward because legislators were elected in a different year from the governor, but the members considered the change necessary to make the interim system work better.

The timing of the decision to establish the interim committee system in 1968 was shaped by a combination of external and internal forces. The effort to rewrite the Kentucky constitution had stirred up interest in legislative reform. There was a national legislative reform movement and a Kentucky citizens' group promoting legislative reform. These may have helped create a climate for reform. More important, for the first time in two decades a Republican was elected governor in 1967.

This reality presented the Democratic majority with a challenge: they needed to be better organized to develop their own alternatives to the governor's program. The new House Speaker, Julian Carroll, and the new lieutenant governor, Wendell Ford, were both experienced legislators and strong leaders with an interest in improving legislative performance (though both would subsequently be strong governors). The director of the Legislative Research Committee, James Fleming, was committed to reform and was imaginative and skillful in devising institutional measures to bring it about. Reapportionment was beginning to bring into the legislature a new group of members with an interest in reform.

Several major judicial decisions have affected the pace and direction of legislative change in Kentucky. The reapportionment decisions of the courts in the early 1960s forced a redistribution of seats in the Kentucky legislature from rural to urban counties. One consequence was the demise of the rotation system in rural counties, making possible longer tenure in office. The expansion in the proportion of seats that were urban probably contributed to the gradual professionalization of the General Assembly.

When the interim committee system was proposed, there were serious doubts about its constitutionality. Because a previous decision of the Kentucky Court of Appeals had legitimized the Legislative Research Commission, the interim committees were made subcommittees of the LRC, a strategy that proved to be successful. In 1984, however, the state Supreme Court made it clear that the LRC could not exercise "legislative powers," and it placed significant limits on the powers of the LRC and its subcommittees to oversee executive agencies. Decisions of the Kentucky Supreme Court in 1984 and 1985 have given the legislature broad latitude in passing a budget, permitting it to suspend legislation through the budgetary process and to specify how the budget would be implemented by the executive branch. On balance, courts have supported the efforts of the Kentucky legislature to utilize the interim committee system, with restraints being imposed only in the area of oversight.

The pace and direction of legislative change have been powerfully affected by the goals, tactics, and skills of successive governors. As we have seen, the interim committee system was established early in Louie Nunn's term as governor, when the Democratic legislative majority and its leadership were able to exercise some independence. Nunn was a strong and skillful governor, however, who was able to win passage of his budget and tax package though the Republicans were in a minority. In fact, Nunn vetoed the bill establishing interim committees, and they were initially set up by the LRC on its own authority. Moreover, in 1969 Nunn strongly opposed the constitutional amendment for annual legislative sessions, and his opposition may have been crucial in its defeat.

From 1971 to 1979, Wendell Ford and Julian Carroll continued the traditionally strong role of the governor in legislative affairs. From 1968 through 1974, as House Speaker and as lieutenant governor, Julian Carroll had helped in the creation and development of the interim committee system. But, as we have described in some detail (chapter 9), Carroll as governor used his knowledge of the legislative process most skillfully to gain passage of the bills he favored and to block those he opposed. He maintained control over the selection of leadership, and he used his influence over the LRC to restrict staff resources available to the Appropriations and Revenue Committee. Carroll professed a commitment to an "independent" legislature, and he made no effort to dismantle the interim committee system. But it seems clear that the legislature's progress toward genuine independence was delayed by the fact that both governors Ford and Carroll exercised their powers so effectively.

The action and inaction of governors John Y. Brown, Jr., and Martha Layne Collins from 1980 through 1987 made possible fundamental changes in the legislative system. Because Brown abandoned the practice of selecting leaders and Collins made no effort to reinstate it, the nature of legislative leadership changed. The leaders gained independent authority, but became directly accountable to the membership, and more particularly to the Democratic members. At any time in the past the legislators could have ignored the governor's advice on leadership selection; but in fact they did not do so until the governor stopped giving advice. It seems most unlikely that any future governor could recapture a powerful voice in leadership selection. Without direct control over the leadership, it becomes much more difficult for the governor to control the legislative timetable, to bargain with members, and to determine the fate of legislation. The governor can no long promise members that their favorite bill will gain committee approval (or threaten to kill it in committee) if the chairmen no longer owe their positions to the governor.

Neither Governor Brown nor Governor Collins proposed a lengthy legislative agenda, and neither was willing to work for passage of legislators' bills. Both lacked the interest or the skill to engage in bargaining with members or to make significant use of the powers of the governor's office on behalf of legislation. As a consequence the legislative process changed: lobbyists focused more attention on the legislature than on the governor's office; committees and their chairmen gained more independent power; the burden of passing legislation was shifted to the Senate and House leadership. But these are changes that are not necessarily permanent nor irreversible. The balance between the governor and the legislature is always in flux. Inevitably, some future governors will have more ambitious agendas, will use their political powers more aggressively, and will bargain more skillfully with members. But they will not be able to regain the dominant positions enjoyed by governors like Ford and Carroll. Stronger governors will confront a stronger legislature, doubtless producing periods of conflict over policy as well as power.

Internal Sources of Change. As we have emphasized, the rigid constitutional limits on sessions forced the legislative reformers to establish a system that would permit members to work effectively during the long interim—studying issues, holding hearings, developing legislation, reviewing budgetary needs, and overseeing the executive branch. They chose to develop an interim committee system as the vehicle for interim activity, rather than special commissions or other devices. They streamlined the regular-session committees and clarified their jurisdiction, and directly linked them to the interim committees. During the 1970s a series of oversight committees were established. Gradually, the committees were provided with larger, more experienced, more specialized staffs.

As a consequence of these developments, the legislature—through its committees—gained sufficient time to study issues and achieved sufficient expertise to make informed judgments about them. The committees gained the potential to become relatively independent centers of decision making. However, until 1980 committee independence was constrained by the governor's role in the selection of leaders and, through them, the committee chairmen. On those issues of concern to the governor, committee chairmen were expected to support the governor and mobilize support for his positions in the committee. The influence of some committees was also weakened by a high level of membership turnover, which eroded experience and expertise.

Since 1980 the committees and their chairmen have gained more independent power. This independence has been greater in the House than in the Senate, because in the latter body the leadership has used the Rules Committee and the caucus more often to constrain committee independence. At the same time, there has been increasing stability of membership on the more important committees. One symptom of the growing power of committees has been the increasing attention paid to them by lobbyists.

The structural and procedural changes developed within the legislature and the political changes originating largely from the governor's office are interrelated. The full impact of these reforms on the operation of the committee system was not felt until the governor's grip on the committee system was loosened. But it is also true that the legislature was better able to take advantage of its new independence in the 1980s because the committee system had already been revitalized.

The changes in the General Assembly have been orchestrated by its leadership. We have noted Speaker Julian Carroll's role in reforming the committee system. Speaker William Kenton, first chosen by Governor Carroll, strengthened the speakership by his ability to build his own coalition and win a third term. He promoted coverage of legislative sessions by Kentucky Educational Television to increase the institution's visibility. He designed and won passage of the constitutional amendment changing the schedule of elections and sessions.

The decline in the governor's influence has strengthened the role of the elected Senate and House leaders; consequently, their tactics and style of leadership have affected the decision-making process. During the 1980s the leaders of the Senate developed a model of independence that emphasized the importance of cohesion among Democratic senators and close coordination between the leadership and committee chairman. In the House, speakers Kenton and Richardson both sought to exercise strong leadership and used the Rules Committee extensively to constrain committee independence. By contrast Speaker Blandford has loosened the reins and encouraged more independence and responsibility by the committees.

In similar fashion individual chairman have influenced the operation of the committee system. Some chairmen are more effective than others in building and maintaining a majority coalition. Some have their own agenda for committee action, and others are more passive. Some try to mediate the demands of interest groups, whereas others go along with whichever groups are strongest or loudest. Some are tough-minded in screening out "bad bills," and others are much more permissive. Anyone who watches the legislative process closely realizes that the effectiveness of committees, and the nature of their outputs, depends very heavily on the skills and priorities of the chairmen. Those who believe that committees do not screen bills rigorously enough usually blame the chairmen. Under the present committee system, chairmen are potentially very powerful; but only those with well-developed political skills are actually powerful.

Perhaps the least obvious and the most illusive force determining the nature of legislative change has been the members themselves. The ambivalence of rank-and-file legislators has slowed the pace of reform, particularly during the 1970s. In the early years, some members were reluctant to devote the time and effort needed to make the interim committee system work. Most Democratic members accepted without question the governor's candidates for leadership posts. Members were willing, and often eager, to trade their votes on issues for district benefits or personal patronage offered by the governor. The same members who asserted the importance of legislative independence urged the governor to use his influence on behalf of their bills.

The attitudes of legislators have gradually been changing. They seem less willing to take instructions from the governor but still willing to bargain over legislation. Many House members have demonstrated a reluctance to follow strong leadership in that chamber.

If there is a growing independence of individual members, it has its roots in their growing political strength. There is a new generation of members who might be described as political professionals. Many members coming to the legislature in the last ten or fifteen years have a long-term interest in a political career and are willing to make sacrifices in their occupation or profession to achieve it. They often plan to stay in the legislature until another political opportunity arises (such as a chance at congressional or statewide office). Some members develop an interest in a long-term legislative career, in large part because the legislature has grown more powerful and the job

more interesting. Members are increasingly willing to devote a large proportion of their time to their legislative job. Members rarely retire after two
to four years unless they are running for another office.

Legislators have developed political techniques that enable them to win
renomination and reelection. They have learned the importance of maintaining contacts with the district and providing services to constituents. They
have learned how to campaign, to raise funds, to use the media. They have
demonstrated a willingness to devote the time that is necessary to serve
their district and build their political base. They have become visible enough
as legislators and skillful enough as politicians so that they seldom are seriously challenged at the polls.

It is this new and different generation of legislators that makes the political reforms work. These are the members who are willing to attend several
interim committee meetings per month and to devote the time necessary
to become specialists in a field. Their willingness and their political ability
to remain in the legislature for a number of terms make possible the stability
and experience that enable the system to work. Not all legislators, of course,
are as committed or as skillful. But most of the fifty or so members who
hold important positions of responsibility in the legislature have that commitment and those skills.

THE CONSEQUENCES OF CHANGE

What are the consequences of the changes for the operation of the legislative system? What have been the effects, if any, on policy outputs? Will
these changes endure? How well does the legislative process work?

There are, of course, no definitive answers to these questions. Perhaps
the clearest, most obvious conclusion to draw is that a broader range of
individuals participates in making legislative decisions. A closely related
point is that the decision-making process has become more public. No longer
is the governor's office the focal point of decision making. Legislation is
initiated not only by the governor and executive agencies and a few interest
groups, but also by legislators and by a wider variety of groups. Those groups
that are trying to pass, or defeat, legislation may seek gubernatorial help,
but they must also enlist the support of the pertinent committees and the
leadership in both houses, and ultimately the rank-and-file members. They
must plead their case in open hearings and in meetings with a wide variety
of legislators, and not behind closed doors in the governor's office. The
number of groups whose lobbyists register and who participate in the legislative process has substantially increased. It is only a slight exaggeration
to say that everyone is represented by a lobbyist in Frankfort.

It is more difficult to pass legislation in the new legislative setting. There are more actors in the legislative process who must be persuaded to provide support. There are now more "veto points" in the system, more places where a powerful group can effectively block legislation, and there is no one who can exercise the political clout once held by the governor that can break a deadlock in the legislature.

We should be more precise about legislative consequences. Actually, some kinds of legislation are no more difficult to pass than used to be the case. An individual member often finds it easier than in the past to win passage of bills that are relatively minor and uncontroversial or bills with a purely local effect. If the bill is well drafted and the member works diligently, the bill is likely to be passed. No longer will the governor or one of his leaders block or delay the bill in an effort to force the member to support administration measures. This is one of the reasons rank-and-file members prefer the new system.

It is also easier for some interest groups to get their bills passed. These are the ones who have established good working relationships with a majority of the members on the pertinent House and Senate committees. They have a good chance of gaining committee approval of their bills, and there is less risk than in the past that the governor, the leadership, or the Rules Committee will be willing and able to block the bills. During the 1985 and 1986 sessions, for example, the Kentucky Education Association had enough influence with the education committees to bring about significant changes in the governor's educational reform package; and the governor was unwilling or unable to keep her original proposals intact.

Very often no single group dominates a committee, and it becomes necessary to compromise. If the major interest groups that are most concerned with an issue are capable of agreeing on a compromise version of legislation, the bill is likely to get passed with the blessing of the appropriate committees and the leadership. Often, committee chairmen and leaders advise the organized interests that no legislation will be passed unless consensus among these interests can be achieved. This was the process by which the major horse racing legislation was passed during the 1986 session. This is the technique that the legislature has used to pass legislation on issues involving labor and management, such as unemployment insurance and workmen's compensation.

Sometimes it is impossible for the major interest groups to reach a compromise on an issue, and the result is a deadlock. This may occur because the issues are too complex, the groups are deeply committed to contradictory positions, or the groups that prefer the status quo are stronger. An example is the deadlock that arose in the 1986 session among the various health organizations on a bill to deal with the problem of financing health care for who lack insurance. Under such conditions a governor may be able to force a break in the deadlock by designing his or her own compromise, putting pressure on legislators to support it, and perhaps mobilizing public support for the legislation. In 1966, after two years of effort, Governor Edward Breathitt won legislative passage of the first comprehensive strip-mine law in the state. Given the entrenched power of the coal interests, it is difficult to believe that the legislature would have passed such a law without intense pressure from the governor. Governor Julian Carroll defeated another powerful interest when he persuaded the legislature to enact a bill severely regulating the bail-bond business.

The most difficult legislation to pass is a bill to raise taxes significantly. For obvious reasons legislators fear that supporting tax increases will be politically costly in the next election. Interest groups may be divided on whether there should be a tax increase, and if so what form it should take. Most tax increases are passed as a direct result of gubernatorial initiatives and pressure. Normally, the governor initiates a tax proposal because he or she decides new revenue is essential to carry out the governor's program. The budget, and the tax increase to finance it, become the governor's highest priority. The governor mobilizes support from organized groups, the media, and the general public by describing what goals can be accomplished with the new revenue. The governor puts pressure on legislators to pass the program, sometimes explaining what projects in their districts must be cut back if there is a shortage of revenue.

The major tax increases in the last three decades have been pushed through the legislature by the governor. It was Bert Combs who won passage of the three-cent sales tax in 1960, and it was Louie Nunn who forced a reluctant legislature (with a Democratic majority) to raise the tax to five cents in 1968. Wendell Ford persuaded the legislature to exempt food and medicine from the sales tax and to make up the revenue by passing a severance tax on minerals—a type of tax that had been repeatedly and unsuccessfully proposed in the legislature.

In 1984 Governor Collins reluctantly proposed a tax increase to finance her education program; the proposal failed because she had not adequately laid the groundwork for either the education program or the tax proposal. The governor revised the proposal to emphasize new taxes on business and agreed to revisions in the education package; both programs were adopted in the 1985 special session that she had called.

In recent years the only exception to the principle that major tax measures require strong gubernatorial support came in 1986 with legislative approval of an increased tax on gasoline. The governor and Speaker Blandford had worked unsuccessfully for this measure in the 1985 special session. But during the 1986 session it was Speaker Blandford who revived the gasoline tax bill and pushed it through the legislature, with some help from the Department of Transportation.

It has frequently been pointed out that the new schedule of legislative elections and sessions makes it more difficult to pass tax legislation or any other bill that may be difficult for members to defend in an election campaign. Under the new schedule, the regular session of the legislature adjourns in mid-April of even-numbered years, and legislative primaries are held only five or six weeks later. Members have been known to remain noncommittal on controversial bills until the filing deadline for the primary had passed and they knew whether they faced any significant opposition. In fact, the legislature moved up the filing deadline from two months to three months before the primary to give members warning about opposition at the polls earlier in the session. It is worth noting that the business tax increase to support educational reform was passed during a special session, almost a year before the legislative primaries.

There is no consensus among those who serve in the legislature or those who observe it about how well the newly independent General Assembly is working. Some believe that stronger gubernatorial leadership is necessary. Some favor strong legislative leadership and a revived Rules Committee; others want more independent committees. Some believe that more party discipline is needed; others believe it is important for legislators to follow their own judgment. Some believe that another effort must be made to amend the constitution and get annual sessions; others believe the present system is working well. Some legislators believe that their job must inevitably become nearly a full-time one; others insist on the advantages of "citizen legislators."

There is no consensus because there is no commonly accepted ideal standard by which to judge legislative performance or accomplishment. There are inherent contradictions between strong leaders and independent committees, between party discipline and members who can make their own decisions.

We believe some of the trends that we have been describing are likely to continue, but others are likely to be reversed or at least change direction. The relatively passive legislative role played by governors between 1980 and 1987 is not likely to be the norm in the future. We expect that most governors will try to use the tools of their office more aggressively to enact their programs, though these tools are less powerful than they used to be in the 1960s and 1970s.

Although the strength of legislative leadership will vary with the individuals occupying the posts, we would expect leaders to become more powerful, as has been the trend in other states. An experienced presiding officer or majority leader, possessing political skills, working as an ally (but not puppet) of the governor, has great potential influence over legislative decisions. The collective leadership, institutionalized as the Legislative Research Commission, has considerable power in the Kentucky system.

Legislative committees now have more time for study, an adequate staff, and reasonable levels of membership stability and expertise. The major uncertainty in committee performance is the qualifications of the chairman. It is sometimes argued that there is a shortage of capable committee chairmen, that there are not enough legislators with the skills and commitment to run committees well. Those committees that have the most capable chairmen are likely to be powerful decision-making bodies, whose recommendations are accepted by the leadership and adopted on the floor. Those committees that are poorly run are likely to be weak, unable to reach decisions or too willing to endorse the recommendations of a few strong interests. Their recommendations are likely to be challenged by the leadership, and either stalled in the Rules Committee, defeated on the floor, or ignored in the other house.

We believe that the legislature is likely to have a significant impact on budgetary decisions as long as the appropriations and revenue committees have strong leaders and a critical mass of committed members. The legislature as a whole is heavily dependent on these committees, and the progress made by the A & R committees in recent years has been remarkable. The governor controls the executive budget and can utilize the item veto if necessary; consequently, it is unlikely that the A & R committees will make drastic changes in the budget, but they will certainly continue to make some changes. And the questions and criticisms raised in the A & R hearings force the executive agencies to pay serious attention to the priorities of the committees.

The success of the oversight committees depends on the same factors that are important for the A & R committees: strong leadership and the commitment of members. These qualities will vary from time to time, of course. If the legislature becomes more professional, members will be able to devote more time to oversight. If annual sessions are adopted, the leverage of oversight committees would be greater because less time would elapse before the next session, in which the committees could seek legislation to overturn administrative actions that they opposed.

The legislative process will be significantly affected by the level of bipartisan competition in Kentucky state politics. Twenty years ago, after reapportionment had occurred and the Republican party had gained additional seats, the legislature appeared to be on the verge of close two-party competition. Today there is no sign of such a trend, and the Republican legislative party is weaker numerically than it was in the late 1960s. If the Republican party were to become closely competitive, or even win an occasional majority in the legislature, the decision-making process would almost inevitably become much more partisan.

Probably the most difficult prediction to make is whether Kentucky senators and representatives will gradually become more nearly full-time legislators. Such a trend is not inevitable. There are only a few states that have truly full-time legislators, whereas a few states have begun to restrict the length of sessions. As long as Kentucky has only biennial sessions, the time demands on members will be less than the national average. Presumably, many Kentuckians believe in the concept of citizen-legislators, and many legislators share that belief.

On the other hand, there are several indications that the time pressures of the legislative job are growing. The problems faced by the state are becoming more complex, requiring better understanding of issues. There are more interest groups seeking to be heard both formally and informally. The budgetary process places heavy demands on A & R Committee members, and the time pressures on oversight committees are growing. During the interim period there are enough meetings of committees, subcommittees, and special task forces so that conscientious members spend at least one day a week on legislative business, although members far from Frankfort may find that travel time raises the average to two days a week. As constituents grow more accustomed to gaining help from state legislators, the burden of constituency service will grow. Sooner or later it is inevitable that annual sessions will come even to Kentucky, requiring members to devote nearly full time to the job for at least three months of each year, though this may lower the workload during the interim.

If this trend continues, members will find it more difficult to balance the time demands of legislative service and their private job or profession or business. Consequently, a larger proportion of legislators will be men and women primarily interested in a political career and willing to subordinate their other work. Such persons are more willing to serve longer terms in the legislature, unless other political opportunities arise, and to raise larger campaign funds, if necessary, to gain reelection. Sooner or later Kentucky legislators will demand an individual staff assistant on a year-round basis. House Majority Leader Stumbo has proposed that each member have a staff assistant during the session.

A claim can be made that career politicians make better legislators. William Muir (1982: 116) argues that this is why California legislators, the most professionalized in the country, are so well informed about issues:

> I believe that California legislators desired knowledge and were willing to work hard to get it because they had adopted the vocation of politics. They were by ambition and circumstance professional politicians. . . . None could reasonably, and few wanted to, count on a dependable future in the assembly. That meant that they had to internalize the benefits of their assembly experience so that they could carry them on to the next stage of their political careers.

It can also be argued, however, as Alan Rosenthal (1979: 21-25) has done, that the growing professionalization of its members can be harmful to the legislature. He says, "There is a tension, even a conflict, between the legislator as an individual and the legislature as an institution," and he identifies several areas of conflict, including the following.

> First, the individual legislator wants more and more opportunities, while the institution needs fewer distractions and more dedicated effort. The individual legislator is concerned with his or her own well-being—in acquiring power, prestige, respect, and satisfaction. . . .
> Second, the individual legislator wants autonomy, while the institution needs teamwork. . . .
> Third, the individual wants at least an equal share of power, while the legislature needs "followers" as well as "leaders." . . .
> Fourth, the individual legislator wants more and more to say Yes while the legislature increasingly needs to say No.

This last point is particularly pertinent to Kentucky. The demands on states are increasing much faster than the tax revenues that are available, and the federal government is pressuring the states to assume more burdens. The legislature, along with the governor, must make hard decisions about budget priorities and about taxes. This requires not only compromises, but intelligent, well-informed, disciplined choices. There is the risk that independent, politically skillful legislators will become too responsive, in the sense of being too responsive to the particular, parochial demands of their districts and the groups that elect them.

Today's legislators are better informed, more experienced, and more independent, and the legislative process is both more open and more efficient. But there is no guarantee that these characteristics will lead to better decision making.

The greatest need in the Kentucky legislature is strong leadership. Rosenthal (1979: 24) has defined this need very well:

> Leadership is required to help pull things together and set priorities, to decide which is more and which is less important. It is required to counsel, stroke, and hold hands as well as take the heat and protect members on occasional issues. It is required to negotiate with the governor on behalf of the legislature and to manage the day-to-day administrative tasks. It is required to take responsibility for the legislature as an institution—strengthening it, managing the staff, and explain its behavior to the press and the people.

There have been many examples of strong legislative leadership in recent years, and some have been described in this volume. Legislative leaders can be credited with developing the interim system and revitalizing the committees. They helped salvage Governor Collins's education program when it appeared doomed, and they pushed the gasoline tax increase when she appeared to have abandoned it. The leaders of the Appropriations and Revenue Committee have consistently explained to all who would listen the fiscal realities facing the state and the need for enhancing revenue sources at a time when gubernatorial candidates have been consistently ignoring these realities and ducking the problems of tax resources.

There is no question that the Kentucky General Assembly has made remarkable progress in the last two decades. The question is whether it has advanced, and can continue to advance, enough to cope with the multitude of economic, environmental, social, and political problems facing the state. The old strong-governor model might offer a quicker way to solve these problems, but it can never be restored. The state needs strong leadership, good judgment, and political courage from both the governor and the legislature if it is to be governed well.

References

Barber, James David. 1965. *The Lawmakers*. New Haven, Conn.: Yale Univ. Press.

Basehart, Hubert H. 1980. "The Effect of Membership Stability on Continuity and Experience in U.S. State Legislative Committees." *Legislative Studies Quarterly* 5: 55-68.

Bernick, E. Lee. 1977. "Legislative Reform and Legislative Turnover." Paper prepared for delivery at 1977 annual meeting of American Political Science Association, September 1-4, Washington, D.C.

Beyle, Thad L. 1982. "The Governor's Formal Power in Kentucky." Unpublished paper.

Bibby, John F. 1966. "Committee Characteristics and Legislative Oversight of Administration." *Midwest Journal of Political Science* 10: 78-98.

Bizzel, Jack E. 1981. "A Profile of Kentucky Lobbyists and Interest Groups: The 1980 General Assembly." Unpublished paper.

————. 1984. "Interest Groups as Perceived by Kentucky State Legislators." Unpublished paper.

Blair, Diane Kincaid, and Ann R. Henry. 1981. "The Family Factor in State Legislative Turnover." *Legislative Studies Quarterly* 6: 55-68.

Boyd, William A. 1982. "Campaign Finance and Electoral Outcomes in Wisconsin and Georgia House Races." Paper presented at the annual meeting of the Midwest Political Science Association.

Calvert, Jerry. 1979. "Revolving Doors: Volunteerism in State Legislatures." *State Government* 52: 174-81.

Clark, Peter B., and James D. Wilson. 1961. "Incentive Systems: A Theory of Organization." *Administrative Science Quarterly* 6: 129-66.

Cooper, Joseph. 1977. "Congress in Organizational Perspective." In *Congress Reconsidered*, ed. Lawrence Dodd and Bruce Oppenheimer, 140-62. New York: Praeger.

Cox, Gary S. 1975. "An Evaluation of the Kentucky Legislative Interim Committee System, 1968-1974." Ph.D. diss., University of Kentucky.

Davidson, Roger, and Walter Oleszek. 1976. "Adaptation and Consolidation: Structural Innovation in the U.S. House of Representatives." *Legislative Studies Quarterly* 1: 37-65.

Drew, Elizabeth. 1983. *Politics and Money: The New Road to Corruption*. New York: Macmillan.

Elling, Richard C. 1979. "The Utility of State Legislative Casework as a Means of Oversight." *Legislative Studies Quarterly* 4: 353-79.

Ethridge, Marcus. 1985. *Legislative Participation in Implementation: Policy through Politics*. New York: Praeger.

Fenno, Richard. 1973. *Congressmen in Committees*. Boston: Little, Brown.

———. 1978. *Home Style: House Members in Their Districts*. Boston: Little, Brown.

Fiorina, Morris. 1977. *Congress: Keystone of the Washington Establishment*. New Haven, Conn.: Yale Univ. Press.

Focus. 1986. "Black Elected Officials in the United States." September.

Foss, Philip O. 1960. *Politics and Grass: The Administration of Grazing on the Public Domain*. Seattle: Univ. of Washington Press.

Francis, Wayne L., and James W. Riddlesperger. 1982. "U.S. State Legislative Committees: Structure, Procedural Efficiency and Party Control." *Legislative Studies Quarterly* 7: 453-73.

Freeman, J. Leiper. 1965. *The Political Process: Executive Bureau-Legislative Committee Relations*. Rev. ed. New York: Random House.

Giles, Michael W., and Anita Pritchard, 1985. "Campaign Expenditures and Legislative Elections in Florida." *Legislative Studies Quarterly* 10: 71-88.

Glantz, Stanton A., Alan I. Abramowitz, and Michael P. Burkart. 1976. "Election Outcomes: Whose Money Matters." *Journal of Politics* 38: 1033-41.

Grau, Craig H. 1981. "Competition in State Legislative Primaries." *Legislative Studies Quarterly* 6: 35-54.

Gray, Virginia. 1976. "Models of Comparative State Politics." *Journal of Politics* 20: 325-57.

Griffin, Patricia E. 1985. "State Senators' Perceptions of their Constituencies and the Role of the Service Function in the State Legislative Process." Ph.D. diss., University of Kentucky.

Hamm, Keith. 1978. "The Effects of Demand Patterns on Committee Decision Making in State Legislatures: A Comparative Analysis." Paper presented at the annual meeting of the Midwest Political Science Association.

———. 1982. "Factors Affecting the Consistency of Committee-Floor Voting in State Legislatures." Paper presented at the annual meeting of the Southwestern Political Science Association.

———. 1984. "Committee Unity and Influence on the Legislative Floor: A Comparative State Assessment." Paper presented at the annual meeting of the American Political Science Association.

———. 1986a. "Measurement of Subsystem Activity from the Committee Perspective: An Exploratory Study of Six Colorado Committees." Paper presented at the annual meeting of the Midwest Political Science Association.

———. 1986b. "Committee Stacking and State Legislative Policy Making: Overrepresentation of Which 'Interesteds'?" Paper presented at the annual meeting of the American Political Science Association.

Hamm, Keith, and Gary Moncrief. 1982. "Effects of Structural Change in Legislative Committee Systems on Their Performance in U.S. States." *Legislative Studies Quarterly* 7: 383-99.

Hamm, Keith E., and Roby D. Robertson. 1981. "Factors Influencing the Adoption of New Methods of Legislative Oversight in the U.S. States." *Legislative Studies Quarterly* 6: 133-50.

Heard, Alexander. 1966. "Introduction—Old Problem, New Context." In *State Legislatures in American Politics*, ed. Alexander Heard. Englewood Cliffs, N.J.: Prentice-Hall.

Hedlund, Ronald D. 1980. "Measuring Legislative Activity or Performance and Developing a Theory of Legislative Change." Paper presented at the annual meeting of the American Political Science Association.

———. 1985. "Organizational Attributes of Legislative Institutions: Structure, Rules, Norms, Resources." In G. Loewenberg, S.C. Patterson, and M.E. Jewell, *Handbook of Legislative Research*, chap. 8. Cambridge: Harvard Univ. Press.

Hedlund, Ronald D., and Keith Hamm. 1975. "Conflict and Perceived Group Benefits from Legislative Rules Changes." Paper presented at the annual meeting of the American Political Science Association.

Hrebenar, Ronald J., and Clive S. Thomas. 1987. *Interest Group Politics in the American West*. Salt Lake City: Univ. of Utah Press.

Insurance Information Institute. 1979. *Occupational Profile of State Legislatures, 1979*. New York: Insurance Information Institute.

Jacobson, Gary C. 1980. *Money in Congressional Elections*. New Haven, Conn.: Yale Univ. Press.

Jacobson, Gary C., and Samuel Kernell. 1981. *Strategy and Choice in Congressional Elections*. New Haven, Conn.: Yale Univ. Press.

Jewell, Malcolm E. 1967. "The Kentucky General Assembly." In Malcolm E. Jewell and Lee S. Green, *The Kentucky and Tennessee Legislatures*. Lexington, Ky.: Department of Political Science, University of Kentucky.

———. 1982. *Representation in State Legislatures*. Lexington: Univ. Press of Kentucky.

———. 1985. "Legislators and Constituents in the Representative Process." In G. Loewenberg, S.C. Patterson, and M.E. Jewell, *Handbook of Legislative Research*. Cambridge: Harvard Univ. Press.

Jewell, Malcolm E., and Everett W. Cunningham. 1968. *Kentucky Politics*. Lexington: Univ. of Kentucky Press.

Jewell, Malcolm E., and Samuel C. Patterson. 1977. *The Legislative Process in the United States*. 3d ed. New York: Random House.

———. 1986. *The Legislative Process in the United States*. 4th ed. New York: Random House.

Jones, Ruth S., and Thomas J. Borris. 1983. "Context and Strategy in Campaign Financing: The Case of Minnesota." Paper presented at the annual meeting of the Western Political Science Association.

———. 1985. "Strategic Contributing in Legislative Campaigns: The Case of Minnesota." *Legislative Studies Quarterly* 10 (February): 89-106.

Kirkpatrick, Samuel A. 1978. *The Legislative Process in Oklahoma*. Norman: Univ. of Oklahoma Press.

Kolasa, Bernard D. 1978. "Party Recruitment in Nonpartisan Nebraska." In *Nonpartisanship in the Legislative Process*. ed. John C. Comer and James B. Johnson. Washington, D.C.: Univ. Press of America.

Kuklinski, James H., and Richard E. Elling. 1977. "Representational Role, Constituency Opinion, and Legislative Roll-Call Behavior." *American Journal of Political Science* 21: 135-47.

McCrone, Donald J., and James H. Kuklinski. 1979. "The Delegate Theory of Representation." *American Journal of Political Science* 23: 278-300.

Mahoney, Mitzi. 1985. "Legislative Oversight of Administrative Policy-making: A Case Study of the Kentucky Administrative Review Subcommittee." Paper presented at the annual meeting of the American Political Science Association.

———. 1987. "The Determinants and Consequences of Decision Making in State Legislative Rule Review Committees." PhD. diss., University of Kentucky.

Mileur, Jerome M., and George T. Sulzner. 1974. *Campaigning for the Massachusetts Senate.* Amherst: Univ. of Massachusetts Press.

Miller, Lawrence W. 1977. "Legislative Turnover and Political Careers: A Study of Texas Legislators, 1969-1975." Ph.D. diss., Texas Tech University.

Miller, Penny. 1986. "Motivations and Continuity of Support of Political Activists in Gubernatorial Primaries." Ph.D. dissertation, Univ. of Kentucky.

Mladenka, Kenneth R., and Kim Quaile Hill. 1986. *Texas Government.* Monterey, Cal.: Brooks/Cole Publishing Co.

Moncrief, Gary F. 1977. "The Consequences of State Legislative Reform." Ph.D. diss., University of Kentucky.

Morehouse, Sarah McCally. 1981. *State Politics, Parties and Policy.* New York: Holt, Rinehart and Winston.

Mueller, Keith J. 1985. "Explaining Variation and Change in Gubernatorial Powers, 1960-1982." *Western Political Quarterly* 38: 424-31.

Muir, William K. 1982. *Legislature: California's School for Politics.* Chicago: Univ. of Chicago Press.

National Conference of State Legislatures. 1979. *A Legislator's Guide to Staffing Patterns.* Denver: National Conference of State Legislatures.

Nechemias, Carol. 1987. "Changes in the Election of Women to U.S. State Legislative Seats." *Legislative Studies Quarterly* 12: 125-42.

Niemi, Richard G., and Laura R. Winsky. 1987. "Membership Turnover in U.S. State Legislatures." *Legislative Studies Quarterly* 12: 115-24.

Ogul, Morris S. 1976. *Congress Oversees the Bureaucracy.* Pittsburgh: Univ. of Pittsburgh Press.

Patterson, Samuel C. 1982. "Campaign Spending in Contests for Governor." *Western Political Quarterly* 35: 457-77.

Payne, James L., Oliver H. Woshinsky, Eric P. Veblen, William H. Coogan, and Gene E. Bigler. 1984. *The Motivation of Politicians.* Chicago: Nelson-Hall Publishers.

Pound, William. 1982. "The State Legislatures." In *The Book of the States 1982-1983,* 181-87. Lexington, Ky.: Council of State Governments.

———. 1984. "The State Legislatures." In *The Book of the States, 1984-85,* 79-83. Lexington, Ky.: Council of State Governments.

Rosenthal, Alan. 1974. *Legislative Performance in the States: Explorations of Committee Behavior.* New York: Free Press.

———. 1979. "Separate Roads: The Legislator as an Individual and the Legislature as an Institution." *State Legislatures* 5: 21-25.

———. 1981a. "Legislative Behavior and Oversight." *Legislative Studies Quarterly* 6: 115-31.

———. 1981b. *Legislative Life.* New York: Harper and Row.

————. 1985. "The Changing Character of State Legislators—Or: Requiem for a Vanishing Breed." *Public Affairs Review*: 80-93.

Sabato, Larry. 1978. *Goodbye to Good-time Charlie*, Lexington, Mass.: Lexington Books.

Scher, Seymour. 1963. "Conditions for Legislative Control." *Journal of Politics* 25: 526-51.

Seligman, Lester G., Michael R. King, Chong Lim Kim, and Roland E. Smith. 1974. *Patterns of Recruitment: A State Chooses Its Lawmakers*. Chicago: Rand McNally.

Shills, Edward A. 1959. "Resentment and Hostilities of Legislators: Sources, Objects, Consequences." In *Legislative Behavior*, ed. John C. Wahlke and Heinz Eulau. New York: Free Press.

Shin, Kwang S., and John S. Jackson III. 1979. "Membership Turnover in U.S. State Legislatures: 1931-1976." *Legislative Studies Quarterly* 4: 95-104.

Smallwood, Frank. 1976. *Free and Independent*. Brattleboro, Vt.: Stephen Greene Press.

Tobin, Richard J., and Edward Keynes. 1975. "Institutional Differences in the Recruitment Process: A Four-State Study." *American Journal of Political Science* 19: 667-82.

Wahlke, John C., Heinz Eulau, William Buchanan, and LeRoy C. Ferguson. 1962. *The Legislative System*. New York: John Wiley and Sons.

Welch, William P. 1980. "The Allocation of Political Monies: Economic Interest Groups." *Public Choice* 35: 37-60.

Zeigler, L. Harmon, and Michael Baer. 1969. *Lobbying*. Belmont Cal.: Wadsworth.

NEWSPAPERS AND MAGAZINES

Courier-Journal. Louisville, Kentucky (July 20, 24, 1986).
Lexington Herald-Leader. Lexington, Kentucky (August 12, 1986).

LEGISLATIVE DOCUMENTS

Kentucky Legislative Record, April 12, 1974, and April 16, 1984.

COURT CASES

Armstrong v. *Collins*. Ky., 709 S.W.2d 437 (1986).
Legislative Research Commission v. *Brown*. Ky., 664 S.W.2d 907 (1984).

Index